FLAUBERT AND THE HISTORICAL NOVEL

Salammbô reassessed

ANNE GREEN

CAMBRIDGE UNIVERSITY PRESS

Cambridge

London   New York   New Rochelle
Melbourne   Sydney

Published by the Press Syndicate of the University of Cambridge
The Pitt Building, Trumpington Street, Cambridge CB2 1RP
32 East 57th Street, New York, NY 10022, USA
296 Beaconsfield Parade, Middle Park, Melbourne 3206, Australia

First published 1982

Printed in Great Britain at the University Press, Cambridge

Library of Congress Catalogue card number 81-6085

British Library Cataloguing in Publication Data
Green, Anne
Flaubert and the historical novel.
1. Historical fiction, French
I. Title
843'.8   PQ2246.S4
ISBN 0 521 23765 3

Contents

Acknowledgements

I am greatly indebted to Professor Alison Fairlie of Girton College, Cambridge, who supervised the thesis on which this book is based, and who has generously offered advice, information and encouragement throughout.

Parts of chapter 6 first appeared in *French Studies*, vol. XXXII (April 1978) and I am grateful to the editors for permission to reprint that material here. I should also like to thank the librarians of the Bibliothèque Nationale, Paris and the Bibliothèque Municipale, Rouen, for kindly allowing me to publish transcriptions from Flaubert's manuscripts.

Introduction

Few literary genres have met with such adverse criticism as the historical novel. Historians tend to despise it for taking liberties with fact, and for inventing and reshaping events without due regard for historical accuracy. Literary critics, on the other hand, are suspicious of the severe constraints it places on itself by purporting to deal with verifiable characters and situations. G. H. Lewes's dismissal of this hybrid genre was typical: 'Idleness – a wish to get at knowledge by a royal route; and a pleasant self-sophistication, that reading such novels is not a "waste of time" – these are the great encouragers of historical novels. What is the consequence? The consequence is that we have false history, and a bad story, palmed upon us for a novel.'[1] Lewes and his fellow critics undoubtedly have a valid point – many inferior works which pass for historical novels do not even begin to satisfy the demands of either history or fiction. Although this is clearly not reason enough to condemn *all* historical novels, the view has been a tenacious one, and the genre has never fully recovered the high reputation it enjoyed in its heyday in the first half of the nineteenth century.

The two most influential works on the subject, Louis Maigron's *Le Roman historique à l'époque romantique* and Georg Lukács's *The historical novel* both, in their different ways, reinforce the old notion that the historical novel died around 1850. For Maigron, the historical novel was a genre peculiar to the Romantic period, a form developed to give expression to a passionate concern with national history and a delight in the picturesque, and which faded once these preoccupations had gone. For Lukács, too, the genre's genesis and decline result from the great social upheavals of the period: there is a fundamental shift in bourgeois ideology after 1848 and the novels written since that crucial date are the works of men now alienated from their historical origins. Detached from the historical process, they find it impossible to reconcile 'the ideological content, the human attitude that is intended and the literary means that are used'.[2] After the upheavals of 1848 it becomes impossible to write a good historical novel.

The obvious weakness in Lukács's and Maigron's approach is their exclusivity. Each starts from a fixed premise, and novels which do not fit the pre-established criteria are disregarded. Consequently, both writers fail to take into account many outstanding historical novels which have proved to be of lasting interest.

When *Salammbô* first appeared in December 1862 it, too, was attacked by critics for not fulfilling what were then considered to be the necessary criteria for a historical novel. Reviewers were bewildered. A second novel from the author of *Madame Bovary* had been widely advertised and eagerly awaited, but instead of a follow-up to the immensely successful novel of provincial life, readers were confronted with a work which did not seem to fit any recognisable category at all. 'Qu'est-ce que *Salammbô?*' asked the reviewer in *La Gazette de France*; 'Poser cette question, c'est déjà faire le procès du livre'.[3] This was indeed the question which contemporary critics were to raise over and over again, trying to find a convenient pigeon-hole for *Salammbô*. They classified it variously as an epic, a prose-poem, a drama, an archaeological *tour de force*, a guide-book to Carthage, and spent far more ink on trying to decide this issue than on giving a considered opinion of its literary merits. On one thing only were they agreed – *Salammbô* did not fit the criteria for a historical novel.

Exactly what these criteria were will be discussed later in this book. Meanwhile it is enough to note the powerful influence of empiricism on literary theory at that time. It presupposed that the past was an objectively existing reality which could be resurrected or replicated by scientific effort; and that the most positively useful contribution to knowledge was gained through direct observation of the external world. Art and literature were valued as a means of conveying such observation. But if the most trustworthy information was that obtained through sense-experience, then an author who wrote about his own period and about what he had personally experienced clearly served a more useful purpose than one v'ho used imagination and fantasy to complete his picture of the past. Novels dealing with periods and events quite outside the author's own experience tended to be viewed with suspicion unless firmly supported by historical documentation.

The gradual infiltration of literary criticism by these philosophical ideas seems to go a long way towards explaining the depths to which the historical novel's reputation sank.[4] And it also explains why readers on the whole still feel more at ease with *Madame Bovary* or *L'Education sentimentale* than with *Salammbô*, even though the first two depict a society and manners which are now history to us. We are reassured by the fact that Flaubert was writing about the kind of people he knew well and set them in familiar and convincing surroundings. They are novels we can trust. But trustworthiness is quite unsatisfactory as the main criterion for assessing a novel, and begs all kinds of questions about the nature of fiction.

When Flaubert came to write *Salammbô* he was worried that his novel would meet with a hostile reaction because it could not possibly give an accurate representation of life in ancient Carthage. But, as will soon become clear, he himself did not consider historical accuracy to be central to his work; and certainly, to a modern reader, the interest of *Salammbô* depends only marginally on the information it imparts about ancient Carthaginian civilisation. Too often, however, the novel is seen merely as a beautiful but sterile monument to aestheticism, a remarkable but puzzling piece of historical recon-struction, or a work of escapism which fits uneasily into the general pattern of Flaubert's writing. But *Salammbô* is much more than this, and my purpose in this book is to present a reassessment of it.

The essential background is the debate about the relation between historical fiction and the history of the historians that engaged both historians and literary critics in France in the first half of the nineteenth century. Flaubert was deeply interested in this debate, and from his correspondence and published writings a reconstruction of his own position on many of the issues is possible. Evidently, these have some bearing on Flaubert's intentions in writing *Salammbô*; but also, the successive manuscript plans make it possible to trace his development of his own method of composing a historical novel.

Side by side, these two elements lead to a new reading of *Salammbô*. Flaubert's treatment of social, political and mythological elements reveals that he chose a distant period and an alien civilisation to examine fundamental problems about the relationship between history and fiction, and about the even more basic problem of the way in which we perceive and make sense of the past, distant or not.

1 Flaubert and historical fiction

Flaubert first became interested in historical fiction through the theatre. The letters he wrote between the ages of eleven and fourteen to his friend Ernest Chevalier continually refer to the plays he is reading, writing, or performing, or to visits to the local theatre in Rouen, and they include sections of the latest theatrical news copied from the review *Art et progrès*.[1] Many of the plays he mentions were the historical dramas then so much in vogue – works such as Dumas's *Catherine Howard*, Victor Herbin's *Jeanne de Flandre*, Casimir Delavigne's *Les Enfants d'Edouard*, Victor Hugo's *Marion de Lorme* and *Ruy Blas*. This last he read barely three weeks after its first performance.

This interest in historical drama influenced Flaubert's early writing. His most substantial work was the five-act play, *Loys XI*, written in 1838, but he also produced a historical drama about *Frédégonde et Brunehaut* (1835), now lost,[2] and the scenario for *Madame d'Ecouy* (1837?). The same influence marks much of his early prose fiction: Dumas's *La Tour de Nesle* was the main source for *Dernière scène de la mort de Marguerite de Bourgogne* (1835), and *Don Juan d'Autriche ou la vocation* by Casimir Delavigne was almost certainly the inspiration behind *Un Secret de Philippe le Prudent* (1836). The historical pieces he wrote up to 1838 repeat many of the commonplaces of the Romantic stage: dramatic duels, assassinations, power struggles, intrigue, disguise and mistaken identity, violence and bloodshed. Royalty or members of the nobility play the central rôles while the populace move in the background: poor, stupid and gullible, scorned by their rulers. These early tales are neither original nor profound and make no rigorous use of historical sources. They are simply colourful and lively attempts to emulate the much-admired dramatic style of writers like Hugo and Dumas.

Flaubert soon outgrew his enthusiasm for the melodramatic intensity of these plays. After 1838 he mentions them rarely, and then always with amused irony. When Pécuchet turns to the theatre, for example, 'Il avala deux Pharamond, trois Clovis, quatre Charlemagne, plusieurs Philippe-Auguste, une foule de Jeanne d'Arc, et bien des marquises de Pompadour, et des conspirations de Cellamare.

Presque toutes lui parurent encore plus bêtes que les romans. Car il
existe pour le théâtre une histoire convenue, que rien ne peut
détruire' (II, 243). As Pécuchet complains, the treatment of historical
subjects in the theatre had tended to become fixed and schematic –
Henri IV was inevitably presented as a jovial monarch and Mary
Queen of Scots as a tragic, weeping queen. But this was much less
true of the historical novel. On the whole, novelists took the concept
of historical fiction more seriously than dramatists did, and throughout
the 1820s and 1830s there were continual attempts to formulate the
purpose and problems of bringing together history and fiction.

Sir Walter Scott, who was undoubtedly the strongest single
influence on French historical novelists in the nineteenth century,
was first translated into French in 1816. By the time *Quentin Durward*
reached France in 1823 his reputation on the continent had been
firmly established. Initially, Scott's method was to write about events
which had happened within living memory and in surroundings he
knew well, and, as he noted in his *Journal*, to select 'the striking and
interesting points out of dull details'.[3] Even when he turned to tales
set in a place and period far from his own immediate experience
he continued to stress the importance of choosing exciting and
picturesque topics, mixing these with 'just so much ordinary feeling
and expression, as render them interesting and intelligible'.[4] Scott
had definite views on what his readers would understand and
appreciate; for him this was a primary criterion in deciding how far
to distort historical fact. He consciously tailored his subject to suit
his readers' supposed taste and was more concerned with this and
with the general flavour of the manners of the period than with
accuracy of historical events or chronology. ('What signify dates in
a true story?', he wrote in his *Journal*.)[5] When the tide of popularity
began to turn against him, however, this was the fault with which
he was most reproached. Characteristically, Bouvard and Pécuchet,
who are at first delighted by Scott's lifelike reconstructions of the past,
are finally disillusioned when they discover his cavalier attitude to
the documented facts of history.

Flaubert knew Scott's writing well. He owned the *Complete Works*
and his correspondence contains references to *The Antiquary*, the
History of Scotland, *The Fair Maid of Perth* and *The Pirate*.[6] This last
he read with particular enthusiasm, saying that it whetted his
appetite for the Oriental tale that he himself was planning to write.
Elsewhere in Flaubert's writing, however, Scott is treated less favour-
ably. Indeed his name is often used simply as a byword to indicate

a character's taste for a certain kind of diluted Romanticism – 'ce romantisme à ogives et à cottes de mailles, qui est à celui de Goethe et de Byron ce qu'est le classique de l'empire au classique du XVIIe siècle, dont Walter Scott a été peut-être le père' (ı, 367). Emma Bovary's passion for things medieval, her dreams of ancient chests, guard-rooms and minstrels, are attributed to her reading of Scott, whose novels form part of Homais's library – a mark of disfavour in itself.

Nevertheless, the immense popularity of Scott's novels inevitably attracted hordes of imitators. Flaubert even has Frédéric Moreau, at the beginning of *L'Education sentimentale*, decide that one day he will become 'le Walter Scott de la France'. But Scott's imitators brought this type of historical novel into disrepute. To write one, as G. H. Lewes commented, an author needed:

no style, no imagination, no fancy, no knowledge of the world, no wit, no pathos; he needs only to study Scott, and the historical novelists; to 'cram' for the necessary information about costumes, antiquated forms of speech, and the leading political events of the epoch chosen; and to add thereto the art, so easily learned, of complicating a plot with adventures, imprisonments and escapes. As for character, he need give himself no trouble about it: his predecessors have already furnished him with *types*; these he can christen anew. Probability he may utterly scorn. If he has any reflections to make, he need only give them a sententious turn; truth, novelty, or depth, are unimportant.[7]

Another equally scornful critic classed Scott's imitators as the 'Wardrobe School of Novelists' – writers who 'give the costume of the time without the life and nerve', and Balzac wrote as early as 1831 that the reading-public were sick and tired of 'l'histoire de France walter-scottée'.[8]

To provide historical fiction with some kind of theoretical formulation was a task taken more seriously in France than elsewhere. Alfred de Vigny perhaps thought most deeply about the problem. He believed that the historical novel could show the hidden movements of history and, moreover, could suggest causes and trace their outcome in a way that was closed to the historian who must rely on already existing material and reproduce 'le vrai' as opposed to 'la vérité' – or what is known to have taken place as opposed to a poetic interpretation of what might have or ought to have happened.[9] In art, he said, probability is far more important than truth; bad historical novels have been produced by copying chronicles and authenticated dialogues where the resulting effect (although 'true') was unconvincing. The novel's great value, according to Vigny, is that it *is* fiction: the novelist is at liberty to invent and to imagine in order to arrive at a more profound and universal truth than is permissible to the historian, and can use literary devices to present this truth in the most effective way.

One can see in Vigny's argument a development of Aristotle's famous claim that the artistic representation of history is more valuable and more important than an exact factual account, since the artist can distil probable and universal truths from specific events. But it was a highly controversial view. Balzac was among those who objected to the stylisation and falsity of Vigny's *Cinq-Mars*; and Sainte-Beuve gave it an unfavourable review on the grounds that it distorted historical truth: 'Monsieur de Vigny,' he wrote, 'n'eut jamais...la première des conditions, le sentiment et la vue de la réalité.'[10]

Flaubert, however, did not agree with these critics. He told Louise Colet that he approved of the way in which Vigny 'faisait de l'historique' and he appreciated the 'jolies pages' of *Cinq-Mars*. Although he was critical of Vigny's handling of recent history in *Servitude et grandeur militaires*, his objections were to the attitudes evinced rather than to Vigny's right to blend fiction with history. Vigny had used his account to make statements about patriotism and duty, and these concepts were of little interest to Flaubert.

He explains to Louise Colet how he would have treated the same period of history himself. What interests him are the extraordinary and fanatical passions it aroused – for example, the absurd, exclusive and sublime adoration of Napoleon – rather than the abstract concept of duty, which he does not consider to be really natural to mankind, or the minor squabbles and skirmishes which he finds too trivial. Battles, he says, are only worth portraying 'lorsque ça fait de grands tableaux avec des fonds rouges'.[11] He is fascinated by the extremes of human nature revealed by such situations and his dislike of Vigny's work is based largely on this difference of attitude to the event: nowhere is there any hint of an objection to the principle of sacrificing factual accuracy to a higher aim.

Nor do Flaubert's criticisms of Victor Hugo's historical writing make any mention of liberties taken with fact. Hugo claimed to be creating a new kind of historical novel to succeed 'le roman pittoresque, mais prosaïque, de Walter Scott'. The terms in which Hugo describes this new type are characteristically grandiose and imprecise – it was to be at once dramatic and epic; picturesque and poetic; real and ideal; true and great – it was to be Walter Scott enshrined in Homer.[12] For Hugo, too, historical accuracy was of minor importance. Writing about his *Notre-Dame de Paris* (1831) where the documentation is both superficial and derivative, he makes no pretence of historicity: any merit the novel might have, he said, came from the fact that it was a work of imagination, caprice and fantasy.[13]

Flaubert's critical comments on Hugo turn mainly upon deficiencies in the novelist's conception of his subject. In spite of his often repeated admiration for *notre dieu* Hugo, Flaubert complains of a fundamental imbalance in *Les Misérables* (1862): it has 'ni vérité, ni grandeur' and contains lengthy accounts of insignificant details while giving no explanation of central points. Moreover, Hugo's philosophy is vague and his characters (especially in *Quatre-vingt-treize*) are unconvincing and wooden.[14] But Flaubert does not object to Hugo's obvious anachronisms and distortions of historical fact. Surprisingly, perhaps, for a writer who spent so much time researching into the background to his own novels and who could boast of reading a 400-page memoir on the pyramidal cypress to furnish a tiny detail for *Salammbô*, Flaubert's view on the issue is that the accuracy of individual details is of relatively minor importance. What does matter is the overall impression, the 'colour and tone' of the novel and, above all, its artistic beauty. As he wrote to George Sand in 1875, 'Je regarde comme très secondaire le détail technique, le renseignement local, enfin le côté historique et exacte des choses. Je recherche par-dessus tout la beauté, dont mes compagnons sont médiocrement en quête.'[15]

Whatever their opinions on the question of historical accuracy, most novelists agreed that the historical novel was properly a vivid account of everyday life in an earlier period, or what Balzac called 'l'histoire des mœurs' as opposed to 'les sèches et rebutantes nomenclatures de faits appelées histoires'.[16] The historian Barante stated that with its new interest in history the novel could go beyond mere relation of the adventures of individuals. Instead, it must present them as live witnesses of the opinions of their time.[17]

Fiction was seen to be better suited to this purpose than history proper. The best novelists, said Balzac, are able to uncover the causes behind events and portray the hidden human passions which are so important in determining the course of history yet which are passed over by historians. Vigny, too, stressed the novelist's privileged position in being able to penetrate to the heart of a period:

L'histoire présente aux hommes le sens philosophique et le spectacle *extérieur* des faits vus dans leur ensemble, le roman historique donne *l'intérieur* de ces mêmes faits examinés dans leur détail. L'un juge les grands résultats du jeu des passions relativement à la marche progressive de l'esprit humain, l'autre représente le mouvement même de cette lutte des passions, l'entrelacement de ses rouages et leur commotion sur leur siècle.[18]

Yet there was considerable disagreement as to how these historically important passions should be treated: to what extent should they be portrayed through real, historical characters?

Scott had worried over this problem, and noted in his *Journal*: 'in my better efforts, while I conducted my story through the agency of historical personages and by connecting it with historical incidents, I have endeavoured to weave them pretty closely together, and in future I will study this more. Must not let the background eclipse the principal figures – the frame overpower the picture.'[19] Yet he was always careful not to allow a historical character to figure too prominently. 'Le roman ne peut admettre qu'en passant une grande figure', commented Balzac, applauding Scott's success in this and admiring, too, his skill in giving detailed explanations of historical incidents by portraying the life and manners of a period through its people rather than by analysing the political events themselves. But in his own novels Balzac was hesitant about the place of the historical figure. In *Sur Catherine de Médicis* they abound; in *Les Chouans* he eliminates them entirely; and in *Une Ténébreuse Affaire* there is one brief appearance of a historical figure, but at a carefully prepared climax in the novel – this was to be the solution he most commonly adopted. Vigny, however, felt that to keep historical figures in the background was merely to sidestep a difficult issue: in Scott's novels the action falls on fictional characters – who can be made to do anything – while a great historical figure occasionally passes in the distance and thus fixes the date of the action and swells the novel's importance. But this, says Vigny, is much too simple a solution. He himself prefers to reverse Scott's method and in *Cinq-Mars* the action is played out among the historical figures while the invented characters provide the background.[20]

Flaubert was aware of the difficulty, but tended to side with Scott and Balzac rather than with Vigny, realising how easily the weighty presence of historical figures could unbalance a novel. He felt that the danger was particularly great in *L'Education sentimentale*. Echoing Scott's 'Must not let the background eclipse the principal figures', he wrote: 'J'ai peur que les fonds ne dévorent les premiers plans; c'est là le défaut du genre historique. Les personnages de l'histoire sont plus intéressants que ceux de la fiction, surtout quand ceux-là ont des passions modérées; on s'intéresse moins à Frédéric qu'à Lamartine.'[21] In *Salammbô*, however, there was less of a problem. The reader, knowing little about the historical figures of such a remote period, has fewer expectations and so the historical imbalance is less likely to occur. Indeed Maxime Du Camp claimed that Flaubert chose his Carthaginian subject for this reason, and that he deliberately set out to foil his earlier critics by writing of a period about which no one knew the first thing.[22] His realism could not then be questioned – another indication, if Du Camp's account is to be believed, of Flaubert's impatience with demands for strict historical accuracy.

One reason for the critics' almost obsessive concern with accuracy and authenticity (and nowhere is this more noticeable than in Frœhner's attack on *Salammbô*) was that many readers had come to see historical novels as an easy and pleasurable way of learning history. Scott himself had encouraged this attitude, saying that it was better to have a smattering of history learnt through reading historical fiction than to have none at all. 'The honey which is put on the edge of the cup induces many to drink up the whole medicinal potion,' he wrote, 'while those who only take a sip of it have, at least, a better chance of benefit than if they had taken none at all.'[23] Mérimée makes fun of this view of the novel in the 'Dialogue entre le lecteur et l'auteur' in his *Chronique du règne de Charles IX*: the 'reader' exclaims how excited he is at the prospect of learning so many new things and being allowed to eavesdrop on great figures from the past; but the author mischievously frustrates these expectations and the chapter ends with this exchange:

– Ah! je m'aperçois que je ne trouverai pas dans votre roman ce que j'y cherchais.
– Je le crains.[24]

Flaubert mocked this widely held view in the *Dictionnaire des idées reçues*. To the commonplace that the reading of novels corrupts the masses he adds the rider: 'Seuls les romans historiques peuvent être tolérés parce qu'ils enseignent l'histoire.'

Although many readers may have liked to believe this, a more common didactic rôle for the historical novel was a vehicle for the author's own ideas. *Les Martyrs* carries a clear religious message, and Chateaubriand claimed to have been persecuted by the Imperial police because of the novel's political allusions; Vigny's prejudice in favour of the nobility colours *Cinq-Mars*; Hugo's preface of 1832 to *Notre-Dame de Paris* makes clear his wish to stimulate public interest in French medieval architecture; the very popular *I promessi sposi* expresses Manzoni's patriotic sentiments; and in *Sur Catherine de Médicis* Balzac uses the events surrounding the massacre of St Bartholomew's Day to state his views on recent events in France, and from the comparison tries to find a pattern underlying all popular revolutions.

Flaubert, however, had little sympathy with overtly didactic novels. God never expresses an opinion, he wrote to George Sand, so what right does a novelist have to express his?[25] His reasons for objecting are primarily aesthetic ones. When his old school friend, the historian and novelist Ernest Feydeau, asked for an opinion about his own latest novel, he was told that he had marred the work by thrusting forward his own ideas and preaching to the reader. 'Tu rentres dans la manie de presque tous les écrivains français,' added Flaubert; 'tu n'as plus en vue le Beau et l'éternel Vrai.'[26]

A passage in the *Education sentimentale* of 1845 is equally critical of writers who distort their presentation of the past, and alter facts and characters in order to put across their own preconceived opinions – these writers, he says, inevitably produce false and lifeless works (I, 358). Here too, as in his statements about accuracy in historical detail, Flaubert is objecting not to an author's right to infuse his work with ideas, but to those cases where the general picture of the period is grossly falsified and the famous 'Beau pur' sacrificed to a didactic aim. As we shall see later, Flaubert projects his own preoccupations and anxieties about contemporary problems into his historical novels, but he does so in a way that is infinitely more delicate and subtle than any of the historical allegories produced while the Romantic historical novel was at its height.

Another of the difficulties facing the historical novelist lay in the choice of language. In attempting to recreate the life and manners of a distant period, should he not also try to reproduce the language of the time? But how to do this without becoming unintelligible to modern readers? Scott had proposed his solution to the problem in the 'Dedicatory Epistle' to *Ivanhoe*: 'He who would imitate an ancient language with success, must attend rather to its grammatical character, turn of expression, and mode of arrangement, than labour to collect extraordinary and antiquated terms.' Scott felt that the introduction of archaic language into his novels 'where the use of peculiar words may add emphasis or vivacity to the composition'[27] was an essential part of the evocation of a distant period, but he relied more on obsolete turns of phrase and syntactical devices than on deliberately archaic vocabulary. Even so, he frequently had to include glosses of unfamiliar terms to help his readers.

Other solutions were tried. Some writers steeped themselves in a bygone idiom in an attempt to create a credible replica; others used rather artificial devices to circumvent the difficulty. For example, in *I promessi sposi* Manzoni elaborately creates the illusion that he is providing a modern translation of an original document, a device also used by Théophile Gautier in *Le Roman de la momie*; and Dumas, in the preface to *Les Trois Mousquetaires*, claims that he is merely publishing a manuscript he found in a library.

In his early historical fiction Flaubert tried a variety of solutions to the problem. *La Mort du duc de Guise* is narrated almost entirely through dialogue, sections of which have been faithfully copied from Chateaubriand's *Analyse raisonné de l'histoire de France* and marked 'historique'; *Dernière scène de la mort de Marguerite de Bourgogne*, *Deux mains sur une couronne* and *Chronique normande du Xe siècle* all begin by appealing to the reader to imagine a bygone age, very different from the present; and in all of them, as in *Un Secret de Philippe le Prudent*, the narrative is carried by the dialogue (another indication, perhaps, of Flaubert's early passion for historical theatre). But his use of inversion, periphrasis and accumulated epithets seems to be an imitation of neo-classical and early Romantic authors rather than a serious attempt to reproduce the flavour of medieval French. It is no different from the style he adopts in his non-historical pieces of 1835–6, and the high proportion of direct speech in his early *contes* diminishes markedly after the end of 1836 when he stopped writing historical tales.

By the time he came to work on his mature historical fiction he had arrived at a compromise solution. *L'Education sentimentale* of course posed no problem on this score, but in *Salammbô*, *La Légende de saint Julien l'hospitalier* and to a lesser extent *Hérodias*, direct speech is reduced to a minimum. When it does occur it is usually in short, simple sentences, the exotic strangeness of the language being conveyed by suggestion. We are not allowed to question the power of Salammbô's words when we are told that 'elle employait simultanément tous les idiomes des Barbares' (1, 698); we are invited to accept Schahabarim's mystical force without being given examples of it: 'Des mots étranges quelquefois lui échappaient, et qui passaient devant Salammbô comme de larges éclairs illuminant les abîmes' (1, 753).

The letters Flaubert wrote while he was working on *Salammbô* make it clear that he was acutely aware of this difficulty. The problem is finding 'la note *juste*', he wrote to Ernest Feydeau: 'pour être entendu, d'ailleurs, il faut faire une sorte de traduction permanente, et quel abîme cela creuse entre l'absolu et l'oeuvre!'[28] The Goncourt brothers record his complaining that he has to 'dilute the local colour like a sauce', and constantly to resort to periphrases because French lacks the precise word he needs: he is caught between giving an accurate but obscure and unreadable account necessitating pages of footnotes, or writing in conventional literary French and being banal.[29] But he resorts to none of the devices used by historical novelists writing earlier in the century. He avoids archaisms and fictitious chronicles, and instead uses unfamiliar and esoteric vocabulary to create a sense of exotic distance in space rather than in time. When we read that Mâtho 'avala du galbanum, du seseli et du venin de vipère' (I, 703), or that Hamilcar's treasure-house contains 'des glossopètres tombés de la lune, des tyanos, des diamants, des sandastrum' (I, 737), the impressive ring of these unintelligible phrases seems to guarantee authenticity, and any meaning they appear to convey derives from their context rather than from a precise referent. Sainte-Beuve complained about this use of language in *Salammbô* and suggested that Flaubert ought to have provided a glossary; Flaubert, however, defended his position strenuously, saying that he had gone to great trouble to avoid technical expressions. When he did have to use an unfamiliar word whose meaning was not clear from the context, he immediately followed it with an explanation. Sainte-Beuve was being 'souverainement injuste'. As he explained to Feydeau, a book will ring true if it is filled to overflowing with its subject. Its colour will then come naturally and inevitably, like a blossoming of the idea itself.[30]

On the whole, Flaubert's reaction to the historical novels of his century was one of dissatisfaction and impatience.[31] Normally a generous critic of other writers, he was never wholeheartedly complimentary about the way in which an author had combined history and fiction, and unfavourable criticisms or dismissive comments were frequent. His own attempts to arrive at a satisfactory solution seem to have derived relatively little from the deliberations of contemporary novelists. They owe more, as we shall see, to the discussions about methodology current among historians.

But it is not only through his correspondence or the comments recorded by his friends that we are able to assess Flaubert's views on the historical novels of his time. On several occasions we find characters in his own novels (normally reliable indicators of contemporary preoccupations) pondering the problems of historical fiction. The most naïve approach is that of Bouvard and Pécuchet. They begin with the assumption that a 'true' historical account is a rigorously scientific accumulation of facts, but as they read through an extensive and indiscriminate selection of historical works they are disconcerted by the contradictions and variations they find in these accounts and come to realise that a truly impartial and objective history is impossible. Unable to unravel the everyday events of their own household, they recognise the futility of attempting to reconstruct the life of the past by the simple accumulation of facts, and so abandon their project of writing the history of the Duc d'Angoulême. This failure brings them to realise that the bare facts of history must be filled out by psychology. They decide that history is defective without imagination, cast aside their history books, and send instead for historical novels. At first they are delighted by the vivid evocations of Scott and Dumas but their enthusiasm wanes as they tire of the stereotyped situations and recognise factual errors and anachronisms. So they pass on to other interests. Their experience is instructive, for it shows the naïvety of all demands for a purely factual, objective account of the distant past. Even more, it illustrates the dangers of fleshing out the bare bones of history with fictional narrative if the resultant work has the superficiality of those historical novels whose characters and plots can so easily be reduced to formulae. If Bouvard and Pécuchet tire of the genre, it is because of the endless repetitions of the same effects:

L'héroïne, ordinairement, vit à la campagne avec son père, et l'amoureux, un enfant volé, est rétabli dans ses droits et triomphe de ses rivaux. Il y a toujours un mendiant philosophe, un châtelain bourru, des jeunes filles pures, des valets facétieux et d'interminables dialogues, une pruderie bête, manque complet de profondeur (II, 243).

In contrast to the deliberately oversimplified and caricatural exposition of the problems of the relationship between history and fiction that we find in *Bouvard et Pécuchet*, the *Education sentimentale* of 1845 has Flaubert discussing these problems fully and seriously, and raising many of the then current questions about the nature of the historical novel as he describes the changes and developments in Jules's ideas. Through his wide reading of history, Jules gradually finds his old prejudices and preconceptions about past ages being undermined. He becomes acutely aware of the gross oversimplifications of most people's idea of any given period, and rejecting these, comes to recognise the infinite complexity of human nature as something which does not change with the passing centuries. He takes delight in discovering weaknesses in great men of the past or traces of greatness in those who are now remembered for their failings; in this he sees the workings of a levelling justice which moderates both pride and humiliation, restoring man to his natural stature. But the benefits of recognising one's own behaviour in the reassuring perspective of a broad historical context can come, Jules believes, only from the study of 'pure' history. Historical facts are diminished when ordered and manipulated by a writer: 'tout ce qui élimine raccourcit...tout ce qui choisit oublie...tout ce qui taille détruit'. Putting forward one of the commonest cases against the historical novel, Jules reverses the Aristotelian dictum and complains of the inadequacies of historical fiction compared with history itself:

Il vit que...les poèmes épiques étaient moins poétiques que l'histoire, et que, pour les romans historiques par exemple, c'était un grand tort de vouloir l'être; celui qui, selon une idée préconçue et pour la loger convenablement quelque part, médite le passé sous d'autres couleurs qu'il n'est venu, refait des faits et rajuste des hommes, arrive à une oeuvre fausse et sans vie; l'histoire est toujours là, qui l'écrase de la hauteur de ses proportions, de toute la plénitude de son ensemble. (1, 358)

Since this passage comes at a point where Jules's education is almost complete, there is good reason to take this criticism of the historical novel as a sincere statement of Flaubert's own attitude in 1845 to the mass of historical fiction already produced in France: Flaubert, like Jules, was as far removed from the *savant* who is interested only in recording facts as he was from the 'rhéteur qui ne songe qu'à embellir'.

His preoccupations with the ambiguous relationship between history and fiction is further reflected in the later *Education sentimentale*, where he shows Frédéric Moreau reading medieval and Renaissance historians and chroniclers – Froissart, Commynes, Pierre de l'Estoile and Brantôme – then feeling the urge to reproduce the vivid historical images in novel form. This is when he aspires to become a French Scott. It is not, however, as a novelist but as a historian that Frédéric later finds peace and satisfaction in writing about the past. Trying to immerse himself emotionally in historical figures and at the same time to achieve an objective account free from personal bias, he reaches a point where he is quite oblivious of his own self – perhaps the only way of avoiding personal suffering, comments Flaubert. For Frédéric, then, the shift from the study of history to the writing of historical fiction and from there to the writing of history is part of a process (as it had been for Jules) of coming to terms with his own problems and of trying to understand his own relationship to a changing world: it is a personal quest for an understanding of the present as much as the past.

It is perhaps this quality more than any other which singles out Flaubert's historical fiction from the rest. In spite of received opinion to the contrary, it is clear that Flaubert's interest in history and his desire to write historical fiction are not simply a turning to the past as an escape from the present. For him, history does not merely provide the novel with settings and subjects rich in excitement and intrigue, or give respectability to a fictional narrative. Rather, it offers a means of understanding the present. Recognising that it is impossible truly to recreate the past, he knows that a historical perspective is firmly rooted in the present, that in a sense a historical 'recreation' is an illusion created by the present – 'l'histoire n'est que la réflexion du présent sur le passé, et voilà pourquoi elle est toujours à refaire'.[32] His sensitivity to the relativity of historical truth and his awareness of its contribution to a fuller understanding of the present are the main factors which distinguish Flaubert's historical fiction. His approach owes less to the debate about the rôle of history in fiction than it does to shifts in the much more serious contemporary debate about the theory of historiography.

2 Flaubert and the historians

Knowledge of the past comes down to us through selected memories and fragmentary records, material sifted and processed by historians. Clearly we can never truly know what it was like to live in any period other than our own. The efforts of a historian to describe the past reflect the values and prejudices of his own day: the 'reality' he tries to seize is only one of many possible interpretations of those facts which, guided by the standards of his age, he has decided to select for scrutiny. Fascinated by the relativity of historical point of view, Flaubert read and compared an enormous number of histories from different periods. His comments on historians, his likes and dislikes, can tell us much about his own developing historical sense and help us to understand the particular attitude to the past which informs his historical fiction.

His interest in historical studies began when he was at school at the Collège Royal de Rouen. Here he was fortunate to have as history master the distinguished historian Adolphe Chéruel, a former pupil of Michelet and later Professor at the Ecole Normale Supérieure in Paris. Chéruel not only taught him at school (where he won several prizes in history) but also gave him private lessons every week, and the period spent under his tuition (1835–9) was probably crucial in stimulating Flaubert's interest and starting to form his critical faculties. The historian Fustel de Coulanges, himself a student of Chéruel in Paris, described how Chéruel inculcated into all his pupils the need for rigour, precision, and the fearless pursuit of truth; and undoubtedly Flaubert's own historical training was founded on similar principles.

Although it was the historians writing in the first half of the nineteenth century who had the most profound effect on Flaubert's views, his reading of Enlightenment historians also contributed to his historical awareness. The notes he took on Voltaire's philosophical world history, the *Essai sur les moeurs*, for example, already indicate his interest in comparative historiography.[1] There, we find him already comparing Voltaire's version of an incident with differing accounts by D'Aubigné and Michelet. For instance, he makes special mention of Voltaire's comment that honour was unknown in the

Middle Ages, and points out that Voltaire's attitude contrasts strikingly with modern historians' view of medieval chivalry.[2]

Another more important idea, which was to become a central theme in Flaubert's writing, was almost certainly derived from his reading of Montesquieu's *Considérations sur les causes de la grandeur des Romains et de leur décadence*. Montesquieu argues that there exist general patterns of human behaviour which always bring about similar consequences. The influence of Montesquieu's view of historical causality is particularly marked in the first *Education sentimentale*, where Flaubert writes of the way in which the same ideas and the same crises periodically return in a chain of cause and effect so evident that it seems to have been planned in advance: he likens the whole historical process to a constantly developing organism which appears to work to a regular pattern (1, 356). This tendency to see history as a series of repetitions, inevitable because human nature never changes, is an essential element in Flaubert's view of the historical process. The events of the present may be confusing and disturbing, but when he sees them in relation to past events they begin to make sense. In the upheaval of 1848 he could find a parallel with the Revolution of 1789, which in turn had its links with the Middle Ages;[3] later, he was to discern the same disturbing pattern in the Commune and wrote to George Sand that it is only our ignorance of history that makes us deplore our own period – 'On a toujours été comme ça.'[4]

In spite of his wide reading of Enlightenment historians and his great admiration for their clarity of style, Flaubert's main interest lay in the history written in his own century. The French Revolution had marked a decisive break with tradition in historical scholarship. Chateaubriand, looking back over the changes in French historiography in the preface to his *Etudes historiques* (1831), saw post-Revolutionary historical writing as falling into two distinct categories which he labelled 'l'histoire *fataliste*' and 'l'histoire *descriptive*'.[5] Although his groupings are somewhat oversimplified, Chateaubriand's division is an interesting and useful one. Not only does it indicate the two very different ways of approaching a study of the past adopted by the foremost historians of the day, but it also happens that one group sums up all that Flaubert was hostile to in historiography, whereas the ideas of the other coincide with his own feelings as to how one should write about the past.

The first of these groups, the so-called 'fatalist' school headed by François-Auguste Mignet and Adolphe Thiers,[6] aimed to explain rather than to narrate, and to present general truths at the expense of colourful details. For these writers the history of the state was of more interest than the history of the individual, and it was to be presented without personal bias. They tended to produce rather circumscribed political histories which concentrated on political institutions and parties, and ignored other questions: intellectual, economic and social.

These historians stressed the need for rigour and authenticity, the need to reproduce the 'vérité des faits eux-mêmes'.[7] This 'factual truth' was felt to reside in state documents and particularly in the personal papers of historical figures, although the historians' use of such documents was not always as extensive and rigorous as they claimed. They also demanded total objectivity. The historian was to stand back from the events to be discussed because only then could he give a true picture of them. Thiers, in the preface to his *Histoire de la révolution française* (1823–7), went so far as to dismiss all previous attempts to write an account of the revolutionary period on the grounds that the authors had been directly or indirectly involved in the events they described: such accounts were to be considered merely as memoirs and lacked the quality of true history.

This insistence on objectivity may in part have been a consequence of growing censorship which a writer could avoid by pretending not to pass any judgements. But it was also a genuine attempt to stand back from the recent and still controversial events of the Revolution and produce an unbiased account.

One of the most penetrating criticisms of the approach was made by Sainte-Beuve. He objected to the way in which these historians wrote with an air of omniscience and infallibility: 'M. Thiers sait tout, tranche tout, parle de tout.' And Guizot's work seemed to him to be history made to seem rational, where every accident becomes a necessity, like a chain from which no link can be removed. 'Guizot's history', he complained, 'is far too logical to be true.'[8]

There was little in all this to appeal to Flaubert. Guizot's *Essais* were, he said, 'capables de faire sécher sur pied tout l'Olympe', and his reaction to Thiers was one of the utmost contempt: 'Peut-on voir un plus triomphant imbécile, un croûtard plus abject, un plus étroniforme bourgeois!' he fulminated to George Sand. 'Non, rien ne peut donner l'idée du vomissement que m'inspire ce vieux melon diplomatique, arrondissant sa bêtise sur le fumier de la bourgeoisie!'[9] What so angered Flaubert was the ineptitude and naïve parochialism with which Thiers expatiated on every conceivable subject. Unsympathetic to Thiers's political ideas, intolerant of his complacency and chauvinism, Flaubert must surely (in view of Chéruel's teaching) also have been impatient with the careless inaccuracies of his historical accounts – Bouvard tells Pécuchet at their first meeting that he has 'noted errors in the works of Monsieur Thiers' (II, 203). Flaubert was equally impatient with the lack of rigour in Sismondi's history, and complained that the *Histoire des Français* was merely a synopsis of all the published material, and that no manuscript sources had been consulted.[10]

A further characteristic of this group of historians is their attempt to isolate the essential features of a period, to select from the mass of circumstantial detail certain constants which would typify the age. Sismondi said that the historian should concentrate on the central points and strip his account of anything which might dissipate the reader's attention;[11] and Guizot, writing more than thirty years later, still characterised his historical approach in terms of a series of high points to be isolated from surrounding detail.[12]

This approach contrasts sharply with Flaubert's. As he had shown in the first *Education sentimentale*, 'tout ce qui élimine raccourcit...tout ce qui choisit oublie...tout ce qui taille détruit' (I, 358): he believed that any attempt to isolate only the main facts of a period must lead to the propagation of *idées reçues*.[13]

The particular kind of objectivity advocated by these so-called 'fatalists' – the unimaginative description of external phenomena in a simple style – was also alien to Flaubert, whose correspondence repeatedly shows his own highly emotional and creative response to the past. He writes of wanting to 'connaître cette vieille antiquité dans la moelle', adding, 'je m'incrusterai dans la couleur de l'objectif et je m'absorberai en lui avec un amour sans partage'.[14] This response can have its own kind of objectivity, as both Jules and Frédéric are made to discover. Through a total absorption into the past the awareness of self is suspended and, with it, judgement and prejudices. This was the very different objectivity that Flaubert sought. It was to bring about this state of self-oblivion that he once advised Mlle Leroyer de Chantepie to identify herself with the lives of people living three thousand years earlier, and to enter into their dreams and sufferings. If she could manage to do this, he told her, 'vous sentirez s'élargir à la fois votre coeur et votre intelligence; une sympathie profonde et démesurée enveloppera, comme un manteau, tous les fantômes et tous les êtres. Tâchez donc de ne plus *vivre en vous*.'[15]

Finally, the very characteristic that caused Chateaubriand to group these historians together under the heading 'fatalistes' was unacceptable to Flaubert. Although Flaubert tended to see historical movements in terms of repeated patterns of behaviour, his view of historical change was organic rather than deterministic. His conception of history allowed for constant change and variation, whereas historians such as Sismondi and Mignet saw the historical process in terms of a strict causal necessity which it was their duty to lay bare as they plotted man's slow but inevitable progress towards the goal assigned to him by Providence.[16]

Clearly, then, Flaubert's reaction to these historians was hostile on every count. Their inaccuracies, their chauvinism, their fatalistic interpretation of history, their deliberately unimaginative and factual accounts and the dullness of their literary style all conflict with Flaubert's own approach to history. There is not one favourable reference to these writers in his work.

From as early as 1835 it was evident that Flaubert's sympathies lay much more with what Chateaubriand had called the 'descriptive' school. One of the primary concerns of this group of writers, headed by Barante and Michelet, was with making history come alive for the reader. Barante said that, unless a historian took more pleasure in description than analysis, the facts would simply wither under his pen. He likened the analytical historian to a cartographer whose map may tell us a great deal about the structure and shape of a region but can never convey the intimate knowledge of a place that comes only from visiting it. The descriptive historian alone is able to paint this fuller picture of the past in all its richness and colour. And, to give his writings this imaginative and dynamic quality, Barante looked towards the historical novel.[17]

It was by no means unknown for historians to turn to the techniques of fiction in order to enliven their accounts. Many of the great *encyclopédistes* – Montesquieu, Voltaire, Diderot, Rousseau, Duclos – had written novels as well as history, and Voltaire had insisted that histories needed to be given the structure of a drama with an exposition, a climax and a dénouement, to prevent them from becoming dry and boring.[18] The Marquis de Sade, writing as a historian rather than novelist, had prefaced his *Histoire secrète d'Isabelle de Bavière* (begun in 1764) with an interesting discussion of the mutual borrowings to be made between history and fiction, although he had warned that, if historians used too many of the novelist's enlivening devices, their histories would lose in dignity.

But the systematic and unashamed borrowing of the techniques of the novel came only after Scott's influence had been felt in France. Augustin Thierry was one of many historians to acknowledge a debt to Scott, whom he called 'the greatest master of all time when it comes to historical divining'.[19] Elsewhere, Thierry said that he had decided to become a professional historian after reading Chateaubriand's *Martyrs*.[20] Barante, too was frank in his admiration for the new historical novel. Since it was history, he said, that had provided these novels with much of their charm, the historian ought to exploit the attractive qualities of his subject by ensuring that his narrative was full, lively and colourful. (Flaubert certainly felt that Barante succeeded in this, and referred to his *Histoire des ducs de Bourgogne* as a masterpiece of history and literature.)[21] Even Flaubert's old friend Ernest Feydeau, who had sharp criticisms to make of the historical novel genre, recognised that historical writing had much to gain by adopting the 'wit, verve and colour of the novel'.[22] And although some writers, Chateaubriand among them, were worried that the historical novel's vivid fictional recreations might overshadow the writing of serious history, most of these 'descriptive' historians recognised that there was room for generous interchange between history and fiction. While historians were producing material which was intrinsically interesting and full of action and drama, their insistence on explaining, on outlining patterns of development, and on showing cause and effect had tended to drain their writing of much of its dramatic value. On the other hand, novelists with devices for creating suspense and capturing the reader's imagination welcomed historical settings and subjects which offered excitement, vigour and intrigue.

Whereas Flaubert was appalled by the dullness of the 'fatalists', the poetic vividness of the 'descriptive' historians delighted him. In a letter to Michelet in 1861 he recalled how he had read many of Michelet's works at school and been so moved by their brilliance and vitality that he had learnt many of their pages by heart: 'ce n'étaient pas des livres pour moi, mais tout un monde'.[23]

Chateaubriand's label, 'école descriptive', does not do justice to the achievements of men like Michelet, Barante, Quinet, Cousin, and Thierry, who were concerned with much more than describing historical events in a simple, vivid style. Rejecting the fatalistic approach to history, they contended that moral judgements should be applied both to present social action and to past history. Michelet made no pretence of impartiality. He demanded a strong emotional involvement with the subject; only then, he believed, could the historian penetrate to the heart of the matter and achieve his '*résurrection de la vie intégrale*, non pas dans ses surfaces, mais dans ses organismes intérieurs et profonds'.[24]

This deeply emotional response to the past was clearly shared by Flaubert. During his journey to Italy in 1845 he wrote to Alfred Le Poittevin: 'Je porte l'amour de l'antiquité dans mes entrailles, je suis touché jusqu'au plus profond de mon être quand je songe aux carènes romaines qui fendaient les vagues', and his sense of affinity with certain historical figures even led him to affect a belief in metempsychosis – he said that he was sure that he had once lived in the Rome of Nero or Caesar.[25] Indeed, his visit to Carthage after starting to write *Salammbô* was as much intended to create an emotional rapport with his subject as to provide specific details of fact.

But Flaubert was critical of the way in which most of these historians passed judgement on the incidents they recounted. Barante alone claimed to let events speak for themselves and said that if the historian was imaginatively and emotionally steeped in his subject, then moral judgements were unnecessary: 'il n'y a rien de si impartial que l'imagination; elle n'a nul besoin de conclure',[26] he wrote, advocating that same kind of objectivity which Flaubert was later to propose to Mlle Leroyer de Chantepie. Just as Flaubert bemoaned the tendency of historical novelists to preach a moral to their readers, so he deplored the way in which historians adopted moral stances. 'Quand est-ce donc que l'on fera de l'histoire comme on doit faire du roman, sans amour ni haine d'aucun des person-nages?' he wrote to Louise Colet in 1852. 'Quand est-ce qu'on écrira les faits au point de vue d'une *blague supérieure*, c'est à dire comme le bon Dieu les voit, d'en haut?'[27]

Nevertheless he did admire the rigorous way in which the best of these historians collected their material. Barante tried to give his accounts an authentic flavour by inserting passages from official documents and contemporary chronicles, but made no attempt to verify the chroniclers' version. Michelet, however, as director of history at the Archives Nationales, had access to unpublished documents which he used, together with (for his *Histoire romaine*) information gleaned from medals, inscriptions, and classical writers. But the newly available mass of documentary evidence was not enough in itself: a '*résurrection de la vie intégrale*' also required first-hand experience. Victor Cousin, who had taught Flaubert's philosophy master, Mallet, as well as Michelet and Quinet, said in his famous lectures of 1828 that the historian must study the country about which he is writing, since the spirit of an age reveals itself not only through its people but also leaves its mark on the physical surroundings.[28] The feeling that a close knowledge of a country was necessary in order to come to a better understanding of its people was of course not new. Montesquieu and Madame de Staël were among those who had shown how environmental factors contributed to a nation's literary output, and Herder (whose ideas Cousin was one of the first to popularise in France) had devoted several chapters of his *Ideen zur Philosophie der Geschichte der Menschheit* (1784–91) to a discussion of the influence of the environment on national genius. Quinet, who translated Herder's *Philosophie* in 1827, adopted this method for his own history of the Italian revolutions: he went first to Italy to be in direct contact with 'la vie réelle du Moyen Age'; he studied documents and chronicles; and only then did he feel ready to begin writing.

The combination of scientific rigour and imaginative insight in these historians' method appealed strongly to Flaubert. The preparations for his own historical writing were based on a similar approach that combined personal memories and travel notes with painstaking research. Although he was always prepared to allow historical novelists to distort the facts as long as he felt that the overall colour of the period was truthfully conveyed, he knew that this 'truth' could only be the result of careful and rigorous documentation. Only then could liberties be taken with the details: as Zola recalled many years later, 'Lorsque Flaubert, après de longs mois d'enragée poursuite, avait enfin réuni tous les documents d'une oeuvre, il n'avait plus pour eux qu'un grand mépris'.[29]

Choice of subject matter was perhaps the most significant difference between the 'fatalist' and 'descriptive' historians. Whereas the fatalists chose to write almost exclusively about France, and to do so from a deliberately limited viewpoint which concentrated on political institutions, the interests of the 'école descriptive' were far more wide-ranging. They tried to include a broad sweep of background information in order to build up a composite picture which, in its complexity, would give a true and profound record of the life of the times. This concern with integral history is largely attributable to the influence of Giambattista Vico, whose *Scienza nuova* (1752) was first translated into French by Michelet in 1827. It was through Michelet's translation that Flaubert came into contact with Vico's work, which he read thoroughly, taking copious notes. One of Vico's most important contributions to historiography was the concept of a Volksgeist, a guiding spirit of the people which pervades all cultural manifestations – language, law, art, folklore, mythology. The historian, he argues, should take all these aspects of life into account in order to isolate general, universal truths.[30] Although Vico was criticised by Barante for drawing general laws from history and for presenting them as predetermined and inevitable, this deterministic side was largely ignored by Michelet – indeed, in the preface to his *Histoire de France* he used Vico's own words in italics to emphasise man's freedom to change and control his development: 'La France a fait la France...Elle est fille de sa liberté. Dans le progrès humain, la part essentielle est à la force vive, qu'on appelle homme. *L'homme est son propre Prométhée.*'[31] Vico's contention that all aspects of a culture must be used to throw light on a historical period was quickly seized on by the 'descriptive' historians and became one of the foremost characteristics of historical writing in the mid nineteenth century. Although Bouvard and Pécuchet had difficulty in understanding the concept ('Comment admettre que des fables soient plus vraies que les vérités des historiens?' asks a confused Bouvard as he struggles with the *Scienza nuova*, II, 240), Flaubert obviously shared the widespread admiration for Vico's approach. His preparations for *Salammbô* bear witness to Vico's influence as he studied the language, mythology, legal system, art and customs of Carthage in addition to its political and military history.

Vico's other main contribution was to influence the way in which nineteenth-century historians viewed the transference of power, a subject that was of particular interest to them in their efforts to understand the forces behind the collapse of the Ancien Régime. Vico's theory was a cyclical one: he saw power ebbing and flowing as one nation climbed to supremacy and then fell into a gradual decline during which another people rose to supremacy. A broadly similar view was developed by Herder, who described the way in which the hegemony of culture passes on from one world-centre to another while individual states flourish and die.

Augustin Thierry was one of the most important of the many historians who assimilated these ideas and used them in an attempt to analyse past revolutions and invasions. His approach was to have a profound influence on Flaubert. Thierry was convinced that the extraordinary course of events in France since the end of the Ancien Régime had put historians in a unique position to understand earlier revolutions. He recognised that the current preoccupation with the study of revolutions and invasions was an attempt to lay a definitive

foundation for a national history; however, he complained that all
the existing analyses of changes in power had one fault in common –
all concentrated on the conquerors and neglected the defeated side.
Unlike his predecessors, Thierry decided to pay equal attention to
victors and vanquished alike. His conclusion was that conquered
peoples, integrated over the years into the victorious nation, come
to form the lowest echelons in that nation's class structure, while the
conquerors survive as a privileged aristocracy.[32]

This somewhat simplistic explanation of the class struggle in terms
of old racial antagonisms met with enthusiastic acclaim and was to
play an important part in forming people's ideas about social
hierarchy and social change. Flaubert was particularly impressed by
Thierry's work and it is significant that when Bouvard and Pécuchet
ask Dumouchel for the best history of France, it is Thierry's *Lettres
sur l'histoire de France* which is sent to them (II, 238). There were two
main aspects of Thierry's view of history which were of special
interest to Flaubert. One was his theory about the racial element in
social structures: we shall meet this theory again in *Salammbô*, where
Flaubert clearly suggests that the class system of Carthage has formed
along the same lines as the old racial hierarchy. The other was
Thierry's view of the way in which power is transferred as nations
progress towards civilisation or decline into decadence and barbarism.
In his *Récits des temps mérovingiens* this process is symbolised by the
changes taking place in three individuals: 'Frédégonde, l'idéal de la
barbarité élémentaire, sans conscience du bien et du mal; Hilpérick,
l'homme de race barbare qui prend les goûts de la civilisation, et se
polit à l'extérieur sans que le réforme aille plus avant; Mummolus,
l'homme civilisé qui se fait barbare et se déprave à plaisir pour être
de son temps.'[33] For Flaubert, these strange oppositions between
barbarism and civilisation were a constant source of speculation.
Again and again his writing touches on the problem as he peels back
man's thin veneer of civilisation to reveal the grossness and cruelty
beneath. In *Salammbô*, of course, the initial differences between the
apparently highly civilised Carthaginians and the barbaric mercenaries are soon shown to be illusory; in his novels of contemporary
society the point is made less explicitly. The notebook he started in
1859, however, shows him planning another contemporary novel
which was to explore the problem openly.

Le grand roman social à écrire (maintenant que les rangs et les castes sont
perdus) doit représenter la lutte ou plutôt la Fusion de la Barbarie et de la
Civilisation...Opposition de moeurs, de paysages et de caractères, tout y

serait. – & le héros principal devrait être un Barbare qui se civilise près d'un civilisé qui se barbarise.[34]

The novel was never written, but the concept of a person continually aspiring to a condition other than his own – whether it be 'un civilisé qui se barbarise', Emma Bovary with her unfulfilled daydreams, saint Antoine struggling to reject the baser human impulses, or Bouvard and Pécuchet restlessly trying to change their lives – is a recurrent theme in Flaubert's work. He often wrote of the aspiration for change as a necessary and healthy one, and believed that there was a need for periodic violent upheavals in order to shake a complacent society out of its lethargy, regardless of whether the crisis brought any significant change. It is not surprising, then, that he should have looked to history for accounts of the changes that man had tried to effect, while at the same time remaining sensitive to those things which can never be altered, those elements of the past which live on in the present.

Through his reading of such a wide variety of history Flaubert's own historical sense developed and his tastes became evident. Hating the dispassionate complacency, the lack of rigour, and the deterministic approach of the 'fatalists', his greatest admiration was for the historians of the 'descriptive' school. In them he found two important qualities: on the one hand, a vivid and imaginative evocation of the past; on the other, a thorough and accurate presentation of carefully documented facts. Theirs was the manner he was to adopt for his historical writing. So, although he wrote to Mlle Leroyer de Chantepie of the need for a deeply emotional and imaginative approach to the past, he could also describe the 'sens historique' to her in uncompromisingly scientific terms which point forward to Zola and the naturalists: 'On va se mettre à étudier les idées comme des faits, et à disséquer les croyances comme des organismes'.[35] This dual approach to historiography is reflected in his fiction.

3 The genesis and development of 'Salammbô'

Salammbô took more than five years to write. It is worth recalling the stages of its preparation and composition, for they provide a vivid illustration of Flaubert's individual approach to historical fiction. They also help to demolish the myth that *Salammbô* is scrupulously faithful to the available documentary information about Carthage. Flaubert himself did much to perpetuate this myth: although admitting to one or two minor liberties in his famous reply to Sainte-Beuve, he strenuously countered Frœhner's criticisms of factual errors and compiled an elaborate dossier of his sources to add substance to his claims.[1] This dossier, which was compiled after the publication of *Salammbô*, gives detailed evidence of the encyclopaedic research undertaken by Flaubert. But, of course, it cannot begin to answer the most important questions: why, after going to great lengths to collect documentation for his subject, was he so strangely selective in deciding which details to use? What were his principles of selection? And how did he achieve his unique blend of fact and imagination? The answers will begin to emerge as we look at the way in which *Salammbô* was put together.

The first reference to *Salammbô* in the published correspondence comes in a letter dated 18 March 1857, in which Flaubert tells Mlle Leroyer de Chantepie of his intention to write a novel set in the third century B.C.[2] By then he had already set about collecting material for the book – that same week he had received replies from Jean Clogenson and Frédéric Baudry giving him information he had requested about the population, topography and flora of Carthage, and about the material available in the Rouen Library.[3] But although he was just beginning seriously to collect information about Carthage in March 1857, we know that for many years before this Flaubert had been amassing a wealth of details – both real and imaginary – about the Orient.

It was a subject which had fascinated him from his early youth. In *Rage et impuissance* (1838), for example, he had described M. Ohmlin's opiate dreams of a fantasy Orient, voluptuous and illusory – an amalgam of dark-eyed beauties and exotic perfumes, flowers and jewels, pagodas and gilded minarets under blue skies and a blazing sun. This was the chimerical, timeless Orient of popular fantasy, the Orient of the *Mille et une nuits* and the *Mille et un jours* which had impressed itself on the imagination of the French Romantics, many of whom had never actually visited the countries they described with such enthusiasm. As Hugo wrote in the first preface to his *Orientales*: 'On s'occupe beaucoup plus de l'Orient qu'on ne l'a jamais fait. Les études orientales n'ont jamais été poussées si avant...l'Orient, soit comme image, soit comme pensée, est devenu...une sorte de préoccupation générale.'[4]

Although serious studies had been undertaken, oriental manuscripts translated, and research on oriental religions and philosophies carried so far that a new Renaissance began to be talked of, the Orient of the Romantic imagination was still a very nebulous and ungeographical concept. For some writers it meant the Arab countries; for others it was Turkey; and while many imagined it stretching out across Africa and India to Japan, there were also those who felt its presence closer to home in Spain and even Gibraltar. Flaubert then was steeped in the exotic and picturesque imagery of an imaginary Orient, and it is this Orient which figures in his early works and which captures the imagination of Jules in the *Education sentimentale* of 1845.

It was about this time that Flaubert started to become seriously interested in the religions and history of the East. He began a systematic programme of reading which reached its peak between September 1845 and October 1846,[5] and, in fact, since the beginning of 1845 he had been thinking of writing a 'conte oriental'. He abandoned this idea, however, in its early stages in order to work on *La Tentation de saint Antoine*, which occupied him right up to the moment he left for his long-anticipated travels in the Orient. So although Flaubert did not begin to gather material specifically for *Salammbô* until 1857, he already had a wealth of fantasy pictures of the Orient, personal travel memories, and factual information from serious reading on which to draw.

By the end of March 1857 Flaubert's research was seriously under way. He made the most of his remaining few weeks in Paris, spending all day reading and taking notes in the library and continuing working at home late into the night. The following month he wrote to Feydeau, asking him to send articles on Eschmoun and Announah from the *Revue archéologique*, and mentioning that his current reading was Aristotle, Procopius and a long poem by Corippus on the Numidian war.[6] At the beginning of May he was still 'perdu dans

[ses] bouquins', reading works on archaeology as well as the 400-page memoir on cypresses, to gather details for his description of the temple courtyard.[7] That month he also read Silius Italicus and very much more, for by the end of May he was complaining, 'j'ai une indigestion de bouquins. Je rote l'in-folio.' Since March, he said, he had already taken notes from fifty-three different works; he was studying the art of war and was satisfied that he could do something new with what he called the 'tourlourou antique';[8] he was working like a Trojan, reading book after book, taking reams of notes.[9] His reading in June included Isidorus, Selden and Braunius, and he claimed to have read and taken notes from eighteen volumes of the Cahen Bible (including the commentaries) in the space of a fortnight.[10] He was making progress: when he received the volume of *L'Encyclopédie catholique* he had asked Crépet for, he found that it could tell him nothing he did not already know.[11] By the beginning of August he had moved on to Pliny, Athenaeus, Plutarch, Xenophon, and five or six memoirs of the Académie des Inscriptions. And then, on 1 September, he began to write.

The difficulties he encountered during the composition of *Salammbô* go a long way towards explaining the difference between this and previous historical novels. The letters he wrote at the time leave a record of his problems and anxieties, they indicate those aspects of his work which most dissatisfied him, and they show the difficulties which continued to trouble him throughout the period of composition. And, as often as not, they show him coming to terms with these problems by adopting the approach of the historians he most admired.

During the earliest planning stages Flaubert's misgivings were for the most part imprecise fears and doubts as to the wisdom of undertaking such an enormous task. He writes of his anguish, of 'Carthage qui [le] tracasse énormément'; it is 'une sale besogne' and the subject itself frightens him 'par son vuide'.[12] He wrote at length about his apprehensions to Louis de Cormenin, and described the painful process of starting to write in hallucinatory terms: 'Un encrier pour beaucoup ne contient que quelques gouttes d'un liquide noir. Mais pour d'autres, c'est un océan, et moi je m'y noie. J'ai le vertige du papier blanc, et l'amas de mes plumes taillées sur ma table me semble parfois un buisson de formidables épines. J'ai déjà bien saigné sur ces petites broussailles-là.'[13] By April of the following year these problems had reached crisis-point. Remembering, perhaps, the recommendations of historians like Cousin and Quinet, Flaubert abandoned everything and set off for Carthage to see for himself the few remaining ruins of the civilisation he was struggling to evoke. The visit had the desired effect. Steeped in the sights and sounds of the Orient, fascinated by the people he met and by the archaeological remains of the area, he felt on his return that he could now write about Carthage with truth and conviction. What little he had already written was discarded. '*Carthage* est complètement à refaire, ou plutôt à faire', he told Feydeau, '*Je démolis tout. C'était absurde! impossible! faux!*'[14]

One of the problems which had been troubling Flaubert and which the Tunisian trip helped to solve was the handling of his characters' psychology. The first indication of trouble had come in April 1857 when he wrote that it was 'le fonds, je veux dire la partie psychologique', that was causing him most difficulty; at the end of May he reported that 'la psychologie se cuit tout doucement, mais c'est une lourde machine à monter'; by the end of June the problem had still not resolved itself and Flaubert was beginning to feel that he had embarked on an interminable task of which he was already weary.[15] It would seem that at this early stage, Flaubert was still too close to the techniques of *Madame Bovary*; towards the end of July, however, he realised that it was a mistake to model *Salammbô* on the psychological novel – instead, he must stand back from his characters and present them in a 'style large et enlevé'.[16] What he was seeking now was that imaginative objectivity which, as both Jules and Frédéric had to discover, can come only when the author is totally immersed in his subject.

Although he realised that his method ran the risk of ending in disastrous sentimental extravagance, he longed to be truly moved by the passions of his Carthaginian characters and thereby achieve impartiality: 'Je crois donc qu'il ne faut *rien aimer*, c'est-à-dire qu'il faut planer impartialement au-dessus de tous les objectifs.'[17] Even with the plans for the novel complete, the psychological element continued to give trouble, and in December, when he was well into his first chapter, he despaired of ever portraying his characters convincingly. As he told Mlle Leroyer de Chantepie, it was his inability to share imaginatively in the experience of his characters that was preventing him from giving an accurate account of the period:

Je *sens* que je suis dans le faux...et que mes personnages n'ont pas dû parler comme cela. Ce n'est pas une petite ambition que de vouloir entrer dans le coeur des hommes, quand ces hommes vivaient il y a plus de deux mille ans et dans une civilisation qui n'a rien d'analogue avec la nôtre. J'entrevois la vérité, mais elle ne me pénètre pas, l'émotion me manque...c'est que je ne palpite pas du sentiment de mes héros, voilà.[18]

But this, written several months before his trip to Tunis, was the last reference to this particular problem. On his return he had not only come to terms with the fact that his characters could not be portrayed with the same realistic complexity as Emma and Charles Bovary had been; he was also overwhelmed by his Carthaginian experience, and, absorbed in his subject, felt confident that he could now successfully create the characters.

There were, however, other problems. The one which preoccupied him longest and most consistently once he began to write was the question of language and style. Problems which he had encountered during the preliminary planning and research period – the fear, for example, of becoming bogged down in topographical detail or of being proved wrong in the minutiae of his resurrection of the past – all faded before his preoccupation with linguistic and stylistic problems. In the very first extant letter written after he began work on chapter 1, he wrote, 'il me semble que je tourne à la tragédie et que j'écris dans un style académique déplorable'. Two months later, he was again deploring the difficulty of striking the right note when describing a period from a distance of two thousand years: 'Pour être entendu, d'ailleurs, il faut faire une sorte de traduction permanente, et quel abîme cela creuse entre l'absolu et l'oeuvre.'[19] On his return from Tunis there was a brief moment of confidence when he believed that he had found the 'ton juste', but his optimism was short-lived. How could he be sure of keeping a middle path between 'la boursouflure et le réel'? Never, he said, had anyone undertaken a work which presented such problems of style. 'A chaque ligne, à chaque mot, la langue me manque et l'insuffisance du vocabulaire est telle, que je suis forcé à changer les détails très souvent.'[20]

He discussed this problem with the Goncourt brothers, and this was when they noted in their Journal that Flaubert was having to use periphrases, and in doing so dilute the effect 'comme une sauce'. The following July Flaubert wrote to them again about the same problem – if the novel were to ring true, it would have to be full of obscure foreign words and annotations; if, on the other hand, he were to write in conventional French, the result would be banal. '"Problème!" comme dirait le père Hugo.' There was also the danger of falling into the style of other writers – Fénelon, Chateaubriand, Delille, and 'tous les écrivains *nobles'* who have ever written an imitation of a Homeric battle scene.[21]

Flaubert was gradually becoming increasingly concerned about the reception his novel would have when it came to be published. The public would find it infuriating and boring – as early as November 1857 he was writing 'Comme ça embêtera le public! j'en tremble d'avance, car il a quelquefois raison de s'embêter', but on the whole he was able to shrug off this fear during the first stages of composition. 'Ce que j'entreprends est insensé et n'aura aucun succès dans le public. N'importe! il faut écrire pour soi, avant tout. C'est la seule chance de faire beau.'[22]

As the chapters advanced, however, worries about the novel's reception became more insistent, and in a letter of July 1860 he confided to Amélie Bosquet just how disturbed he was at the thought of being misunderstood and undervalued. His novel would bore the reader to death, he felt, and 'si un roman est aussi embêtant qu'un bouquin scientifique, bonsoir, il n'y a plus d'Art'. His reading public would be irritated by it, and therefore unsympathetic; defects abounded, and although a few discerning readers might appreciate the beauties of *Salammbô*, Flaubert felt that his original prediction would be justified: 'Mon bouquin ne fera pas grand effet.'[23] Wearied by forebodings of the stupid comments his book would attract, as the end approached he drew near to despair. '*Je n'en peux plus!*' It was repetitious, boring, even the plan now seemed faulty but it was too late to do anything about that. Flaubert was physically exhausted, and the Goncourt brothers feared for his sanity.[24] But the final corrections were made to the manuscript at the beginning of July 1862, and, in a spirit of resignation rather than relief, Flaubert wrote to Jules Duplan, 'Je me résigne à regarder comme fini un travail interminable. Je viens de relire pour la huitième fois ma copie en y trouvant des taches nouvelles que je corrigerai sur les épreuves. Donc maintenant je n'ai plus rien à faire.'[25]

Most of the *Salammbô* manuscripts are now in the Bibliothèque Nationale, Paris. The notes and rough drafts, Flaubert's final autograph version and the copyist's manuscript for the printer form five hefty volumes, and in June 1980 the library also acquired a collection of Flaubert's notes on books he read in preparation for his Carthaginian novel.[26] In the same year, seven additional *Salammbô* folios came to light in the Bibliothèque Municipale, Rouen.[27] That manuscripts are continuing to turn up in this way must be a warning to scholars to be wary of drawing conclusions based on incomplete material (part of this book has had to be revised at the last moment to take the Rouen manuscripts into account), and a reminder that we cannot be sure that the sixty folios of plans and early notes in the Bibliothèque Nationale, together with the two scenarios included in the Rouen papers, constitute all the plans for the novel. Nor can we be at all certain of the order in which the plans were composed. And the issue is further confused by a librarian's note to the effect that the volume of papers was dropped before being numbered and that the subsequent pagination is therefore somewhat arbitrary. Nevertheless, these folios are invaluable in showing how this highly complex novel was gradually constructed. In particular, they throw light on Flaubert's attitude to his historical material and show to what extent he accepted or adapted the testimony of his most important source, Polybius' *Histoire*.

The plans may be divided into three categories. First, the folios containing a plan of the novel from beginning to end; second, the folios containing expanded notes on a shorter section of the novel; and last, the folios containing scattered notes not referring to any one part of the plot. The folios which fall into the first and perhaps most interesting category are in BN Mss. n. a. fr. 23.662 (unless otherwise stated, all folio references are to this volume) and Rouen Mss. g322. They can be placed in chronological order without much difficulty, as changes in the characters' names and in the way they are spelled indicate the probable sequence. Thus Salammbô is originally called Pyra or Pyrra (or Pyrha, Pyrrha and even Phyrrra) before becoming Hanna and finally Sallambô, Sallambo or Sallammbô, whereas Mâtho starts out as Mathos (the Polybian spelling) in folio 181 and thereafter appears as Matho, Mathô and Mâtho: the position or existence of his circumflex remains undecided until a much later stage of the manuscripts. In folio 181 Giscon is five times 'Gescon' (again, the Polybian spelling) and 'Giscon' only once, but in the subsequent scenarios he always appears under his definitive name. (In my discussion of the scenarios, I follow Flaubert's spelling of the characters' names as they appear in each folio.) In view of these changes it would seem that the scenarios were written in the order 181, g322A*, 219–20, 238, 182, 180 and g322B*.

Folios marked with an asterisk are published for the first time in the appendix. In transcribing the manuscripts I have used obliques (/.../) to indicate Flaubert's interlinear additions, and pointed brackets (⟨...⟩) to indicate his deletions.

(1) Folio 181

When we examine the seven plans which cover the plot in its entirety, we see immediately that the outline of the novel changed rapidly in the few months between Flaubert's first mention of his intentions and the start of the novel proper. Unlike the first scenario of *Madame Bovary*, which had concentrated on thumbnail sketches of characters, their backgrounds, their appearance, folio 181 of *Salammbô* sees Flaubert working to fit together the events of his narrative. This is not altogether surprising, since a novel dealing with the whole span of the Mercenary War was obviously to be more eventful than an account of the triviality of Emma Bovary's existence in a small provincial town. Nevertheless, the incidents related in folio 181 bear little direct relation to the course of the war as recounted by Polybius and the other historians consulted by Flaubert, and the implication is that he already had a firm idea of the historical background against which the novel was to be set. The first few lines serve simply as an *aide-mémoire* to be extended later into a picture of the social and political background:

Etat politique (deux partis distincts) et résumé de Carthage au retour des mercenaires.
Ce qu'ils étaient – effet /vertigineuse/ de Carthage sur eux.
Comment ils s'y conduisent. Ils sont logés autour de la ville – et dans les jardins, dans les arrière-cours des riches.

At this point the scenario turns away from recorded history to the fictional plot surrounding Mathos and Pyra, prototype of Salammbô, and daughter of a rich, unnamed senator. The fictional side now becomes the guiding line for the historical events which are not detailed here, but which one must assume to have been already considered by Flaubert:

tout se démoralise dans Carthage, à mesure que la /description de la/ maison du sénateur se relâche.

The absence of the fictitious senator and the behaviour of Mathos and Pyra are seen to be in some measure responsible for the growing insubordination of the mercenaries. Political events impinge again only after the peplos has been stolen, when, in a scene somewhat reminiscent of the end of Act II of Hugo's *Hernani*, Mathos and Pyra are forced to part as the Carthaginians expel the mercenaries from the city. Here again, fictional demands dictate to fact: it is necessary that Mathos should have some personal motive for hating Gescon, and so Flaubert invents one:

Les merc. sont forcés de partir par un stratagème quelconque de Gescon (dont on aura parlé, qui leur aura fait des représentations) – aussi de là plus tard la haine personnelle de Mathos contre Gescon.

The nature of Gescon's stratagem has not been decided on, but its very existence is determined by psychological necessity. (This is more like the technique of the first *Madame Bovary* scenario where Flaubert was clearly less concerned with events in themselves than with the way in which they were brought about by the interaction of the characters.)

After the mercenaries' departure the *séance de nuit* is sketched in, with the note 'mesures à prendre – disputes'. At this stage Hamilcar and Pyra's father are two separate people, the senator belonging to the moderates whereas Hamilcar is violently hostile to the mercenaries. But again, action is subservient to character, and the *séance* ends with personal invective rather than political argument. Flaubert is primarily concerned here with working out personal relationships, the interplay of characters, and above all, their motivation. Mathos's reasons for stealing the veil, for hating Gescon, the mercenaries' reasons for leaving the city, Hamilcar's reasons for taking command and entering the war, and Spendius's reasons for detesting Gescon – are all suggested in this first scenario. They form essential pivots for the action, although they are modified as the novel develops.

Twice in this scenario the mercenaries' prostitutes are mentioned – first, when they leave Carthage with the soldiers; and again, when the mercenaries send them away and they return to the city. An explanatory note says, 'ils chassent les femmes du camp par regret des bourgeoises de Carthage'. In each case, the note is closely linked to a reference to Pyra. It is she who watches the prostitutes leave Carthage, and later, when they are expelled from the camp, Mathos dreams of her. In this scenario she appears as little more than a sexual symbol – she is the reason why Mathos wants to conquer Carthage; she is 'ennivrée du feu mystico-hystérique d'Astarté', the goddess of love and fertility; this is, as yet, her only rôle. The character's religious implications are otherwise totally absent: the goddess Astarté is merely the source of Pyra's sexuality and none of the more complex mytho-religious forces have yet appeared in the plan. Even the opening words. 'Etat politique (deux partis distincts)', suggest that Carthage revolves around two *political* factions rather than a dual religion.

From the point where Spendius conceives his plan to enter Carthage and steal the veil, the scenario sketches in subsequent events with great rapidity. Mathos fails to find the peplos (a marginal note suggests that Gescon may have had a hand in restoring it to a temple, thus providing yet another motive for Mathos's hostility towards him). Pyra refuses to follow him. The mercenaries' violence becomes uncontrollable – 'la foule déborde les héros qui la conduisent – elle est ivre de sang versé'. Then follow the sacrifice to Moloch, the siege of Carthage (only at this stage does Hamilcar take command, a step which Flaubert is careful to motivate: a stone flung from a catapult lands in the grounds of his palace and constitutes a personal insult), the cannibalism of the mercenaries, the massacre, the crucifixion of Spendius and torture of Mathos. And finally, 'repas patricien – geste de Pyra'. There has been no mention of the elaborate tactical manoeuvres, of the rivalry between Hamilcar and Hannon, or of Hamilcar's murdering the deputation of mercenary leaders. All these points are contained in Polybius, and Flaubert presumably always intended to use them. At this stage of composition, however, he is primarily concerned with setting down the outlines of the creative, episodic part of his novel, and even the characterisation is at a minimum, with only a brief marginal note which runs:

Gescon – modéré, sage.
Hamilcar gd homme
le père bourgeois furieux, /sanguinolent/
Mathos le vrai homme
Spendius, ⟨pâle⟩ avisé et féroce.

A clear-cut structural duality runs through this scenario. Politics are schematised into 'deux partis distincts'; a neat distinction is made between the conditions of the mercenaries in Carthage and in their desert camps: 'inquiets – mélancholie – quelle différence d'avec la veille!'; and contrasts are frequently drawn between pairs of characters: 'Mathos & Spendius – leurs caractères différents'; 'amour de Mathos & de Pyra – grâce de la force, terreur de la grâce'. At one stage, Mathos is set against Gescon by the invention of a motive to account for his antagonism: 'aussi de là plus tard la haine personnelle de Mathos contre Gescon'; later, it is Spendius who is opposed to him: 'Giscon peut être mêlé à cette restitution pr. que ⟨M⟩ Sp. l'exècre', while the 'rapports du père & de la fille' remain to be elaborated. The tendency towards a bi-partite structure, already emerging clearly from this early manuscript, is akin to what Thibaudet saw as

Flaubert's 'vision binoculaire', a pattern which also runs through the early plans for *L'Education sentimentale*.[28]

There are interesting comparisons to be made, too, between this scenario and the first known sketch for *Madame Bovary*. Surprisingly, the satire of a certain type of bourgeoisie which was later to become one of the main themes of *Madame Bovary* is totally missing from the first plan. The same is true of this first *Salammbô* scenario: the satire will come later. However, something of what is in store is hinted at in the unexpected references to the Carthaginian bourgeoisie: '/ils chassent les femmes du camp par regret des ⟨fem⟩ bourgeoises de Carthage/'; 'bassesses des bourgeois'; and finally the 'père bourgeois furieux /sanguinolent/'. Although the word *bourgeois* is not entirely out of place here, given its original meaning 'citizen of a borough', it does nonetheless strike one as an anachronism. None of Flaubert's historical sources uses it, and he is careful to omit it from the finished novel. Its particular use in this folio suggests that, for him, it already carried perjorative connotations: the bourgeoisie commit 'bassesses'; and Pyra's father, the 'père bourgeois furieux /sanguinolent/', has the outraged reactions of the stereotyped *bon père de famille*. Its repetition here is one of the first indications that Flaubert was already viewing Carthaginian society in the light of his contemporary preoccupations – preoccupations which will become increasingly apparent as the novel progresses.

Whereas the *Madame Bovary* fragment had sketched the characters of the novel and indicated the plot outline as a necessary consequence of the interaction of their mentalities, at this early stage *Salammbô* treads a more uneasy path between character and plot. With the historical course of events pre-imposing a well-defined narrative outline on his novel, what Flaubert is trying to do now is to build his own imaginative structure around it, forging links between the given and the invented, establishing a firm framework before beginning to elaborate on it.

(2) Folio g322A*

Folio g322A*, from the newly discovered Rouen papers, provides another fascinating insight into the earliest stages of the novel's genesis. Unlike all the other plans, this one is divided into two sections. On one side of the small, blue sheet of paper is an outline of the historical background to the novel; on the reverse is a brief plan of the fictional plot. The only point of contact between the two synopses, apart from the recurrence of four proper names – Sicca, Hamilcar, Naravase and Matho – is that both start with the mercenaries in Carthage, and both mention Matho's death at the end. Flaubert's task in subsequent plans is to bring together these two sides of the plot, to produce a novel in which history and fiction merge imperceptibly.

The historical outline of this folio is in fact a much condensed summary of chapters 15 to 18 of Polybius' *Histoire*, which Flaubert referred to as his infallible authority on historical facts. I shall return later to Flaubert's borrowings from Polybius; for the present, however, it is enough to note Flaubert making a straightforward chronological *aide-mémoire*, and tentatively grouping his notes into sections by means of brackets in the margin.

On the reverse of the page we find Flaubert summarising his fictional plot, giving the briefest of outlines of the events planned in folio 181 with only one alteration – Hamilcar is now Pyra's father, and Pyra is on the side of the mercenaries:

Pyra /est du parti des mercenaires qui à la fin vont trop loin/ – indécise.

From this point on the plan is terse and allusive, with only the monosyllabic 'lares' to indicate the ritual surrounding Hamilcar's homecoming; 'nuit dans le camp' to summarise the heroine's visit to Matho's tent and the recovery of the veil; and 'chute' to cover all that happens after fortune swings back to the Carthaginians.

Unconcerned here with developing the events planned in folio 181, Flaubert is simply establishing two brief memoranda of fact and fiction. With the historical and fictional strands outlined in parallel, however sketchily, he returns to the task of weaving them together.

(3) Folios 219–20

The third scenario, written on a small double sheet of paper, and comprising folios 219 recto and verso and folio 220, constitutes a considerable advance on the two previous plans. The situation at the beginning, before the mercenaries leave Carthage, is sketched in greater detail and is treated as a complex and shifting network of relationships. Naravas appears for the first time as more than just a name; with him is introduced the theme of jealousy and fear which runs strongly though through this scenario. He, Matho and Pyra are all living in Hamilcar's house which serves as a close confine to the action as the atmosphere of jealousy and fear builds up. (The words

'peur' or 'terreur' recur four times in the first few lines.) Then,
'enfin – pris d'une folie subite', Matho steals the veil and so initiates
the action. The emphasis on these emotions is important since they
not only determine the behaviour of the characters towards one
another, but also help to bring about a political situation which will
correspond to historical demands: Naravas is afraid of Matho who
loves Pyra; Pyra is afraid of both Naravas and Matho, but recognises
that Matho is holding his soldiers in check because of his feelings for
her, and as a result less damage is done in Hamilcar's house than
elsewhere – 'ce sera même plus tard un des motifs de jalousie et
d'accusations de la part des sénateurs contre Hamilcar'.

Naravas's fear and jealousy eventually make him leave; Matho
continues to inspire Pyra more with fear than love; and Pyra herself
is bluntly described as 'une patricienne qui a surtout peur de se
compromettre'. This phrase, 'peur de se compromettre', casts Pyra
firmly in the mould of a nineteenth-century French bourgeoise. It is
a phrase which recurs frequently in Flaubert's letters and rough
notes.[29] And, of course, the fear of being compromised is a strong
motivating force behind the behaviour of both Madame Arnoux and
Madame Dambreuse in *L'Education sentimentale*. This bourgeois side
to Salammbô's character is brought out very clearly in the scenarios:
after the 'baisade', 'elle redevient patricienne' (folio 200); 'Salammbô
était devenue bourgeoise. Plus d'exaltation' (folio 202 verso).
Although the final version contains no overt references to Salammbô
as a bourgeoise, the relevant characteristics are nevertheless present
in a subtler and more insidious form in the finished work.

With its concentration on the motives and emotions of the
characters, this second scenario shows Flaubert directing his attention
more towards a psychological study and less towards an outline of
the action – in this respect it resembles the first scenario of *Madame
Bovary*.

Flaubert's psychological explorations take a particularly revealing
turn in another reference to Pyra. In spite of her fear of him, the
'patricienne' is not indifferent to Matho:

curiosités de la femme civilisée – attrait du Barbare – elle ne s'en rend pas
compte.

While this is clearly a comment on the nature of the relationship
between Pyra and the mercenary leader, it also points to a theme
which had long fascinated Flaubert and which was to be of great
significance in the finished novel – the relationship between the

'primitive' and the 'civilised'. He was aware of elements of both in his own personality ('la civilisation n'a point usé chez moi la bosse du sauvage, et...je crois qu'il y a en moi du Tartare et du Scythe', he wrote to Louise Colet).[30] Several of his early writings raised the question in more general terms. *Quidquid volueris* (1837) deals with the contrast between a primitive being and civilised society, suggesting that the savage can be more sensitive, more capable of real passion, than the civilised man. And in *Smarh*, written two years later, a similar theme is touched on as the savage is tempted by Satan with promises of sophisticated women, new weapons, rich clothes and luxurious palaces – the same temptations which attract the mercenaries to Carthage. *Smarh*, as Flaubert told Ernest Chevalier, is the story of how the barbarian races are 'civilised'. However, Flaubert was interested not only in the transition from barbarism to civilisation; the reverse process also fascinated him. The novel he planned to write about the modern East was to have included scenes in both Paris and the Orient and explore the strange oppositions between the gradual civilising of Oriental man, and European man's return to the savage state. Although Flaubert never carried out his plan, the idea behind it underlies much of his writing; and when the *Salammbô* note is seen in this context it clearly indicates not only the way in which the civilised woman is drawn towards the barbarian, but also has wider implications for the whole novel. Since we know that Flaubert was interested in the idea of the gradual breakdown of distinctions between contemporary Western civilisation and the 'Barbarie' of the Orient during the period when he was working on *Salammbô*, we must see the Mercenary–Carthaginian struggle in the same light. So once again it appears that Flaubert's vision of Carthage was bound up with his view of contemporary French 'civilisation' and its tendency to return, as he said to the Goncourts, 'à l'état sauvage'.

In the first scenario the heroine had played the coquette, seeming to encourage Mathos's advances until, suddenly, 'lâcheté de Pyra. elle ne veut plus le suivre'. In the second, however, she is less aware of the nature of her feelings for him. The discrepancy between conscious and subconscious desires and motivations increases as the scenarios develop. But in this second one there is still no explicit reference to the pull of Tanit, and the mystical reasons for Pyra's going to the mercenary camp are barely hinted at:

la jeune fille prend, après mille luttes, la résolution de sauver la ville, en reprenant le voile – elle y touchera, elle mourra, mais Carthage sera sauvée par une femme.

The motive is ostensibly a patriotic one, with a touch of romantic martyrdom; but Flaubert is also interested in the problem of the frustrated woman who is prevented by the strictures of society from experiencing the excitement and intensity of the active life open to men.[31] Salammbô is like Madame Bovary, 'reléguée dans l'étroite enceinte d'un village';[32] like Madame Arnoux, restricted in her behaviour by a sense of duty towards her family; like Félicité, living vicariously by following the progress of men who are free to travel to distant parts. As the novel expands, additional layers of potential motives and self-deceptions will be built up, and come to interlock so perfectly that it becomes impossible to distinguish a true motive from a spurious one.

This might be called the Pyra scenario, for it centres on her. Although at this stage Flaubert still intended calling his novel *Carthage*, the supreme importance of the main character is already apparent, and is even greater here than in the finished work, since she has not yet been associated with Tanit, and is influential in her own right.

This scenario contains even less historical detail than the first, although it does mention Naravas's going over to the Carthaginian side and his betrothal to Pyra. But with the brief note, 'développer et coordonner les événements historiques qui ne sont qu'un accessoire du roman', Flaubert passes over the violence of the mercenaries, the sacrifice to Moloch, the siege of Carthage, and the final débâcle in the *défilé de la Hache*. Did Flaubert really believe that the historical events were only an accessory to his novel? At this stage, certainly, he is more concerned with developing the motives and interplay of character than with analysing the historical details. Yet it is clear from folio g322A* that the sequence of events during the course of the war is firmly fixed in his mind, and that they form the underlying structure on which the novel builds. What this note does seem to indicate is the relative unimportance of the historical events compared with the fictional development. Right from this early stage Flaubert evidently envisages his book as something very far removed from a straightforward reconstruction of a specific historical period, and reminds himself that the real meaning of the work is not centred on the Mercenary War.

(4) Folio 238

The next scenario is a small blue sheet numbered folio 238. Shorter than the previous ones, it is simply an *aide-mémoire* briefly setting out the main events of the plot in their order, and corresponding to the finished novel with one minor exception: Giscon is still represented as helping Hanna in some measure to steal the veil and to escape from Matho's tent, whereas in the final version he refuses even to point to the direction in which she should flee. The 'importance et influence de Spendius' is noted – a factor which will be greatly expanded in the next scenario; but the main concern in this very brief synopsis of the plot seems to be to trace the interactions of the characters. In particular, Flaubert plans the way in which they are to interact spatially – arrivals and departures are repeatedly mentioned and the scene shifts between Carthage and the mercenaries' camps. But this scenario constitutes little significant development on the previous ones, and the religious element is still very slight.

(5) Folio 182

The fifth scenario does, however, represent a considerable advance. Much fuller than the previous one, it now shows Flaubert beginning to work out the historical coordination he mentioned in folio 220, and tracing some of the political intrigue to add yet another layer of motivation to the action. Spendius has become far more important. His past is alluded to, coinciding with Polybius' and later historians' accounts, but he is given added significance because it is he who motivates Hamilcar's anger with his overseers:

fers brisés dont plus tard s'aperçoit Hamilcar. C'est là le commenc. de sa fureur contre ses intend.

Throughout, the military and political movements are linked to the fictional elements of the plot in a more consistent way than before. The orgy in Hamilcar's garden is referred to, with the marginal addition:

pendant tout ce temps-là il arrive des mercenaires de Sicile – un nouveau régiment, le soir de l'orgie.

Not only are the historical movements clearer, but all the elements of the plot are more carefully orchestrated, with battles and manoeuvres inserted at specific points in the narrative.

Naravas, like Spendius, has developed considerably. His departure

from Carthage is specifically attributed to his fear and jealousy of
Matho, who has received 'quelques preuves d'amour' from Hanna.
But he has become more devious, and his duplicity is hinted at more
than once – it is he, now, who is instrumental in having the
mercenaries sent away:

on les congédie (ce qui est l'oeuvre secrète de Naravas.
il a fait des rapports...)

And his defection is also mentioned.

In this scenario the psychology of the mercenaries is also given
some attention. Once they have left Carthage we follow their
uncertainty, the effect of Spendius's strength of will ('propositions
d'Hann. Math. est indécis mais Spendius le dissuade – il se dessine'),
and their sudden revolt. After the capture of Giscon, the theft of the
peplos and Hanna's refusal to follow Matho are coordinated with the
rising of the provincial towns and Naravas's coming over to the
mercenaries' side. Naravas's motives for his change of heart are not
discussed at this point; Flaubert has simply written 'pourquoi?' here,
and then scored it out.

From then on, the scenario follows the historical account with the
addition of one or two details which will later be developed into
important themes in the novel. Hamilcar returns, the Senate discuss
the situation and Hamilcar 'boude le gouvernement. Un motif
personnel le force à prendre part à la guerre'. But meantime Flaubert
has jotted down his intentions of showing Hamilcar being presented
with an inventory of his possessions, his confrontation with his
daughter, their mutual refusal to face the truth ('ils se comprennent
à demi-mot, ou ils ont peur de se comprendre'), and an impression
of the 'état religieux' of Carthage. This is the first scenario where
religion plays any significant part, and in a note at the top of the
page Flaubert has schematised its nature:

la religion roule sur deux idées. Baal et Astarté le terrible, sanguinaire, et
le voluptueux, l'orgiaque.

But having outlined the historical situation in Carthage, Flaubert
swings back to his invented plot. Hanna visits the mercenary camp
and stays there for several days ('ce sera une occasion de *décrire* le
camp et les moeurs des mercenaires'), but she is interrupted in the
'joie de la fouterie mystique' by the hideous apparition of Giscon, who
curses her but also plays an as yet undetermined part in the recovery
of the peplos.[33] Once the veil has been restored to Carthage, the plot
follows the course of history:

défection de Naravas. Consentement d'Hanna – les mercenaires sont battus. supplice de Giscon – farces cruelles. siège de Carthage. sacrifice à Moloch. réconciliation d'Hamilcar et d'Hannon (le fils). Revers des mercenaires – défilé de la Hache – prise de Matho. supplice. festin – mort.

With the exception of the feast at the end and the name attributed to Hamilcar's daughter, all this final section corresponds with the account given by Polybius. It can unwind now that Flaubert has released the triggers of the fictional motives.

Gradually, it is becoming apparent that each of these scenarios concentrates on a different aspect of the novel and its structure. Whereas the first one was mainly concerned with outlining the fictional events which Flaubert was to add to the historical account of the war, the second one gave brief and separate summaries of the historical and fictional strands, while the third plan tended more to develop the characters in relation to the rôles they must play. The fourth one was little more than an *aide-mémoire* orchestrating the interrelation of characters and their movements. In this fifth scenario, the historical and invented plots are drawn together and coordinated.

(6) Folio 180

Large brackets in the margins of folio 180 separate the notes roughly into chapters, and all the main scenes are indicated. There are indications, too, of some of the themes which will be worked around the skeleton of the plot: a note at the top of the page says,

Ce qu'était Carth. description physique (position seulement) – descript. morale: races – religion. politique.

The idea of starting the novel with a lengthy description of the city was later abandoned, but its elements – race, religion and politics – were of course retained and developed to become three of the most important themes in the book.

It is in this folio, too, that the rôle of Naravase becomes more important. He is in mysterious collusion with Giscon:

Naravase s'esquive avec Giscon. Manoeuvres de Naravase indirectement racontés...Départ pour ⟨Cirtha⟩ /Sicca/ avec Naravas qui les [the mercenaries] emmène.

Giscon himself presented problems to Flaubert. In a letter to Feydeau dated 19 December 1858, he admitted that he was in a quandary because he found that he had to describe in chapter 3 a situation already treated in chapter 2. Whereas a cunning novelist might have used some trick to get round the problem, Flaubert was refusing to take the easy way out: 'Je vais lourdement m'épater tout au milieu, comme un boeuf', he wrote, 'tel est mon système'.³⁴ The difficulty referred to (and found in chapters 2 and 4 of the finished novel) is already foreseen in this scenario:

bien différencier les 2 tumultes dans le camp, à propos d'Hannon & à propos de Giscon. Hannon n'y fait qu'une visite & Giscon y reste plusieurs fois avant qu'on l'enchaîne.

This is of course one of the problems of basing a narrative on a historical episode – how can one achieve an artistically satisfying structure when the real sequence of events imposes its own less acceptable pattern? Flaubert succeeds in overcoming this particular difficulty by making the attitudes and temperaments of Hannon and Giscon so very different that the two incidents, far from being confusingly repetitive, form a suggestive parallel to one another.

This scenario now begins to explore the possibilities offered by the large number of different races taking part in the war. The idea had first been introduced in folio 182, where Flaubert noted that each race reacted differently when intoxicated with wine. This sixth scenario contains several references to the many races in Carthage and to their national characteristics. In a note at the top Flaubert has indicated his intention of using the races of Carthage as part of the 'description morale' of the city; when the towns begin to revolt he seizes the opportunity of presenting a 'dénombrement épique et pittoresque des peuples de l'Afrique'; part of his 'tableau du champ de bataille' will be a description of the 'funérailles diverses'; and in a little scribbled note apparently unrelated to the rest of the text he writes 'tables de changeurs – descriptions des médailles des peuples différents'.³⁵ The grandeur of vision implied by these notes, the desire to paint a huge canvas, drawing distinctions not between individuals but between whole nations, reflects Flaubert's demands for 'gigantic epics';³⁶ and the 'dénombrement épique' assumes vast proportions in later drafts, with lists of notes on the physique, weapons, armour and customs of countless tribes and nations. Sometimes the lists are merely strings of figures, so enormous as to be virtually meaningless, yet precise to the last digit – a characteristic of the classical epic.

The above note about money-changers introduces into the scenario of folio 180 yet another theme which will assume great importance in the final novel, but which is barely touched on in the early scenarios: the theme of money and greed. In the present plan we see the mercenaries at Sicca bored and homesick rather than coveting the wealth of Carthage for its own sake:

> on s'embête. /rêves de retraite et de patrie/ calculs.

But gradually the demands increase. When the bourgeois visit the mercenary camp there are 'querelles pr. la taxe des vivres' and the soldiers' jokes 'vont en crescendo et deviennent effrayantes comme les exigences'. As in the fifth scenario, 'Hamilcar...se fait rendre ses comptes', an episode which, in the novel itself, will come before the *séance de nuit* – his wealth is one of his first concerns on returning after a long absence. For the rest, however, this scenario ends like the previous ones, with the final details of the siege, the sacrifice to Moloch, the *défilé de la Hache*, and Mâtho's capture, torture and eventual death no more than catalogued. Salammbô's death is not referred to, and it seems likely that Flaubert's enthusiasm for his subject and his desire to start writing meant that he was more concerned with planning the opening sections of the book and still content to leave the end in its bald outlines.

(7) Folio g322B*

Folio g322B* seems to be the last total plan made by Flaubert before embarking on the novel proper. Closely written on both sides of a large sheet of paper (39 × 30 cm), with additional notes squeezed between the lines or festooning the margins, it is also by far the most detailed. The notes are now divided into chapters more systematically than in folio 180, and the sections are numbered – there are fifteen of them, although the ground covered in each does not correspond to the contents of the fifteen chapters of the finished novel. As was the case in previous plans, far more weight is given to the earlier part of the plot. Hamilcar's return and the *séance de nuit*, for example, which come in chapter 7 of the final version, are here described in the twelfth section, and all that follows is condensed into the last three sections. On the other hand the banquet with which the novel opens is not introduced until the third section of this scenario.

Section 1 is an expansion of the marginal note at the top of folio 180 – a description of Carthage, a 'vue d'ensemble', to include not only its topographical position but also details of religion, race and politics. And, consolidating the references to cupidity scattered through folio 180, the description of Carthage is now also to cover 'commerce monopole proie'.

The second section continues to sketch in background, both historical ('état de Carthage après la 1ère guerre punique') and descriptive (the bald statement that the mercenaries are 'logés dans la maison civile d'Hamilcar à Mégara' is now filled out: '/ce qu'elle était. palais – magasins – communs – parc – métairie. viviers. animaux. étoiles/'). Indeed, one of the most striking features of this scenario is its attention to such details. The previous scenario already had all the novel's major episodes in place; the present one elaborates, clarifies, and adds details of atmosphere and mood. And here, for the first time, Flaubert notes that the mercenaries' banquet is entirely Sallambo's idea: 'Sallambo a l'idée de leur donner un festin.'

The third section outlines the banquet in very much more detail than before and stresses the relationship between Matho and Naravas even before Sallambo arrives on the scene:

/parallelisme de Matho et de Naravas et contraste/ /éblouissement de l'un, jalousie de l'autre/.

Subsequent events – Sallambo's song, her dance, her offer of the drink to Matho, and her flight in the mule-driven chariot – are sketched in rapidly, and the description of the sun rising over the aftermath of the orgy is also indicated. But the final detail of the section (Matho's search for Sallambo inside the house, including a description of her room) will be dropped from the final version, presumably to avoid repetition when he later visits her as she sleeps.

Sections IV and V continue to flesh out the bare bones of the narrative with vivid touches of detail conveying moods, such as Spendius's exhilaration as he 'se balance sur son chameau ivre de liberté'. The boredom of the mercenaries at Sicca is also sketched in:

S'embêtent. /peu de vivres – changement de régime – regrettent Carth./ Calculent sur le sable. (...) /rêves de retraite – pas de nouvelles – rien! rien – on s'impatiente/

This frustration brought about by enforced inactivity is in sharp contrast to their mood at the end of section VI, after they have rejected Hannon:

les Mercenaires plient les tentes /il fait beau/ & se mettent en marche brusquement. /joie. on reprend de l'air, on va se battre, on rentre dans la vie active./

One of the significant advances made in this scenario is in the portrayal of Hannon. Previous plans said little about him, but his grotesque appearance and general incompetence are now clearly spelled out both in section VI (at some length), and later, in section XI where Flaubert stresses the ease with which the mercenaries defeat him at Utica.

The rest of the scenario continues in much the same way, following the plot outline established in earlier scenarios, even repeating word for word key phrases from folio 180 which act as landmarks in the narrative:

Arrivée d'Hannon...propositions...Révolte...députation des bourgeois... Giscon...vol du peplos...Fureur de Matho...Hannon battu à Utique. joie des mercenaires...Retour d'Hamilcar...Hamilcar dans sa maison se fait rendre ses comptes. le père et la fille...

But those guiding phrases are always filled out with new descriptive detail to convey a texture, to give a sense of how things feel and look, or to evoke atmosphere and mood. Sometimes, too, Flaubert adds little notes to himself about how he should handle specific incidents: of the enumeration of African races, he writes, '/ceci à mettre plus tard au siège de Carthage/'; he notes that at the battle of Utica he must 'insister sur la revanche & la facilité avec laquelle ils battent Hannon'; and in describing the battle of the Macar he reminds himself to 'insister sur la stratégie'.

But at several points this scenario breaks new ground in a more significant way. Surprisingly, this is the first plan to mention the aqueduct, either as a means of entry into Carthage (section IX) or as a weapon against the Carthaginians: '/Sp. a l'idée de couper l'aqueduc/' (section IX) and 'Siège de Carthage – on coupe l'aqueduc. – soif de tout un peuple' (section XV). Moreover, although previous scenarios mentioned the siege and the sacrifice to Moloch, it is only now that we find a reference to Hannibal: '/la ville tendue de noir/ – Moloch /H. est obligé de donner un des enfants. – convulsion d'Annibal. H. le regarde dormir./' (section XV).

From the siege of Carthage to the end, the plan is very much fuller than any previous one although the information is compressed into one single section. There are details of the starving mercenary leaders in Hamilcar's tent, 'avec des yeux rouges comme des loups affamés' and the final sequence is charted with some care:

M. s'avance. mouvement de S. M. expire. Elle se reçoit. on la félicite. Naravas élève sa coupe (tous l'imitent) & boit au génie de Carthage /en lui passant le bras gauche sous la taille)/ – Sall. lève la sienne. Mais elle retombe, morte, pr. avoir touché au peplos d'Astarté.

Strikingly, these final words already bear the cadence of the final sentence of the finished novel. With the rhythm of the ending already echoing through his mind, we must assume that Flaubert then felt able to turn to writing the novel proper.

This survey of the *Salammbô* scenarios gives us some idea of the kind of demands made on Flaubert by his historical subject. If we compare them with the scenarios for *Madame Bovary* the difference of treatment becomes more apparent. Preparing his first major novel, Flaubert had concentrated above all on the psychological details of his characters and had paid little attention to the novel's ultimate structure – Claudine Gothot-Mersch, in her detailed genetic study of *Madame Bovary*, has shown how the novel was allowed to develop freely and organically, following the changes of Flaubert's inspiration rather than adhering to any pre-planned structure.[37] The case of *Salammbô* is very different. In the period spent on the scenarios (nearly five months as compared to the seven weeks devoted to planning *Madame Bovary*) Flaubert was concerned with much more than psychological detail. In spite of his experiments with various ways of expanding the plot, it was never allowed to develop freely: it is constantly underpinned by the historical framework. These seven 'total' plans show his concern for coordinating the events of the war with imaginary events which multiply the motives and implications of the historical ones.

It is in the partial plans and notes, however, that the central themes are worked out. In them Flaubert expands scenes or character sketches or merely jots down a few words to indicate a possible line of development; and since these rough preliminary notes express his ideas in their barest form without heed for style or *bienséance*, they frequently reveal his preoccupations more readily than do their carefully transformed counterparts in the finished novel. This can best be seen when certain of the central themes of the novel are extracted from the mass of scattered notes and examined in isolation; when these fragmentary notes and plans are studied, we can discern the gradual crystallisation of detail around certain key aspects.

One of the most extensively worked themes is the religious influence in Carthage. This was an aspect which received little attention in the earliest plans, and it is only in the fifth (folio 182) that the religious element shows signs of becoming an important factor in the structure of the novel:

la religion roule sur deux idées. Baal & Astarté le terrible, sanguinaire, et le voluptueux, l'orgiaque.

Flaubert did not anticipate that this aspect would present many problems: when he had completed his plan of the novel he wrote to Frédéric Baudry that 'le côté religieux se fera'.[38] But, as we can see from the remaining plans and notes, the religious element was worked out with considerably less ease than Flaubert had hoped. It is expanded into an extensive study with a proliferation of details relating to religious rituals and beliefs, the function and appearance of the priesthood, religious involvement in the affairs of state, and so on, of which only some have found their way into the finished novel.

The sexual element in the religion of Carthage, which Flaubert hinted at in the complete scenarios, is intensified in the later notes. At the beginning of the novel the two choirs of white-robed eunuch-priests which flank Salammbô reflect her chastity (folio 187v), but after the 'baisade' there is the 'Feu d'Astarté' (folio 188)[39] which creates the link with the ferocity and virility of the religion of Moloch, his association with fire and flames, and his priests, 'rouges de vêtement & de teint, forts, comme des bouchers pontificaux' (folio 204).[40] As religious details accumulate, this polarisation becomes increasingly evident; the priesthoood requires virgins to come and prostitute themselves in the Temple of Tanit (folio 200) and the influence of the moon extends to 'l'enfantement des femmes' (folio 189).

As a logical development from the emphasis on the sexual influence of the Carthaginian gods, the notes also make clear their human qualities. They are treated by the Carthaginians as having normal human feelings – jealousy, *amour-propre*, and appetite for food.

on tâche d'exciter la jalousie du dieu et de le prendre par l'amour-propre afin qu'on ne dise pas parmi les nations: où est leur Dieu? (folio 204)

haine du dieu ennemi qui se nourrit mieux que nous. on y croit, parce qu'il fait peur. Mais on l'exècre. on voudrait le tuer. (folio 215*)

These are characteristics equally applicable to the Carthaginians themselves, who transfer their own mental processes to their deities. It is not surprising, then, to find the ferocity of the Carthaginian mentality recurring within the religious framework: the description of the high priest of Moloch tearing out Mâtho's heart, in folio 204, is only one example of the intensity of violence perpetrated by the priesthood – violence which is every bit as dreadful as the atrocities of the battlefield.

Flaubert does devote a large part of the plans to details of exotic religious ritual and superstition, thus preventing the human aspects of the gods from dominating completely. But although noting the mystical and spiritual bases of the Carthaginian religions, he stresses, even at this early stage, their worldly aspects and their close affinities with those traits in the Carthaginian mentality that he wished to emphasise. His sifting of material for details which corroborate his preconceived view becomes increasingly apparent.

This tendency emerges even more clearly if we look at the use he made of his primary source, Polybius' *Histoire*. There have been several detailed studies of Flaubert's borrowings from Polybius. Critics have stressed Flaubert's fidelity to his source, pointing out that he used Polybius' account of the Mercenary War not only for the general outline of the historical events but also for many minor details, and that there are very few of Polybius' statements which do not find their way into *Salammbô*. L. F. Benedetto, in *Le origini di 'Salammbô'*, even goes so far as to criticise Flaubert for keeping too close to the Polybian source and thereby distorting the artistic balance of the novel's structure.[41] In their search for Flaubert's borrowings, however, these critics have largely ignored the question of how Flaubert used his source. More interesting from our point of view than enumerating the Polybian details in *Salammbô* is to examine how Flaubert has dominated this material and integrated it into his novel in such a way that he could claim that the historical events 'ne sont qu'un accessoire du roman'.

It is true that Flaubert does recount virtually every fact given by Polybius, but it is an important feature of his method that he also greatly alters the importance of events in relation to one another. He adds to them, he changes their significance by introducing fictitious characters whose lives they are to affect, or by altering the traits of a 'real' character; and since he does not share Polybius' attitudes and prejudices, he deviates considerably from the *Histoire* and moulds the facts to suit the demands of his fiction. The significance of his note, 'coordonner les événements historiques', becomes clear when we see how he has expanded or fused or subtly twisted events to follow the movement of the fictional narrative.

The opening banquet-scene provides a good example. Polybius merely states that, with the mercenaries in Carthage, disorder and licentiousness were widespread both day and night. Folard in his commentary insists on this detail, stressing the fact that the troops' idleness was a dangerous factor contributing to corruption and violent disorder in the city. Flaubert, however, has taken up these very general references, illustrated them in the specific context of a banquet, and adapted them in such a way as to point to most of the important themes in the novel. The mercenaries' gluttony in consuming exotic foods and drink at the feast is in ironic contrast to the hunger which will later drive them to eat human flesh in the *défilé de la Hache*; the chaos of the soldiers contrasts with the order of Salammbô and her two files of priests and with the symmetry of the topiary work and geometric flower-beds in Hamilcar's garden, all suggesting a Carthage which has not yet started to disintegrate. While providing a suitably dramatic setting to launch the non-historical Mâtho–Salammbô intrigue, this opening also enables Flaubert to outline, largely through snatches of conversation, the historical situation up to that point. The details of this historical background are, of course, to be found in Polybius.

The scenes of barbarian disorder are counterbalanced when Flaubert describes the visit of the Carthaginians to the mercenary camp and their surprise at the order and discipline they see there. The visit is not mentioned in Polybius but it is typical of the way in which Flaubert adds scenes which will not only prepare the way for future, authenticated events, but will also reflect back to a parallel or opposing scene earlier in the novel. In this instance the discipline of the camp gives a foretaste of the unity of the mercenaries and the efficiency of Mâtho's command, both details which are corroborated by Polybius. Moreover, it contrasts with the earlier scenes of chaos at the banquet: the detail tells us much about the Carthaginians' attitudes and prejudices, and emphasises the similarities between the apparently civilised townspeople and the 'barbarian' mercenaries.

With one exception, all the historical figures mentioned in the relevant chapters of the *Histoire* reappear in *Salammbô*. The exception is Polybius' general, Hannibal, whom Flaubert conflates with other historical generals to create the fictitious Hannon. Yet, although none of the historical generals suffered from his dreadful disease, Flaubert's grotesque invention does have a probable source in Polybius: again, we find Flaubert picking up any detail which coincides with his vision of Carthage and adapting it to suit his purpose. In this instance it is a moralising passage in Polybius which seems to have captured Flaubert's imagination. Polybius writes:

n'est-il pas vrai de dire que si le corps humain est sujet à certains maux qui s'irritent quelquefois jusqu'à devenir incurables, l'âme en est encore beaucoup plus susceptible? Comme dans le corps il se forme des ulcères que les remèdes enveniment, & dont ils ne font que hâter les progrès, & qui d'un autre côté laissez à eux-mêmes ne cessent de ronger les parties voisines, jusqu'à ce qu'il ne reste plus rien à dévorer: de même dans l'âme il s'élève certaines vapeurs malignes, il s'y glisse certaine corruption qui porte les hommes à des excès dont on ne voit pas d'exemples parmi les animaux les plus féroces.[42]

This vivid image of physical and moral decay is given concrete form in the novel, where Hannon's physical corruption progresses as the war becomes increasingly brutal. Moreover, Hannon's obsession with material wealth and personal luxury is shown to be one of the symptoms of the disease, and he comes to symbolise the progressive moral corruption of the Carthaginians. Characteristically, Flaubert elaborates on his theme and integrates it into not only the historical but also the mythological element. The notes explore the possibilities of Hannon's elephantiasis and give it a special significance: 'l'élé-phant est consacré au soleil. rapport de l'éléph. et de l'éléphantiasis' (folio 201v*), thus associating Hannon with the sun-god Moloch, the source of his sickness. He is also identified with the themes of sexual lust ('rage du coït' is one of his symptoms – folio 201v*), corruption, decadent luxury, and hypocrisy as he smears himself with perfumes and gold dust to hide the worst of his hideous disease. He is a truly Flaubertian figure – gross and ridiculous, but not without pathos – in whom Flaubert can indulge his most grotesque and extreme descriptive powers; as such he is a more suitable correlative to the degenerate Carthaginian civilisation than his historical proto-type could ever have been.

The *Salammbô* scenarios frequently reveal the way in which Flaubert picks out one of Polybius' facts, only to embroider or distort it until it fits perfectly into the desired pattern. To take but one example: for Polybius, Naravase is a brave, honourable and generous soldier who has always admired the Carthaginians and whose devotion increases as he recognises Hamilcar's outstanding qualities. Flaubert's version, however, is strikingly different. The first significant mention of Naravas, in folio 219, introduces him into the plot far earlier than the Polybian version would suggest – he, Matho and Pyra are together in Hamilcar's house, where Naravas is already playing 'un rôle assez sot', he is cowardly and jealous, and by the next scenario, folio 238, Flaubert has clearly decided to make him a cunning, devious figure. Folio 201v* summarises the full extent of his duplicity:

⟨Narr'havas voulait faire révolter toute l'Afriq. & se créer un royaume indépendant. Mais voyant H. le plus fort il se rangea de son côté. En prévision de toute éventualité il n'avait pas voulu (rappeler cela) faire le siège de Carth. ce qui eût été une folie alors. & il allégua près d'Hamilcar que c'était grâce à lui qu'on ne l'avait pas fait. il voulait toujours se ménager une retraite...Il a attaqué les deux villes ⟨voi⟩ Utique & Hippo-Zaryte, voisines de son pays.⟩ ⟨ c'est ce qu'il dit à Ham. en se donnant à lui dans sa tente⟩

Polybius remarks that Hamilcar was initially suspicious of the unknown adventurer, and this may well have prompted Flaubert's decision to make Narr'havas into a cunning opportunist. But, taking up Polybius' passing reference, he has invented reasons and motives for it which are a vital part of the fictional plot. Significantly, these invented motives are ones of which Flaubert had been very conscious during the political upheavals of 1848, and the widespread opportunism born of self-interest, jealousy and fear were later to be described in the characters of L'*Education sentimentale*. In this respect Narr'havas has much in common with Dambreuse and Sénécal.

The section dealing with Spendius and Mâtho's penetration into Carthage, their violation of the temple of the goddess who is believed to be supreme protectress of the city, and the theft of the veil, has no source in Polybius. Its position in the novel does, however, reveal much about the way in which Flaubert used his historical source and throws light on his attempts to 'coordonner les événements historiques'. For he has inserted this fictitious incident immediately after an historical incident which it parallels: the barbarians burst into the tent of Giscon, whom they had once respected and who had symbolised for them the authority of Carthage; they torture him and steal the silver they find in the tent. So the historically authentic account of the barbarians forcing their way into a place which had once been the symbol of protection and authority, abusing the figure they had once revered, and stealing from him, lends substance to the fictional account of the mercenary leaders' similar behaviour towards Tanit. The thematic parallel also increases the sense of widespread insubordination and the rejection of established authority – it points to the beginning of the end of Carthage's supreme domination.[43]

Another way in which Flaubert uses Polybius is to take an incident which the historian recounts in its baldest outline, and then to develop it into a major section of the novel. The siege of Carthage is a good example. Polybius' account simply says that:

Mathos et Spendius, après ces événements, portèrent leur ambition jusqu'à vouloir mettre le siège devant Carthage même. Amilcar alors s'associa dans

le commandement Annibal... Il prit encore avec soi Naravase, et accompagné
de ces deux Capitaines, il bat la campagne pour couper les vivres à Mathos
et à Spendius.[44]

Then, after telling about the help brought by Naravase, Hiéron and
the Romans, Polybius concludes:

Tous ces secours mirent les Carthaginois en état de défendre leur ville contre
les efforts de Mathos et de Spendius, qui d'ailleurs étoient là aussi assiégez
pour le moins qu'assiégeans. Car Amilcar les réduisoit à une si grande disette
de vivres, qu'ils furent obligez de lever le siège.[45]

In *Salammbô* these events are spread over two chapters, and the
sketchiness of the Polybian version enables Flaubert to elaborate the
fictional side of the story without contradicting any of the historical
facts. So he weaves in the episodes of the destruction of the aqueduct
and the holocaust to Moloch, knowing full well that the aqueduct is
an anachronism but one which does not interfere with the historical
outline.[46] The only other major disruption of chronology is his
alteration of the date of the treaty with Rome: whereas in Polybius
this comes in the middle of the siege, in *Salammbô* it is announced
immediately after Narr'havas has raised the siege. As always, this
kind of deviation from the source has a specific function. The
suggestion here is that, with one piece of good fortune following on
another for the Carthaginians, the tide has turned in their favour and
the holocaust has succeeded in placating Moloch. And the long
description of the holocaust itself again shows Flaubert using his
device of thematic parallels: the frenzy of self-destructive slaughter
as the Carthaginians offer their sons to Moloch has its counterpart
in the self-destruction of the barbarians both by cannibalism (which
Polybius describes) and by armed combat. This description of the
barbarians killing one another at Hamilcar's orders is a detail not to
be found in the source work, but its inclusion in the novel serves to
underline the parallel with the children's sacrifice and at the same
time stresses the irony of the situation: soldiers who up to this point
have fought savagely against the Carthaginians now have to kill each
other for the privilege of serving in a Carthaginian army.

Polybius' attitude to the war is quite different from that of Flaubert.
Polybius sees the whole affair as stemming from the Carthaginians'
unfortunate failure to rid themselves of the mercenaries immediately
the peace with Rome has been concluded. Once the mercenaries and
Carthaginians are at war, Polybius' sympathies with the latter are
obvious. In spite of their heavy losses, he says, the Carthaginians

emerge from the war covered in glory; not only have they recaptured the African provinces, they have also meted out a just punishment to the seditious barbarians.[47] Flaubert, on the other hand, ostensibly allows the events to speak for themselves. In his view, however, there is clearly little glory for the Carthaginians. His version is less a fictionalised reconstruction of a historical period than an exploration of the base and violent impulses inherent in man and which, although normally held in check, must break out in certain circumstances.

So Flaubert's use of his primary source seems to bear out the indications given by his notes and scenarios. Starting from Polybius' outline, the novel develops in a determined direction. It is clear that Flaubert is less concerned with strict observance of the given historical details than with following a preconceived idea. When information from the historical sources happens to coincide with his already-formed concept, Flaubert seizes on it and integrates it into the novel to illuminate a period which he believed to be close, in many respects, to mid nineteenth-century France.

4 'Salammbô' and nineteenth-century French society

One of the accusations most commonly levelled against *Salammbô* is that it is a novel of escape whose historicism is evidence of a deliberate attempt by Flaubert to isolate himself from contemporary problems. Georg Lukács claims that Flaubert set out 'to reawaken a vanished world of no concern to us', a world which would have no connection, direct or indirect, with his own; Victor Brombert says that Flaubert is interested in history only in so far as it implies absence and distance, or a closing-in on itself; Dennis Porter argues that *Salammbô* is a fictional dead-end where history is used for purely aesthetic purposes; and Albert Thibaudet calls it a novel deliberately detached from life where history is used as a distancing effect in order to present 'un bloc de passé pur, une sorte d'astre mort comme la lune'. Jean-Paul Sartre sees this kind of escape into the past as a characteristic response of Flaubert's – headlong flight into a long-vanished world is his only recourse when real life threatens.[1]

It is certainly true that Flaubert delighted in history and derived enormous pleasure from reading accounts of life in the distant past; but to suggest that *Salammbô* is simply the indulgence of an escapist imagination is grossly to underestimate the significance of this complex novel. We have seen how Flaubert painstakingly scanned hundreds of volumes of historical source material and then, from the vast amount of documentation, began to select a comparatively restricted range of detail to be included in the finished work. Faithful after a fashion to historical truth (his inaccuracies are generally sins of omission rather than of commission) he knew that he had probably done as much research into the history of Carthage as anyone else in France; he could be confident that the reading public would not be offended by blatant errors or anachronisms. It could pass as a historical novel set against a convincingly accurate background of the Mercenary wars. But if this were all, *Salammbô* would deserve the comparative neglect into which it has fallen. Flaubert, however, has attempted something far more ambitious. Like any great novelist, he challenges the way in which the reader sees the world around him; he offers a new perspective. If that perspective were limited to a remote and almost forgotten civilisation its interest would indeed be slight, as hostile critics were quick to point out. Instead, however, Flaubert is making a statement which is as applicable to the time at which he was writing as it is to ancient Carthage. In order to appreciate the novel fully, we must consider it in relation to the social and political climate in which it was written.

Why, first, did a novel portraying Carthage at the height of its decadence, threatened by barbarian hordes, suggest itself to Flaubert's imagination? His claim that he simply wanted to escape from the horrors of the present is clearly only part of the truth, for those aspects of contemporary French society which he found so distasteful emerge even more vividly in *Salammbô*. Their presence is far from being the 'modernisation' which Georg Lukács roundly condemned as resulting from a failure of imagination on Flaubert's part;[2] it is not that Flaubert is so emotionally and intellectually a product of nineteenth-century France as to be incapable of avoiding anachronistic modernisms. Rather, he has chosen to examine, in an unfamiliar context, some of his own feelings and anxieties about contemporary France.

During the first part of the nineteenth century comments on conditions in France followed two opposing tendencies. On the one hand there were frequent expressions of faith and pride in the country's economic development and in technological advances which inspired confidence in future progress; on the other, there were accusations of decadence. As the century advanced, it was the awareness of the symptoms of decadence which gained ground. By 1852, Frédéric Ozanam, one of the foremost Catholic historians of the period, was writing that the best minds of his time believed in the decadence of France and felt that the idea of progress had become totally discredited.[3] And of course Flaubert in his *Dictionnaire des idées reçues* shows just how commonplace this view of contemporary society had become: 'EPOQUE (la nôtre) – Tonner contre elle. Se plaindre de ce qu'elle n'est pas poétique. L'appeler époque de transition, de décadence' (II, 308).

Significantly, critics of this phenomenon often looked to the great cities of antiquity at the period of their decline as a shameful model of what was happening to France. When Eugène Pelletan vehemently attacked what he saw as the mediocrity, greed and moral turpitude of Parisians, the venality of the Press, and the vulgarity of literature in Second Empire Paris, he called his book *La Nouvelle Babylone*; Thomas Couture's painting *Les Romains de la décadence* was the

sensation of the 1847 Salon; Taine likened Paris to Alexandria and
Rome in his *Essai sur La Fontaine*, and Edgar Quinet, one of the more
alarmist commentators on the state of the nation, gave dire warnings
of disaster for France unless the country could rouse itself out of its
moral and political apathy and avoid sharing the fate of the Rome
of the late Empire. Like Babylon, Rome and Alexandria, Carthage was
repeatedly evoked as just such a warning – Balzac, Janin, Mercier,
Beauchesne, Bertin, Lecouturier and Berthet were among those who
pointed to the fall of Carthage as a gloomy portent of the future of
Paris.[4]

Others found more specific parallels. In 1840 Guizot pleaded the
cause of peace with the words: 'Vous voulez faire les Romains, et
vous avez la Constitution de Carthage!' When Guizot was subsequently appointed Minister for Foreign Affairs, Pierre Leroux recalled
that remark, and commented that Thiers's '*eunuchisme* guerrier' had
simply given way to Guizot's equally ineffectual '*eunuchisme* pacifique
et législateur'.[5] It goes without saying that in *Salammbô*, also, the
eunuchs represent the passivity and quiescence of one element of a
highly civilised society, and that the Carthaginian eunuchs were
historically authentic. Flaubert has included them not merely to provide a touch of exotic local colour but as an imaginative symbol which
already carried similar political connotations for his own period.

By 1862 it was a commonplace opinion that France was in a state
of degeneration – after her accumulation of power and prestige
during the Napoleonic period, an apparently inevitable decline
seemed to have set in. The rot was spreading from within. Commentators were predicting the destruction of France in terms which
again anticipate *Salammbô*: Paris, the capital of a nineteenth-century
late Empire in moral and spiritual decline, was in danger of being
destroyed by barbarians who would emerge from within France
herself.[6] The words 'barbare' and 'barbarie' were frequent in
polemical writing of the mid-century, a scornful label applied to any
faction in society which seemed to contradict the values of the
polemicist. As in *Salammbô*, where men of widely differing nationalities, creeds and motives are united under the term 'Barbares', so
in the mid nineteenth century the word was applied to almost
anything that was seen as a threat.

Yet the terms were not always used pejoratively. There were some
who welcomed the power and vitality inherent in any group capable
of disrupting the status quo. Michelet, for example, noted that the
rise of the working classes was often compared to a barbarian invasion

and he seized on the analogy with enthusiasm. 'Barbares! Oui, c'est-à-dire pleins d'une sève nouvelle, vivante et rajeunissante. Barbares, c'est-à-dire voyageurs en marche vers la Rome de l'avenir.'[7] Leconte de Lisle's Poèmes barbares, too, express admiration for those distant, primitive, passionate and violent times, and Flaubert, while sharing the common belief that France was in a precarious position, in danger of being toppled back into an uncultured, savage and barbaric state, nevertheless also admired the energy and intensity he associated with 'la barbarie'.

His comments on the 1848 revolution in his notes for L'Education sentimentale indicate the ambiguity of his attitude – on the one hand the fabric of French civilisation is threatened with destruction: 'Nouveaux barbares sous les coups desquels la famille, la religion, la liberté, la patrie, la civilisation toute [sic] entière, était menacée de périr.' Yet he also suggests that this can have a cathartic effect: 'Soulagement comme après une invasion de barbares.'[8] Although in letters to friends Flaubert often complained that France was passing through a phase of outright barbarity, at the same time he could also appreciate the need for some such savage upheaval to shake an otherwise dull society out of its complacent lethargy. 'Nous avons peut-être besoin des barbares', he wrote to Louise Colet in 1852; 'L'humanité...prend à ses agonies périodiques des infusions de sang.'[9]

So in a social and political climate where France's future was constantly likened to the downfall of the great decadent civilisations of antiquity, where even inter-party wrangles were described in terms of the age-old struggle between the Orient and the Western world, between barbarism and civilisation, Flaubert's choice of subject for his second major novel inevitably suggests his concern with contemporary problems and gives the lie to the assumption that he merely wanted to escape from the present. To draw parallels between nineteenth-century France and a degenerate antique society was as commonplace as the prediction of a barbarian invasion, and to liken Paris specifically to ancient Carthage was nothing new. Salammbô, however, is the first sustained exploration of the similarities between these two societies.

In describing the decline of Carthage, Flaubert used the simple technique of accompanying the city's moral and political corruption with a gradually increasing physical corruption, a theme which runs through the whole book. It is first introduced at the feast, when, at the height of the orgy, panic spreads among the mercenaries as the rumour goes round that the Grand Council has poisoned them. This detail is of particular significance not only because it is the first intimation of a sickness both physical and moral which will gradually envelop the whole army; but also because it has a striking precedent in mid nineteenth-century France.

It was in 1848 that one of the worst cholera epidemics of the century hit France, claiming nearly twenty thousand victims in the capital alone and provoking bitter resentment at the government's handling of the situation. As in the previous severe outbreak of 1832, suspicions were rife – in 1832 all Paris police stations had received a circular from the Préfet de Police warning them that the 'éternels ennemis de l'ordre' were spreading a false rumour that the epidemic had been started deliberately by the authorities, who were using poison to reduce the population and divert attention from current political problems.[10] The *Salammbô* incident has no source in antiquity: it is only one of many instances of Flaubert's way of taking an observed response to a contemporary situation and then fitting it perfectly into his Carthaginian novel.

The insidious encroachment of sickness and corruption, of which the poison scare was only a foretaste, is accompanied by the buzzing of flies. They first appear clustering on the putrefying corpses of the lions which the mercenaries come upon when they first leave the city. It is at this point that the real sickness begins in the army: 'Ils étaient, d'ailleurs, les hommes du Nord surtout, vaguement inquiets, troublés, malades déjà...de grands moustiques bourdonnaient à leurs oreilles, et les dysenteries commençaient dans l'armée' (I, 702). Later when Spendius is haranguing the mercenaries, the manuscript bears a note to the effect that 'de temps à autres il s'interrompait pour reprendre haleine; et l'on n'entendait que le bourdonnement des mouches'.[11] Even in moments of apparent serenity Flaubert uses the buzzing of flies to indicate that all is not well. In the silence of the chamber where Salammbô is asleep, 'un long moustique bourdonnait' (I, 720); the manuscript notes that there are flies buzzing in the temple of Moloch, attracted by the smell of meat (folio 197); and when Hamilcar returns to Carthage after his long absence, 'dans le silence des appartemens, tous ses souvenirs bourdonnent comme des mouches'.[12]

The whole course of the war is treated as a kind of creeping sickness – the barbarians fall prey to many different types of disease – 'maladies de peau', 'maladies nerveuses' and so on, before the dreadful ending in the *défilé de la Hache*; Carthage itself resembles a city struck by the plague;[13] and even Salammbô's disguise as she crosses the desert to the mercenaries' camp accords with the prevailing situation: she is passed off as a sick boy travelling to a distant temple in search of a cure (1, 757). The corruption of Carthage itself is symbolised by Hannon's decaying body, carefully but ineffectually smeared with precious ointments and perfumes in an attempt to conceal the rot – a metaphor which recalls Gautier's poem 'Paris' where he describes the French capital as

> Une société qui retombe au chaos,
> Du rouge sur la joue et la gangrène aux os![14]

In a sense the mercenary soldiers were right when they claimed to have been poisoned by the Carthaginians, since the corruption – the greed, the selfishness and ruthlessness – has spread to them. It is no coincidence that their skin diseases are said to be like Hannon's.

Flaubert's analogy between the moral corruption of Carthage and widespread physical sickness was one which had frequently been used to express uneasiness about the state of nineteenth-century French society, and accusations of corruption abounded. Writers often described corruption – whether in government or in the private sector – as a malignant disease spreading out from Paris. Balzac refers to Paris as 'ce grand chancre qu'ils voyaient étendu à leurs pieds, ardent et fumeux, dans la vallée de la Seine', and Berthet has the Seine exclaim, 'Oh! qui me délivrera de Paris, cet ulcère de mes flancs?' in his poem 'La Malédiction de Paris' (1852).[15] The opening speech at the Rouen reform banquet in December 1847, at which Flaubert was present, took 'La Corruption' as its main theme, and the announcement of the topic drew thunderous applause from the audience. Duvergier de Hauranne's address to the same assembly referred to the then existing electoral system as a kind of corruption spreading over France – nothing was being done to check the government's policies, he complained, 'et en attendant, le flot monte, la gangrène gagne';[16] it was, as Flaubert himself described it later, 'une si fétide époque'.[17]

Contemporary statistics show that it was during the period of revolution in the mid-century that the highest death rate occurred in France, with 36.7 deaths per thousand inhabitants recorded in 1849.[18] This figure was due in part to the cholera outbreak of 1848–9 which medical authorities attributed to polluted drinking-water and inefficient drainage and sewerage. As a result the need for extensive civil engineering works was recognised and public controversy arose over the means of providing a sufficient supply of pure drinking-water. Flaubert describes a similar predicament in *Salammbô*, where the lack of drinking-water is the cause of many deaths, both of Carthaginians during the siege, and of mercenaries trapped in the desert.[19] During the period that Flaubert was writing his novel, Haussmann's re-organisation of the water supply to Paris was arousing intense public interest, which focused particularly on one of his favourite projects – the construction, first proposed in 1854, of a 107-mile-long aqueduct carrying fresh water to Paris from the Somme–Soude springs. It is surely more than a coincidence that Flaubert should have introduced a great aqueduct into his novel – an aqueduct which, on his own admission, was a complete anachronism: 'Aveu! mon opinion *secrète* est qu'il n'y avait point d'aqueduc à Carthage, malgré les ruines actuelles de l'aqueduc...Le souvenir de Bélisaire coupant l'aqueduc romain de Carthage m'a poursuivi, et puis c'était une belle entrée de Spendius et Mâtho. N'importe! mon aqueduc est une lâcheté! *Confiteor.*'[20] It is more than likely that the 'lâcheté' was suggested to him by the current interest in the great Paris scheme quite as much as by his recollection of the story of Belisarius.

Also at this time, Haussmann's plans for the redesigning and rebuilding of Paris were causing violent reaction in the French public. A number of novels written under the Second Empire are set against a background of the rapidly changing capital, and it is estimated that about ninety miles of new roads were driven through the city during Napoleon III's reign, transforming its appearance as well as the lives of thousands of people whose homes had to be torn down to make way for the new streets, open spaces and public monuments.

This is yet another feature of contemporary Paris which coincides with the Carthage of *Salammbô*: the face of Carthage is changing as quickly as the French capital, where crowded areas of medieval houses clustering round a network of narrow, winding alleyways were being cleared away under the Second Empire. As in Paris, the cramped, old quarters of Flaubert's Carthage are swept away, boundaries disappear, and the ancient walls are torn down so that their stones can be used to rebuild the ramparts. Other building is going on in the city – when Hannon reads out the list of government expenditures to the mercenaries, heading his account are sums spent on rebuilding temples and paving streets, and the novel dwells at length on descriptions of the architecture and topography of the city, and on the geometricality of its layout. But in Carthage the superficial order and symmetry of the city cannot hide its moral and political disintegration.[21]

This is a contrast which is fundamental to the novel. The beautiful symmetry of the novel's structure as a whole effectively stresses the unease and disorder of the society about which Flaubert is writing, since this order and symmetry are constantly threatened, laying bare the flaws in an apparently highly organised civilisation. In spite of the oppositions which are repeatedly set up between the ordered Carthaginians and the disorganised barbarian rabble, these contrasts are temporary and shifting. When the mercenaries set up camp outside Sicca after the confusion of the banquet and the pell-mell departure from Carthage, the geometricality of their organisation comes as something of a surprise: 'Les Grecs alignèrent sur des rangs parallèles leurs tentes de peaux; les Ibériens disposèrent en cercle leurs pavillons de toile; les Gaulois se firent des baraques de planches' (I, 702). And later, when the Carthaginians visit the mercenary camp, 'Au lieu de la confusion qu'ils avaient imaginée, partout c'était un ordre et un silence effrayants' (I, 711). Similarly, the apparently random manoeuvres ordered by Hamilcar in the crossing of the Macar turn out to have a hidden order which wins through in the end. But more often the reverse is the case. The geometricality of the garden is soon destroyed and the internal dividing walls of Carthage are pulled down; and although Hamilcar, on his return by sea, passes through the outer harbour full of rotting flotsam into the yet uncorrupted inner sanctum – the inner basin surrounding his island palace where the water is so pure that the white pebbles on the sea-bed are clearly visible – there is an indication, in the lucid, symmetrical description, that the distinction between the corruption outside and the still centre of purity will soon disintegrate. The process has already begun with the decay of the old triremes, unusable now with their rotting timbers and peeling paint. The order and symmetry of the positioning of the members of the *séance de nuit*, echoed by the geometrical architecture of the Temple of Moloch, is undermined by dissension among the *Cent*, while the satanic figure of Spendius moves through the novel provoking disorder and delighting in the consequences. When we read in the final chapter that 'partout on sentait l'ordre rétabli, une existence nouvelle qui commençait' (I, 794), we are ready to appreciate the irony: order is felt to have been restored, the veil of Tanit has been returned and the barbarians annihilated, but the reader has been made aware of the instability of such 'order', and knows that it cannot and will not last.

In May 1841 there appeared in the *Revue des Deux Mondes* a long and important article by Saint-Marc Girardin entitled 'De la Domination des Carthaginois et des Romains en Afrique comparée avec la domination française'. Like Guizot and Leroux, Saint-Marc Girardin was struck by the similarities between the Carthaginian and French attitudes to war, and it is possible that this article may have served, directly or indirectly, as yet another source for *Salammbô*: the parallels drawn between the French and Carthaginian colonisation of North Africa are closely argued and recur (although never explicitly) in the novel.

One of Saint-Marc Girardin's main points is that Carthage employed mercenaries from different countries in order to diminish the likelihood of conspiracies. Since the men had no ties of affection for the country that engaged them, sedition was not uncommon; but this was thought to be less dangerous than a revolt of a national army. All countries which have subsequently conquered North Africa have adopted the same strategy, he observes, and to prove his point he cites the latest statistics from the *Tableau des établissements français en Algérie* showing the number of native soldiers in the French army in North Africa. The other main point of comparison which he uses are the systems of land-ownership or of tribute-raising. He advocates the Carthaginian system whereby the colonisers owned and cultivated the land on the coastal strips but merely exacted tributes from inland towns. This was the system described by Polybius. In *Salammbô* Flaubert describes the cruelty and ruthlessness necessary for the successful operation of this scheme:

Carthage exténuait ces peuples. Elle en tirait des impôts exorbitants; et les fers, la hache ou la croix punissaient les retards et jusqu'aux murmures. Il fallait cultiver ce qui convenait à la République, fournir ce qu'elle demandait...Puis, au-delà des régions directement soumises à Carthage, s'étendaient les alliés ne payant qu'un médiocre tribut; derrière les alliés vagabondaient les Nomades, qu'on pouvait lâcher sur eux. Par ce système les récoltes étaient toujours abondantes, les haras savamment conduits, les plantations superbes. (I, 722)

The system he describes is identical to the one which French colonisers were later to adopt in Algeria, and which Saint-Marc Girardin writes of approvingly:

Autour d'Alger, les Européens sont propriétaires, car là nous pouvons aisément défendre et cultiver la terre; et l'administration supérieure a eu raison, je crois, en 1837, d'annuler un arrêté de général Damrément qui interdisait aux Européens, dans la province d'Alger, le droit d'acquérir des terres. Dans la province de Constantine, au contraire, qui est une province intérieure, les Européens ne peuvent pas posséder. Là, nous nous contentons de gouverner et de lever le tribut.[22]

That this article, drawing its parallels between the colonising policies of Carthage and contemporary France, should have been published in such a respected and widely circulating journal as the *Revue des Deux Mondes* is further evidence of the fact that in deciding to set his novel in ancient Carthage, Flaubert was choosing a background which for many of his readers must have held associations with specific aspects of their own society.

The associations are further strengthened when one considers the treatment of slaves by the two communities. On 26 May 1840, a commission was set up by royal command to look into the question of slavery in the French colonies, and the Act abolishing slavery was the first reform passed by the provisional government when it came to power in February 1848. Similarly, one of the first actions of Flaubert's mercenaries in Carthage, once they feel themselves to be in a position of strength, is to free the slaves from the dungeons. But in both cases the promised freedom is illusory. We know from contemporary reports (and Flaubert knew from first-hand experience) that although slavery had been nominally abolished, the inhabitants of many of the implanted villages in the North African colonies led lives of virtual serfdom. Millesimo, for example, was described by Flaubert on his return from Carthage in 1858 as:

Village atroce, tout droit; ligne d'acacias devant les maisons basses, petites clôtures: c'est la civilisation par son plus ignoble côté...des femmes, dans les champs, labourent ou sarclent en vestes et en chapeaux d'hommes, portières de Paris transportées au pays des Moresques, la crasse de la banlieue dans le soleil d'Afrique. Et les misères qu'il doit y avoir là dedans, les rages, les souvenirs, et la fièvre, la fièvre pâle et famélique! (II, 719)

The similarities between these politically inspired villages, created in the same spirit as the National Workshops, and the villages under Carthaginian control described in *Salammbô* will be discussed in the next chapter, but what is particularly relevant here is that although slavery had been officially abolished in the French colonies, the lives of people like the women Flaubert saw in Millesimo were unchanged. The government hailed its abolition of slavery as a symbol of the new freedom it would bring to society, and yet it was prepared to use the inhabitants of these implanted villages as slaves in all but name. The pattern of expectation and disillusion accompanying the 1848 revolution and described so tellingly in *L'Education sentimentale*, runs just as clearly through *Salammbô*, beginning with the symbolic freeing of the slaves: the course of the novel shows that this action is an empty gesture rather than a symbol of a new freedom. Flaubert suggests that in such a society there can be no real liberty. Behind the historically accurate account of the way in which each side eventually finds itself confined and besieged, he is drawing attention to man's perverse impulse to enslave himself to his own destructive greed and false ambitions. 'Il y a si peu de gens qui aiment la liberté par le temps qui court!' he complained as he worked on *Salammbô*.[23]

The novel also reflects Flaubert's assimilation of current ideas on race and nationality. The manuscripts reveal how carefully he researched into the differences between men of various races – they abound in detailed lists of national characteristics, differences in dress, in behaviour, in weapons, together with notes on the origins of and relationships between different races. Worked into the finished novel these details serve to clarify the changing racial structures within Carthage. During its rise to power and prosperity the city has attracted men of many nationalities, from the Indians who ride the war elephants to the 'hommes de race chananéenne' who have a monopoly of Carthaginian trade (I, 723). Gradually, the old social structure which had been based on a racial hierarchy breaks down (Flaubert had noted in a preliminary sketch that the different districts of the city had originally been built by different races, with Byrsa the oldest, folio 217*), and instead gives way to a hierarchy based on wealth. A short passage at the centre of the novel describes how, in order to obtain stone for reinforcing the ramparts, Hamilcar orders the demolition of the old walls which had once separated the different racial groupings, and how, the walls gone, 'la différence des fortunes, remplaçant la hiérarchie des races, continuait à maintenir séparés les fils des vaincus et ceux des conquérants; aussi les patriciens virent d'un oeil irrité la destruction de ce ruines, tandis que la plèbe, sans trop savoir pourquoi, s'en réjouissait' (I, 741). In effect, Flaubert is here echoing Augustin Thierry's theories about the historical development of social structures, and showing how the class system within the city has formed along the same lines as the old racial hierarchy. In his comment on the patricians' discomfiture at the destruction of the dividing walls, Flaubert is clearly indicating the start of a class struggle, the beginning of the end of Carthage's established social hierarchy.

The mercenary army, on the other hand, is composed of small, clearly identified ethnic groups characterised by an intense energy and vigour, a primitive life-force that makes them capable of almost superhuman feats of strength and violence. Each group preserves much of its national identity, but, because of having lived and fought together for so long, these identities are beginning to merge. Religious beliefs spread from one group to another. Moreover the mercenaries' contact with the decadent luxuries of Carthage has a debilitating effect on them – as they leave the city to make their way through the hinterland Flaubert describes the 'commencement de l'inquiétude motivé par le désert. Ils ont été amollis par la ville' (folio 178).

In *Salammbô* Flaubert can indulge his distaste for the milk-and-water contemporary man with his lack of drive and energy – men like Léon Dupuis and Frédéric Moreau who may well be sensitive and even moderately passionate individuals, but who nevertheless are incapable of sustained and vigorous action. In contrast, *Salammbô* shows scenes of unconstrained ferocity and intense passion in the confrontations between mercenaries and Carthaginians.[24]

In the first half of the nineteenth century many people firmly believed that the human race had degenerated from some primitive, superior stock, losing both physical and moral energy as time passed. As a nation became more civilised, so its vigour was thought to decline. This view is summed up in Leconte de Lisle's poem addressed 'Aux Modernes':

> Vous vivez lâchement, sans rêve, sans dessein,
> Plus vieux, plus décrépits que la terre inféconde,
> Châtrés dès le berceau par le siècle assassin
> De toute passion vigoureuse et profonde.[25]

It was already a commonplace by the time that Flaubert was writing, yet for him the fascination of this primitive energy is an ambiguous one. For although Mâtho, for instance, is capable of phenomenal feats of strength and endurance, these often achieve nothing. One night he plunges into the sea and swims continuously for three hours until he reaches the foot of the Mappales cliffs, but this trial of strength merely results in bloodied knees and broken fingernails: he returns to the water and swims back. The energy of the mercenary army, too, is presented ambiguously. All too often it takes the form of unchannelled savagery, quite unlike the noble vigour of a stereotyped 'primitive' as imagined by those who saw city life as an enervating influence.

Flaubert seems also to believe that something very like this primitive savagery soon manifests itself when men come together in

large crowds. They are then particularly prone to violent changes of
mood. Crowd behaviour and reaction in 1848 as described in
L'Education sentimentale often follows a pattern very similar to their
equivalents in *Salammbô*. In the later novel the crowd's respect and
admiration for Professor Samuel Rondelot suddenly gives way to
hatred and vituperation when they see him as a representative of
authority, just as the mercenaries suddenly turn violently against
Giscon whom they had welcomed with wild applause only moments
earlier. In each case Flaubert portrays the same stupidity and
fickleness and savagery of an angry crowd resorting to its ability
to shout down opposition instead of putting forward a rational
argument. The degeneration of dialogue into a meaningless animal
noise is exploited in both novels. Examples from the barbarians are
legion, but it is significant that this also happens at a dinner party
given by Dambreuse, where an inane conversation ends with the
exchange: 'Ah! bah! – Eh! Eh!' (II, 66). Later, Frédéric leaves the
political meeting at which he has tried to present himself as a
candidate, while the crowd listens in uncomprehending admiration
to a flow of Spanish. In describing crowd behaviour in *Salammbô*
Flaubert is developing to the full a literary technique which he is the
first to use to this extent. He treats the crowd as an entity, with all
the characteristics of a hot-tempered, inconstant and unreflecting
individual. Nevertheless, in the very spontaneity and impetuosity
shown by large groups, he obviously saw traces of the kind of energy
that he regretted had faded from contemporary behaviour – he was
not being entirely facetious when he told Louise Colet that he liked
the masses only when they were rioting.[26]

Flaubert's interest in questions of race and nationality was shared
by a great many writers of the period. It was a time of unprecedented
preoccupation with the physical characteristics of racial types in the
belief that these would provide a key to a wider understanding of
social dynamics. Interest in concepts of race had grown rapidly
during the first half of the nineteenth century and left few areas
untouched. Subjects as different as linguistics and natural sciences
were affected; Dr Gall's new science of phrenology enjoyed great
popularity; and in the ecclesiastical field concern with distant races
led to a surge of evangelistic missions. In a review of contemporary
studies on the history of races written in 1848, Alphonse Esquiros
claimed that writers on race fell into two distinct categories – the
physiologists, like Serres or the Abbé Frère, who studied anatomical
characteristics and tried to find connections between a nation's moral

and intellectual progress and the development of the nervous system;
and the historians, who looked on the ancient customs, language and
literature of a race as the prime factor in understanding its distant
past.[27] Among the latter were such distinguished historians as
Michelet and Guizot, both of whom traced national characteristics
back to a country's constituent races.[28] Augustin Thierry, who took
these ideas further, based his theory of history on the intermingling
of races. The origins of France's troubles could, he believed, be traced
back to the moment when the barbarians infiltrated Gaul after the
collapse of the Roman Empire in the sixth century, and it was in this
clash of nationalities, with one people asserting its superiority over
another, that Thierry saw the origins of the class struggle.[29]

One of the more controversial writers on the subject was Joseph-
Arthur, comte de Gobineau, whose *Essai sur l'inégalité des races
humaines* was first published in 1853–5. In this work he came to the
conclusion that: 'la question ethnique domine tous les autres
problèmes de l'Histoire, en tient la clef, et que l'inégalité des races dont
le concours forme une nation, suffit à expliquer tout l'enchaînement
des destinées des peuples'.[30] Using this ethnological key to help him
predict the future of France, Gobineau made a pessimistic forecast
based on his theory of the inevitable debilitating effect of racial
intermingling. The social changes he foresaw were not dissimilar to
the changes Flaubert has shown to be taking place in Carthage:
France, said Gobineau, is a great nation, conquering, expanding,
wealthy and attracting foreign immigrants who settle there to enjoy
the many advantages she has to offer. Gradually, then, her ethnic
structure changes and her social structure comes to depend not on
racial distinctions but on those of wealth and class. But as a hierarchy
of class imposes itself and racial distinctions disappear, so the 'pure'
national stock becomes hopelessly diluted and weakened. Gobineau
used the downfall of Carthage as an example to prove his theory:
he saw Carthaginian civilisation as doomed from the outset because
of the inherent political inferiority of the Phoenician race: 'En tant
qu'appartenant à la souche phénicienne, souche inférieure en vertus
politiques aux races d'où sortaient les soldats de Scipion, l'issue
contraire de la bataille de Zama ne pouvait rien changer à leur sort.
Heureux un jour, le lendemain les aurait vus tomber devant une
revanche', and so the ultimate downfall of the civilisation becomes
inevitable.[31] *Salammbô* contains this same sense of the inevitability
of Carthage's collapse, describing a civilisation which has passed its
peak and is moving into the period of religious fanaticism, excessive

luxury, immorality and decadence which Gobineau believed to be symptomatic of the last stages of national decline.

The changes taking place among Flaubert's barbarians also reflect contemporary ideas about the factors governing variations in racial characteristics. Hippolyte Taine's famous survey of the relationship between the development of a nation and the literature it produces was typical of current ideas in its definition of race in terms of innate, hereditary qualities which are modified by environmental factors.[32] When a race migrates, Taine argued, the change in climate necessarily affects its corporate intellect and its social structure – an idea which is illustrated by Flaubert's barbarian groups who find themselves outside Carthage, far from their countries of origin, and bewildered by their strange new environment. Living in clearly defined ethnic groupings at the beginning of the novel, the barbarians are shown gradually to lose their individuality as they re-adapt to their alien surroundings and assimilate new beliefs: 'Le camp, pour la plupart, remplaçait la patrie' (I, 787). In the context of contemporary ideas on race which Flaubert has used in his novel, the merging of nationalities among the barbarians marks the beginning of the long process of civilisation. The Carthaginians, on the other hand, have almost reached the end of that process and are soon to disappear. The implications for the nineteenth century are obvious. As Flaubert commented to Louise Colet, 'il n'y a plus de race!...Si rien ne change (et c'est possible) avant un demi-siècle peut-être l'Europe languira dans de grandes ténèbres.'[33]

Clearly, then, we canot take at face value the letter to Mlle Leroyer de Chantepie which is frequently quoted as proof that *Salammbô* is a work of escapism, a retreat into a distant world that had no connection with his own.[34] When Flaubert said that he wanted to write a novel set in the third century B.C. because he wanted to escape from the modern world, and that he found it as wearisome to write about contemporary society as to live in it, he was telling only part of the truth. After all, the letter was written at the very beginning of his preparations for the novel, and even if he did feel at the time that he needed to escape into the past, the creative process was soon underway and the need to 'sortir du monde moderne' was not mentioned again. Moreover, if he was prompted, at the outset, to choose the Carthaginian subject because of his revulsion for contemporary society, the choice must be seen as a reflection on his own period. It is a natural extension of his distaste for and bewilderment at the present rather than a complete withdrawal from it.

5 *Political and economic parallels*

It is now evident that in writing *Salammbô* Flaubert was influenced by many of the ideas currently circulating in France. Contemporary preoccupations have been assimilated and reworked into the Carthaginian framework to produce a novel that consistently touches on problems affecting the society in which he was writing. Nowhere is this more true than in the field of politics.

Flaubert's habit of expressing totally opposing points of view makes it difficult to reduce his views on the changing political situation in France to a coherent whole, and the comments of his contemporaries are of little help. 'Absolu et versatile, voulant mourir pour sa patrie et vivant fort bien avec tout le monde, vainqueurs et vaincus, il n'avait aucune conviction politique', wrote Princesse Mathilde. 'Tantôt il demandait toutes les répressions, tantôt il n'en admettait aucune.'[1] Maxime Du Camp portrays Flaubert as totally uninterested in the complicated political situation that followed the 1948 revolution, and equally unconcerned by the *coup d'état* of 1851;[2] the Goncourts record that he shared the feelings of their many literary friends who had become completely disillusioned about politics and had a *laissez-faire* attitude towards whoever was in power. But the testimonies of these contemporaries should be treated with some suspicion. Although they are unanimous about his lack of interest in politics, Flaubert's own letters (quite apart from the evident political awareness of *L'Education sentimentale* and *Bouvard et Pécuchet*) argue against them. The probable reason for this discrepancy is that there was a marked difference between what Flaubert said to his friends and what he wrote – and it is the written statements which are likely to be more reliable, since we know that Flaubert tended to let himself be carried away by his own eloquence, often making wild statements which he might well not wholeheartedly believe, merely for the sake of provoking a reaction in his listeners.

Nevertheless, the letters written before 1848 show little evidence of any interest in politics. Although Flaubert did travel to Paris with Louis Bouilhet to witness the end of the violent February Days (which culminated in Louis-Philippe's abdication) and take notes on what he saw, his preoccupations that year were not political ones. Whereas some of his closest friends became involved in the crisis – Louis Bouilhet entered the lists for election and Louis de Cormenin put himself forward as a candidate for the Legislative Assembly, subsequently standing down in favour of Lamartine – Flaubert's letters show him overwhelmed by the crises in his own life. That year his oldest and closest friend, Alfred Le Poittevin, died; his relationship with Louise Colet came to an end; he was alarmed by the rapid mental deterioration of his brother-in-law, Hamard; and was struggling to finish *La Tentation*. His departure for the Orient in October of the following year further removed him from any possible involvement in the rapidly changing political scene in France.

But the revolution of 1848 had the most profound and long-lasting influence on Flaubert in spite of his apparent indifference at the time. The intensity of his reaction to the Commune in 1871, which he saw as a repetition of the bitter fighting of the June Days,[3] is a measure of his awareness of the importance of the 'rendez-vous manqué' of 1848, and Sartre has argued convincingly in *L'Idiot de la famille* that the revolution of 1848 marked a deep and permanent split in Flaubert's life.[4]

After 1848 Flaubert's letters frequently refer to the contemporary situation, and a definite consistency of attitude begins to emerge. His political views are based on his hatred of any form of constriction, any political dogma which attempts to force society into its mould. Even more, he fears the stultifying effects of a régime which seeks to level society by crushing individualism and minority groups, and which he believes can lead only to utilitarianism and mediocrity. At times he comes close to advocating either a kind of enlightened despotism by an intellectual élite, or, failing that, total anarchy.[5] The fact that he could vacillate between two such opposing poles of thought is evidence of his adamant refusal to opt for any one system which would always risk becoming a restrictive and confining force: 'La médiocrité chérit la Règle; moi je la hais. Je me sens contre elle et contre toute restriction, corporation, caste, hiérarchie, niveau, troupeau, une exécration qui m'emplit l'âme.'[6] He is opposed to the socialists, whom he regards as old-fashioned and authoritarian; he is opposed to universal suffrage, which he considers to be 'aussi bête que le droit divin, quoiqu'un peu moins odieux!'; he abhors any kind of despotism.[7] Yet basically he believes that the new régime is likely to be neither better nor worse than the old. He welcomes the change for its own sake, but feels that the same human weaknesses will always reassert themselves: 'c'est déplorable. Républicains, réaction-

naires, rouges, bleus, tricolores, tout cela concourt d'ineptie. Il y a
de quoi faire vomir les honnêtes gens, comme disait le Garçon.'[8]
Unable to envisage any possible solution to the problems he saw
overtaking society, he nevertheless recognised, and felt he had to
write about, those trends he most detested. Much of this frustration
and pent-up anger was focused on the events surrounding the
downfall of the bourgeois monarchy.

As one constantly finds in Flaubert's writing, however, experiences
and impressions had to be allowed to sink in and mature for a long
time in his mind before he could come to terms with them sufficiently
to transpose them into his work: only when distanced from them in
time, he said, could he recreate experiences imaginatively, ideally –
and only then did he feel he could handle them in safety.[9]

This was never more true than with the revolution of 1848. At
the end of his life Flaubert was still preoccupied by these events,
devoting one of the most important chapters of *Bouvard et Pécuchet*
to a caricature of the wild enthusiasms and muddled thinking of the
period; twenty years after the revolution, it received its fullest
treatment in *L'Education sentimentale*; and I believe that *Salammbô*,
ostensibly plunging back into the distant and exotic past, is in fact
Flaubert's first serious attempt to come to terms with the implications
of the political events which had followed one another with confusing
rapidity in 1848. That the Mercenary War had a more than
incidental significance for him can be clearly demonstrated by
reviewing the course of events in the novel in conjunction with the
circumstances of the downfall of the July Monarchy.

Flaubert uses the first few pages of *Salammbô* to outline Carthage's
political situation against a background of the mercenary banquet
in the gardens of Hamilcar. In his meticulous study of the sources
of *Salammbô*, L. F. Benedetto remarks on Flaubert's predilection for
describing banquet scenes, and refers to many instances of these in
the other novels and the correspondence; but he can find no
authentic historical basis for this one.[10] There are, of course, practical
reasons which must have prompted Flaubert to begin his novel in this
way, since the scene provides a perfect opportunity for the introduction
of several important themes: the gluttony, which is unsatisfied even
by the abundance of exotic foods and drinks, not only hints at the
mercenaries' insatiable greed but also anticipates their desperate
hunger in the *défilé de la Hache*, where they have to resort to eating
human flesh; the order and symmetry of the garden first contrasts

with and then succumbs to the barbarian chaos; the first act of sacrilege is committed with the killing of the sacred fish, and Salammbô's entrance between the rows of eunuch-priests introduces the mystical element. But Flaubert's reasons for choosing this particular scene were more complex, and if we turn to France in 1848 analogies immediately spring to mind.

A vogue for reform banquets was sweeping through the country as demands for electoral reform grew stronger. One of the requests was for an extension of the franchise. The right to vote was solicited for all the National Guard, for people with certain educational qualifications, and for taxpayers who were respectable citizens even though not wealthy enough to qualify for the right to vote under the existing system. Significantly, the manuscripts of *Salammbô* reveal that Flaubert originally intended that one of the demands of the mercenaries, once they begin to realise that they are in a position to attempt to bargain with the Carthaginian bourgeoisie, is that they should be entitled to representation in the Senate (folio 187v).

The first of the French reform banquets was held on 9 July 1847, in the gardens of the Château Rouge at Montmartre. They quickly grew in popularity: Flaubert himself was among the eighteen hundred guests at one of these assemblies held in Rouen on 25 December of the same year. In a letter to Louise Colet he has left a vivid account of this nine-hour meeting held over a banquet of veal, cold turkey and roast sucking-pig; he describes the 'cris d'admiration qui partaient de tous les côtés de la salle aux hurlements vertueux de M. Odilon Barot et aux éplorements de M. Crémieux sur l'état de nos finances'.[11] When he decided to open his novel with the great banquet, it seems likely that Flaubert remembered this huge gathering where political ambitions were voiced with such ardour over copious food and drink.

Further evidence of this comes in the manuscript plans where Flaubert notes that 'les Clubs politiques de C. avaient prêté leurs cuisines autant par peur des mercenaires que pr. faire une farce à Hamilcar' (folio 193). The expression 'Clubs politiques' is obviously contemporary jargon, a shorthand phrase which Flaubert would not intend to transfer to the novel, but which nevertheless points to a link with his own period. The ambiguous and complex motives of the 'Clubs politiques' in lending their kitchens have certain similarities to some of the attitudes evinced by the parliamentary opposition in 1848. Although they wished to strike a blow at the government, several factions feared the consequence of a massive and perhaps violent demonstration. For this reason the plans for the famous banquet of the *XIIe arrondissement* (which was finally cancelled on the eve of the February Days) underwent various modifications. Eventually, the place, date and price of the banquet were altered, to discourage the participation of the most troublesome and extreme elements. The details are quite different from *Salammbô*, but in both cases there is a similarity of attitude, a similar ambivalence – each of the banquets is simultaneously an act of defiance (and approved of by the governmental opposition as such) and a definite threat, feared by all.

Our suspicions that Flaubert had the unruly reform banquets in mind when writing this scene are confirmed by a strange similarity of detail in a episode in *L'Education sentimentale*. He describes how crowds of 'réformistes' gathered outside the Madeleine to attend the banquet, not realising that the government had ordered its cancellation: 'La foule augmentait de plus en plus, quand tout à coup vibra dans les airs le refrain de *la Marseillaise*. C'était la colonne des étudiants qui arrivait. Ils marchaient au pas, sur deux files, en bon ordre (II, 109). Cento shows beyond doubt that this was an accurate description of an actual episode, and indicates several sources which could have supplied Flaubert with his information.[12] But before being used in *L'Education sentimentale*, the dramatic entry of the students finds itself transposed into *Salammbô*: the crowds at the mercenary banquet are interrupted by sounds of music – Salammbô enters, and following her are two orderly files of priests who sing a hymn to the divinity of Carthage. The banquet, the interruption of a disorderly crowd by two orderly files of men, singing in praise of their nation – these parallels are too close to be coincidental. Although they add little, if anything, to the meaning of *Salammbô*, the fact that Flaubert was prepared to use the dramatic effects of an episode from the February revolution in describing an incident at the mercenary banquet again shows that the Carthaginian novel was written at a time when his imagination was working within the context of 1848.

As the banquet scene unfolds, we learn more about Carthage's political and economic situation. The Republic has waged a long, sometimes glorious war against its hereditary enemy, Rome. The war, however, has been ended by the signing of treaties which the Carthaginians feel to be humiliating and 'plus funeste[s] que vingt batailles' (I, 731) in order to extablish a suitable climate for trade and commerce.[13] There is nostalgia for the vanished glories of a once great city:'Ah! pauvre Carthage! lamentable ville! Tu n'as plus pour te défendre les hommes forts d'autrefois, qui allaient au-delà des océans bâtir des temples sur les rivages. Tous les pays travaillaient autour de toi, et les plaines de la mer, labourées par tes rames, balançaient tes moissons' (ɪ, 697–8).

All this is strikingly similar to the position that France found herself in in 1848. The fact that Louis-Napoleon, an otherwise mediocre candidate, was able to have himself elected President that year largely on the strength of his associations with the great Napoleon is an indication of the extent to which the old myth of lost grandeur lingered on in the minds of the French. Many Frenchmen still felt that their national pride had suffered at the signing of what they called the 'shameful treaties' of 1814 and 1815. They were also deeply resentful of Guizot's appeasement of England during the war scare in the 1840s and looked back to the Napoleonic era as one of glory and greatness, when there was plentiful opportunity for their own 'hommes forts', and when their armies ranged from Moscow to Madrid, while Rome, Amsterdam, Ragusa and Hamburg were all cities of the French Empire.

Yet by 1848 France was isolated. In his *Avertissement au pays*, Quinet had warned his countrymen that they had been abandoned by all their former allies and were now the focus of suspicion and hatred for the surrounding peoples.[14] At the beginning of the novel Carthage is in precisely the same position of political isolation, hated by Tunis, betrayed by almost all the towns of Lybia, and with Utica and Hippo-Zaryte covertly hostile but attempting to maintain an apprehensive neutrality.

The main reason for the Carthaginians' readiness to agree to the humiliating terms of the treaty with Rome was their wish to have peace in order to favour their commercial interests. As early as 1797 Chateaubriand had drawn parallels between Carthage and modern France, basing his comparison on the similarities in commercial interests and obsession with money in the two communities. Michelet, too, stresses the Carthaginians' fierce commercial spirit in his history of the period: war to the Carthaginians was a kind of business speculation where victory would mean new commercial outlets and possibly the acquisition of land with valuable mineral deposits to be exploited, and where the lives of thousands of mercenaries was considered a fair price to pay for good financial returns.[15] A note in the *Salammbô* manuscripts shows Flaubert taking up this point, describing the ruthless commercial drive of the Carthaginians who treat their mercenaries like any other marketable commodity:

c'était une marchandise qui leur servait à en gagner d'autres...Magdassen
un homme à figure dure – /fabricateur/ marchand d'eunuques et d'ébène
exprima le sentiment de tous.
– Périssent vingt mille Barbares plutôt qu'un seul d'entre nous. on en
rachète. Voilà tout. tant que nous aurons de l'argent. pas si bête.[16]

But Flaubert also shows the alternative attitude to war, an attitude
equally dictated by commercial interests, when he has Carthaginian
merchants argue for peace in the knowledge that trade prospers in
peacetime. The clash of interests must have been a familiar one to
Flaubert's readers. The very treaties which seemed dishonourable and
weak had been pressed for by those Frenchmen who had vested
interests in the commercial prosperity of the country. An era of peace
and stability was needed if trade and commerce were to flourish, and
the fact that quotations of French government securities had risen
at the news of the defeat at Waterloo indicates with what eagerness
the end of the war was awaited by the French middle classes. These
two opposing attitudes lasted on into the 1840s and beyond: the
feeling that France must have peace at all costs if she was to build
up her economy and become a prosperous, thriving nation
('Enrichissez-vous' was Guizot's famous advice); and the incompatible
regret for the glories of a great war, accentuated by shame at the
memory of the annihilation of the Grande Armée and the occupation
of French soil by Cossack troops. This memory, together with the
experience in the Crimea, strengthened the notion that Russia was
France's hereditary enemy as Rome was to Carthage.

Quinet's analysis of the problem facing France in 1840 is equally
applicable to the situation in Flaubert's Carthage.[17] France, he said,
is a great and prosperous nation, rich in industry, agriculture and
manpower; but in spite of its enormous potential its vitality is being
sapped by ruinous policies at home and abroad. Unable to recover
from the defeat of 1815, the country is incapable of taking the
decisive action needed to re-establish itself as a major power. Quinet's
regrets about France's loss of vigour have their counterpart in
Salammbô's lament for the fading of Carthage's energies; but in both
France and Carthage the overwhelming support was initially for a
non-aggressive policy which would favour trade and increase
prosperity.[18]

It was ironic, then, that in both cases the commercial, materialistic
ruling factions defeated their own ends, concentrating their energies
on increasing their own wealth without taking into consideration the
far-reaching consequences this might have. For France was soon to

find herself forced into what was virtually civil war, with her capital in a state of siege and her troops alerted, just as Carthage was to be pushed reluctantly into a war with what had once been the mainstay of her underpaid army.

In short, Flaubert has selected for his novel a state seemingly remote in distance and time, yet whose political situation offers striking parallels with that of France on the eve of the 1848 revolution.

'C'était à Mégara, faubourg de Carthage, dans les jardins d'Hamilcar' – the famous opening sentence hints at the analogy the reader will be invited to draw, since to anyone of Flaubert's generation the word *faubourg* carried with it connotations of simmering dissension and the threat of popular revolt. So when we are told of the banquet that has been provided for the mercenaries in an attempt to placate them, and allow the associations evoked by the word *faubourg* to linger on, we began to discover richer layers of meaning in the narrative.

We learn that the mercenaries have been flattered and fêted, and that Hamilcar has repeatedly made them exorbitant, if vague, promises. They hope for a share in the treasures of Carthage, and the longer they wait in the city the higher their aspirations become: rumours circulate about the fabulous wealth won by great warriors of the past, and they remember tales of ordinary soldiers crowned with diadems. Although payment is postponed, they are hailed as the saviours of Carthage. But soon the mercenaries find themselves reviled and expelled from the city. Not surprisingly, when they realise that Carthage has betrayed their trust, they are all the more indignant for having entertained false hopes.

Flaubert is here using a behaviour-pattern typical of the beginning of almost any revolution, and he has Polybius' account to support him. The mercenaries, writes Polybius, 'se rappellant les promesses qu'on leur avoit faites dans les occasions périlleuses, fondoient là-dessus de grandes espérances, & en attendoient de grands avantages'.[19] Yet the phenomenon described by Flaubert was one which he might well have noticed in the events leading up to 1848 – it was certainly a reaction which had caught Victor Hugo's attention, causing him to reflect at some length in his journal that when the deprived come into contact with luxury, they are fired with envy and a deep sense of injustice. Rather than simply demanding adequate food, housing and employment, they crave luxuries for themselves.

But more particularly, the mercenaries' resentment has close parallels in the behaviour of the members of the *ateliers nationaux* and their treatment by the French authorities. These National Workshops had been set up when the provisional government came to power in February, and were intended to solve the unemployment problem while providing a fluid, cheap and convenient labour-force to undertake various public schemes. Supposedly restricted to Parisians, the Workshops also attracted men from the provinces; the checks were inadequate and since the numbers were far greater than anticipated, many ineligible workers were able to infiltrate the official groups. Often they had done little or no work, but received payment. In spite of the inefficiency, the lack of work for the men, and the organisational problems, the scheme was continued for some time. Emile Thomas, the official in charge of the Workshops, recounts a conversation he had with a government minister which gives a clue to why they persisted as long as they did. The minister had insisted that he must be able to have workers at his disposal on any given day, and asked whether they were armed, adding that it was essential they should be, and offering help in procuring weapons.[20] So it would seem that the provisional government intended to use the National Workshops as an emergency militia, instantly available to suppress uprisings. If this was their plan, it misfired violently.

When the government did eventually disband the Workshops, it was faced with the problem of thousands of angry, disillusioned, unemployed men centred on the capital. Like the mercenaries, they had been flattered: only a short time previously they had heard themselves acclaimed as 'Peuple magnanime, peuple héroïque, peuple souverain',[21] but now they knew that they were resented and scorned. Thiers was calling them 'Cette vile multitude';[22] and the government was taking steps to disperse them by any means possible. And so they were faced with the prospect of being sent off to the provinces, or (in the case of the younger workers) of being forcibly conscripted into the army. A hundred thousand unemployed were to be expatriated, it was decided; in fact 13,000 were sent to Algeria, to forty-two centres where the scheme was a total failure because of sickness and the inability of most of the Parisian workmen to adapt to working on the land in an unaccustomed climate.

Both the mercenaries and the members of the *ateliers nationaux* form large groups in Carthage and Paris; at first they are a useful asset to the governments, by providing a potential defence force, but later they become a financial embarrassment and a threat. Both groups are showered with flattery and promises; both are expelled from the capital, becoming embittered and vengeful as a result. When an initial payment is made to the mercenaries those who turn up to collect it include impostors, just as ineligible workers had collected wages from the *ateliers*: 'ceux qui avaient reçu leur solde en demandaient une autre pour leurs chevaux; et les vagabonds, les bannis, prenant les armes des soldats, affirmaient qu'on les oubliait' (I, 713–14). Once their suspicions of having been cheated give way to anger, the mercenaries of course pose a much more violent and immediate threat than did the disbanded National Workshops, yet the similarity of situation is clear. The solutions lighted on by the respective governments are also similar. Both issued ultimatums, sending the hordes out of the city, refusing to give them any more money. And like the Parisians who were sent to North Africa, many of the mercenaries are totally unadapted to living in the desert. Although they set out relatively optimistically, they are soon overcome by the unaccustomed conditions and terrain, disease spreads among them, and they begin to long for home.

Flaubert has included in *Salammbô* two significant details about the financial affairs of the mercenaries which have no basis in the historical sources. They do, however, have analogies with the French crisis of 1848. When the provisional government came to power it faced a sudden lack of confidence in paper money. Panic spread, and within the space of a fortnight the gold reserves of the Banque de France had fallen by 50 per cent; on 15 March alone the Bank paid out ten million gold francs in exchange for notes. Flaubert has imagined a similar situation in Carthage when the mercenaries' distrust of the Republic causes them to stipulate 'qu'on leur payât en argent (en pièces d'argent et non en monnaie de cuir)' (I, 712).

Later, when news comes to the provincial cities that support is needed for the mercenaries in their attack on Carthage, Flaubert describes the people's infectious generosity as they offer work or gifts to the emergency fund – the children sharpen javelins, the women give their jewellery, everyone wants to contribute to the destruction of Carthage. Although the hatred motivating the gesture has no direct parallel in 1848, Flaubert may well have remembered the fund set up that year by the new Finance Minister, Garnier-Pagès, to receive 'patriotic gifts', and the enthusiasm with which many people contributed to it or offered one or more days' work to the government.

In France as in Carthage, the fear of a food shortage, whether real or anticipated, was a source of tension and unrest which contributed to the threat of open rebellion. The high cost of food, its scarcity, and the heavy taxes levied on it, all play a part in inciting the mercenaries to take up arms against Carthage, and in urging the provinces to lend them their support. Hannon complains about the steep rise in prices and the lack of certain commodities, and Flaubert notes in the manuscript that one of the details to be described when the Carthaginians visit the mercenary camp is 'Querelles pr. la taxe des vivres' (folio 180). Moreover, the food shortage will come to play a vital part in the subsequent course of the war, as both sides have to resort to eating carrion in order to avoid starvation until the total deprivation of the *défilé de la Hache* brings the struggle to an end.

The situation in France never developed to such desperate extremes, but it is generally agreed that one of the factors contributing to the revolution of 1848 was the severe hardship caused by food shortages. Food prices had continued to rise gradually during the first half of the century; home production of wheat could not keep pace with demands, and France had to rely more and more on imports – the average yearly import between 1815 and 1839 was 733,000 hectolitres, whereas it rose to 1,133,000 hectolitres in 1840–1.[23] The bad harvests of 1845–7 brought the situation to famine point. It is even recorded that in some of the worst-hit areas dead horses and contaminated cattle were dug up for food, and this was one of the causes of the typhus and cholera epidemics of 1846–8.

Moreover, in both France and Carthage the food shortage induced fraudulent dealings in corn. When the Africans demand the corn they have been promised by the *Grand Conseil*, Giscon goes through the accounts and discovers to his horror that the prices entered have been falsified by the *Anciens*. Ridiculously low corn prices have been recorded even at the height of the war when supplies were at their most precarious.

In France public scandals had been caused by similar deceptions – notably by the *affaire Bénier* which is mentioned in *L'Education sentimentale*. Bénier, in charge of government food supplies, had submitted false accounts over a long period and speculated with the money embezzled. The scandal broke when it was discovered that there was a deficit of 14,000 hundredweight of corn in the stores.

The accumulation of all these grievances finally causes the mercenaries to turn against Carthage. News of their revolt quickly spreads to the provinces where it is is greeted with universal delight, coupled with outbursts of violence against the representatives of the Republic: 'Sans rien attendre, on étrangla dans les bains les intendants des maisons et les fonctionnaires de la République' (I, 722). (Here, Flaubert's original plan was to have these *intendants* not strangled but stabbed in the baths[24] – a detail which would inevitably have recalled the fate of Marat.) As the news travels across the desert, reinforcements for the rebel forces come from far and wide.

Just as the Carthaginian colonies followed the mercenaries' example, so, as the unrest in France grew in 1847–8, the French provinces began to emulate Paris and show their dissatisfaction. There were many violent outbursts: the country's economic difficulties turned the people's anger against wealthy landowners, and in Alsace the homes of rich Jews were pillaged. In the south, forests were set on fire; and even before the uprising had begun in the capital, civil war seemed imminent in the provinces. In Paris itself, the political climate attracted revolutionaries of many different nationalities who not only worked towards a change of régime in France, but also used Paris as a centre for projecting a similar change in their own countries. Among the international groups working in the French capital in 1848 were the *Club de l'émigration polonaise*, the *Club démocratique ibérique*, the *Société suisse du Grütli*, the *Réunion allemande de Paris*, the *Club des émigrés italiens*, the *Société patriotique belge*, the *Société démocratique allemande*, and the *Club des ouvriers allemands*. Furthermore, when the news of the February revolution arrived from Paris there was widespread jubilation in the provinces – particularly in Alsace and Strasburg – and this triumphant enthusiasm spread out across Europe to most of France's neighbours.

Although Polybius does mention the cooperation of the African colonies in the mercenary revolt, he describes it in a very different way, with little suggestion of the universal enthusiasm and anticipation that was a feature of both France in 1848 and Flaubert's version of Carthage. Polybius simply states that Mathos sends to African towns to ask them to support him: 'Presque tous les Africains entrèrent dans cette révolte. On envoia des vivres & des troupes, qui se partageant, une partie mit le siège devant Utique, & l'autre devant Hippone-Zaryte, parce que ces deux villes n'avoient pas voulu prendre part à leur rébellion.'[25] The enthusiasm, the violence, the convergence on Carthage of hundreds of foreign supporters all smack more of 1848 than they do of Polybius' *Histoire*.

News of the mercenary rebellion exacerbates the tensions that already exist among the rulers of Carthage. There is an uneasy balance of power in the Republic, where the Assembly of Ancients, 'Les Cent', is countered by two suffetes, 'ces restes de rois, moindres que des consuls' (1, 723). The *Grand Conseil* is constantly on its guard against a seizure of power by the suffetes, and they hate Giscon for this reason: 'ils redoutaient le hasard d'un maître et, par terreur de la monarchie, s'efforçaient d'atténuer ce qui en subsistait ou la pouvait rétablir' (1, 711). For the same reason, it is only when the words 'Il veut se faire roi!' are pronounced at the *séance de nuit* that the Ancients are so enraged that they unsheath their forbidden daggers and threaten Hamilcar.

The Carthaginian *Conseil* is fragmented. In a manuscript note, Flaubert has jotted down a reminder that at the *séance de nuit* there are to be 'individus qui parlent d'après leur intérêt personnel'.[26] Hamilcar is well aware of the rifts within the Senate – he deliberately stays away from Carthage 'pour que les choses s'embrouillent',[27] and his calculations are for a while successful. By devious means he manages to deprive the *Grand Conseil* of its legal rights to appoint his generals, and the Ancients are powerless in the face of such genius. So the struggle continues, with the Ancients refusing their support when Hamilcar seems to be becoming too powerful, and with Hannon doing his best to hinder his progress through jealousy and envy. This deliberate non-cooperation almost results in Carthage being defeated by the barbarians.

A similarly uneasy balance of power existed in France after Louis-Philippe's removal. Just as the Carthaginian Assembly of Ancients was alert to any possibility of the suffetes becoming too dominant, the French Assembly was wary lest the President should attempt to convert his office into that of monarch, and so it was decided that the presidency would be a four-year span of office without the possibility of re-election. Looking back on the aftermath of the 1848 revolution, Maxime Du Camp wrote:

les journaux quotidiens ne cessaient de répéter: 'L'horizon politique se rembrunit.' Il se rembrunissait, on peut en convenir. Le dualisme créé par la constitution de 1848 avait logiquement produit le résultat que l'on n'avait pas prévu. Entre le pouvoir législatif représenté par une assemblée unique, c'est-à-dire sans contrepoids ni contrôle, et le pouvoir exécutif représenté par un président issu du suffrage universel, nommé pour quatre ans et non rééligible, la lutte était inévitable. Elle avait éclaté et elle était alors dans toute son ardeur...L'Assemblée était divisée, ou plutôt morcelée en plusieurs partis, qui tous avaient des aspirations différentes...C'était l'impuissance dans la diversité et la confusion dans le désordre.[28]

This strained balance between the fragmented Legislative Assembly and the President characterised the short life of the Republic, until the *coup d'état* finally resolved the issue.

Polybius and other historians of the Mercenary War frequently refer to the dissensions and hostilities among the rulers in Carthage, and Flaubert's account obviously has authentic sources, but this in no way invalidates the argument. For his way with history, it is becoming clear, is to select from his source material those details which fit into his own notion of a revolutionary situation conceived after the manner of 1848, and to weave his tissue of associations into a convincing historical framework.

This is what he has done with his description of the siege. The siege of Carthage was of course a historical fact, and very different from the siege of Paris in 1848 – different in the intensity of its violence, different in strategy, different in duration (the siege of Paris really lasted only four days, although the state of siege was not officially declared until the second day and was not revoked until long after). Nevertheless certain similarities do persist between the two situations and Flaubert has made full use of them.

In both cases the circumstances were such that the entire populations were involved very directly in the crisis taking place around them – all sections of the community took part in the struggle. In Carthage, the townspeople are drawn into the fighting which before had been for them something remote, undertaken by soldiers, and affecting them directly only when they had to pay taxes and make the other financial sacrifices necessary to pay for the course of the war. But during the siege the situation is quite different. Everyone has to contribute to the effort: the arsenals are emptied, the slaves are armed, and each citizen is allotted a rôle. All the remaining Roman defectors are made captains; and carpenters, armourers, blacksmiths and goldsmiths are sent to man the war machines. On the rebel side the same exigencies apply, with even the women and children gathering stones and earth for military use.

It was the same in Paris in 1848. The rebel forces included cabinet-makers, mechanics, carpenters, metal-workers and gold-smiths, and several women were killed on the barricades. In both cases barricades have to be erected and torn down, and the vulnerable areas have to be fortified as well as possible. In Carthage there is a bustle of building activity, with the transportation of stones and wood and rubble; it was the same, on a smaller scale, in Paris, where barricades were built with a skill and precision that won the admiration of the soldiers sent to demolish them.

In preparation for the mercenaries' attack, the townspeople of Carthage undertake a programme of military training which is reminiscent of the training of the National Guard in 1848. Flaubert must have known about this from first-hand experience, since he was mobilised in April, after the government had decided that membership of the National Guard would be extended to all male citizens. He gives an amusing caricature of a parade of the newly enlisted guards in *Bouvard et Pécuchet*:

Le soir même on commença les exercices. C'était sur la pelouse, devant l'église. Gorju, en bourgeron bleu, une cravate autour des reins, exécutait les mouvements d'une façon automatique. Sa voix, quand il commandait, était brutale. 'Rentrez les ventres!' Et tout de suite, Bouvard, s'empêchant de respirer, creusait son abdomen, tendait la croupe. 'On ne vous dit pas de faire un arc, nom de Dieu!'
Pécuchet confondait les files et les rangs, demi-tour à droite, demi-tour à gauche; mais le plus lamentable était l'instituteur: débile et de taille exigüe, avec un collier de barbe blonde, il chancelait sous le poids de son fusil, dont la baïonnette incommodait ses voisins. (II, 251)

But this scene already had a counterpart in Flaubert's description of the Carthaginian *Riches* beginning their training:

Les Riches, dès le chant des coqs, s'alignaient le long des Mappales; et, retroussant leurs robes, ils s'exerçaient à manier la pique. Mais, faute d'instructeur, on se disputait. Ils s'asseyaient essoufflés sur les tombes, puis recommençaient. Plusieurs même s'imposèrent un régime. Les uns, s'imaginant qu'il fallait beaucoup manger pour acquérir des forces, se gorgeaient, et d'autres, incommodés par leur corpulence, s'exténuaient de jeûnes pour se faire maigrir. (I, 723)

There is the same incompetence, the contrast between the fat and the thin, the tucked-up tunics, and even the fact that Bouvard and Pécuchet's manoeuvres take place outside the church, while the exhausted Carthaginians collapse on tombstones. One cannot help wondering whether Flaubert has transposed into both novels the memory of some such exercise in which he once took part.

And just as the provisional government abolished recruitment restrictions for the National Guard, making all citizens eligible, so it becomes necessary for Hamilcar to decide that enrolment in the army is the duty of all able-bodied men, regardless of their social class: 'les citoyens eurent chacun leur poste et leur emploi' (I, 769).

J.-J. Mayoux, one of the few critics to suggest any connection between *Salammbô* and France, sees Hamilcar as a transposition of Napoleon I: 'Hamilcar, c'est Bonaparte. Il débarque brusquement, comme l'autre reviendra d'Egypte; il se querelle violemment avec les politiciens de l'Assemblée, forme des armées, repousse les invasions ("l'esprit d'Hamilcar emplissait la République"), et, dans son caractère manifeste la même énergie infatigable, la même rigueur inflexible, avec les mêmes colères nerveuses.'[29] Elsewhere, Spendius is compared to the members of the triumvirate of the Terror: 'Il est sarcastique et haineux comme s'il parlait au club des Jacobins: on croirait entendre Couthon ou Saint-Just.'[30] It is, however, misleading to draw such direct analogies between characters from the novel and individual figures in France. Very general similarities do exist, but these are based on traits which Flaubert must have observed and transferred to his characters, rather than on any deliberate attempt to portray specific nineteenth-century figures against a Carthaginian background.

The clearest indication of his method comes in a letter to Ernest Feydeau: 'A propos de Carthage, j'entre maintenant à la séance des *Cent* dans le temple de Moloch, où on engueule M. Hamilcar Barca lequel doit répondre avec une éloquence digne d'Odilon Barrot, ou plutôt du général Foy.'[31] It is significant that Flaubert should have chosen to compare Hamilcar to these two politicians, both celebrated for their oratory, for they both appear elsewhere in his writings as caricatural figures whose portraits symbolise the complex political affiliations of the French. In Dambreuse's study, a portait of Foy (the famous Napoleonic general who was seven times *député* between 1819 and his death in 1825) hangs opposite one of Louis-Philippe; and in a note made when he was visiting an inn to check details for the Fontainebleau episode of *L'Education sentimentale*, Flaubert found it worth recording that 'dans la salle de l'auberge, caricature de Bellangé, portraits de 1830, Lamennais, Odilon Barrot'.[32]

The comparison of Hamilcar to Odilon Barrot is of particular interest. Barrot was notorious for his florid oratory, and Flaubert had himself witnessed a sample of it at the Rouen reform banquet in 1847. Maxime Du Camp, also present, gives this description: '[Barrot], se frappant sur la cuisse, croisant les bras, se démenant comme un lion et agitant sa tête sans crinière, parla de tout – du char de l'Etat – de la coupe décevante de la popularité – de l'hydre de l'anarchie – du fatal aveuglement du pouvoir – de la stérile ambition qui sème les torches de la discorde – de la moralisation des classes pauvres – de l'humble argile humaine ennoblie par la pensée.'[33] Although

Hamilcar is far from being a Carthaginian replica of Odilon Barrot,
he nevertheless displays many of Barrot's oratorical characteristics.
The frequent reworkings of the *séance de nuit* section, which is much
shorter in the finished version than in the preliminary sketches,
indicates Flaubert's determination to do full justice to the scene. It
is the passage which contains the most direct speech in the novel
– the problems of writing a convincing dialogue doubtless contributed
to the lengthy reworking – but Flaubert has found a way round his
difficulty by making clever and extensive use of gesture. Like Barrot,
Hamilcar faces his audience with his arms crossed;[34] as his speech
becomes more impassioned, the *Cent*, again like Barrot, 'se battaient
la cuisse droite pour marquer leur scandale', while Hamilcar,
'emporté par un esprit, continuait, debout sur la plus haute marche
de l'autel, frémissant, terrible; il levait les bras, et les rayons du
candélabre qui brûlait derrière lui passaient entre ses doigts comme
des javelots d'or' (I, 732). The alternation of wild rhetoric ('Eh! tu
déclames comme un rhéteur', shouts one of his audience) and
extravagant gesture continues until the end of the session, rising to
a climax as he pronounces his anathema.

Another contemporary trait which is suggested in *Salammbô* is the
philistinism of the Carthaginians. The political climate in Carthage
is shown to be inconducive to works of artistic merit, and Flaubert
notes in one of the drafts that 'La poésie qui devait être nulle
(littérature utilitaire, traité d'agriculture) devait virtuellement se
reporter sur la religion–mysticisme' (folio 192). Flaubert was scathing
about the lack of aesthetic interest shown by the reading public of
his own day, complaining that their minds were occupied by
thoughts of railways, rubber composition and Great Exhibitions;
poetry, art and beauty were all foreign to them.[35] Many others shared
his feelings and deprecated the mediocrity of France's literary output.
Some of the most promising writers had turned from 'pure' literature
to politics at the July revolution; the practice of pre-publication
announcements forced writers to produce more quickly; and in
general the standard was felt to have declined sharply for reasons
that were attributed to the contemporary political climate. Sainte-
Beuve fulminated against the mediocrity of what he called 'la
littérature industrielle', and Eugène Pelletan saw this literary decline
as an indication of France's barbarity.[36] According to Maxime Du
Camp, Flaubert had long been convinced that the political climate
was suppressing literature: 'Ils ne savent qu'imaginer pour nous
tourmenter; ils ne seront heureux que lorsqu'il n'y aura plus ni

écrivains, ni dramaturges, ni livres, ni théâtre.'[37] It is interesting that
Flaubert should describe Carthage as a city where the political
situation has discouraged all but the most utilitarian literature,
especially since this is in complete opposition to Chateaubriand's
evidence. Far from producing only utilitarian works, claims Chateaubriand, Carthage made great progress in the arts though it actually
forbade the study of the sciences as being of Greek influence.[38] So
it seems that once again Flaubert has taken a contemporary trait and
transposed it into his vision of Carthage.

There was another area of contemporary experience, not directly
connected with the revolution, which several of Flaubert's friends
believed to have influenced the Carthaginian novel. This was the
Algerian war. Du Camp commented that the description of the *défilé
de la Hache* was an exact portrayal of one of the *chotts* (salt lakes)
that had been frequently written about during the most recent
Algerian insurrection; and after the Goncourt brothers had listened
to Flaubert read part of *Salammbô* at a dinner party, they noted in
their *Journal* that 'Flaubert voit l'Orient, et l'Orient antique, sous
l'aspect des étagères algériennes.'[39]

An expedition had been led against Algeria in 1830, and achieved
its aim within three weeks. French occupation was gradually extended
in North Africa, until the Arab chief, Abd-el-Kadar, organised an
armed attempt to check its progress in 1839. It took an army of some
88,000 men, several years' campaigning, and a long series of
massacres and atrocities before Abd-el-Kadar was finally defeated
and captured in 1847.

The French reaction to this particularly bloodthirsty war was
mixed. Some, like Louise Colet, were moved to rousing expressions
of patriotism: in 1845 she wrote a poem entitled 'Le Marabout de
Sidi-Brahim', and dedicated it to the French army.[40] This poem
glorifies the heroism of a small French band of men besieged and
eventually massacred by a far larger force of Arabs, but the story
bears a remarkable similarity to the massacre in the *défilé de la Hache*.
Most of the French battalion have been killed:

> Ils avaient massacré, jusques aux derniers rangs,
> Notre beau bataillon des chasseurs d'Orléans.

and the survivors are besieged in the desert. They are in

> ...cette étroite redoute
> Où, cernés par l'Emir, sans vivres, sans secours,
> Notre faible cohorte a combattu trois jours.

The siege continues until the lack of food becomes desperate:

> Or, le troisième jour, plus faibles, nous sentîmes
> Que de la faim bientôt nous serions victimes;
> Et nous fûmes réduits en ces extrémités,
> A de vils aliments par l'homme rejetés.

Eventually the Arab force swoops down and the French are completely outnumbered:

> Nous étions quatre-vingts, ils étaient quatre mille!...
> Alors le désespoir s'empara de nos âmes,
> En nous disant adieu nous nous précipitâmes
> La baïonnette au poing pour vendre chèrement
> Dans ce dernier combat notre dernier moment.

There ensues a terrible slaughter from which only twelve French soldiers escape with their lives:

> Ce fut des deux côtés une affreuse tuerie!...
> Le capitaine mort!...plus que quatorze en vie!
> Dont douze seulement se sont sauvés enfin:
> C'est nous, frères, voyez! nous expirons de faim.

And the poem ends with a dedication comparing the courage of these soldiers to the most glorious exploits of the heroes of antiquity.

But many did not share Louise Colet's enthusiasm, especially when the French began to commit even worse atrocities. French prisoners had been murdered by the Arabs in Algeria, and the French army's reaction was to take immediate revenge in the form of *razzias*, systematic massacres of native population. This, too, corresponds with the course of events in *Salammbô*, where the murder of the Carthaginian prisoners by the barbarians is the impulse which drives the Carthaginians to commit the most cruel atrocities: 'ils déclarèrent qu'il n'y avait plus désormais, entre les Carthaginois et les Barbares, ni foi, ni pitié, ni dieux, qu'ils se refusaient d'avance à toutes les ouvertures et que l'on renverrait les parlementaires avec les mains coupées' (I, 765). In France, Lamartine was one of many who reacted with horror to the news of the *razzias*. 'C'est à nous à donner l'exemple de la générosité, bien loin de prendre des leçons de cruauté', he declared to the Chamber on 10 June 1846. However, the reaction of Bugeaud, the general in charge in Algeria, and of his followers was similar to that of Flaubert's Carthaginians – they persisted in the belief that such shows of force raised French prestige in the eyes of the native population, and made them more ready to submit to the colonisers.[41]

Several contemporary commentators compared the methods of colonisation adopted by the French in North Africa to those of the Carthaginians. We have already noted how Saint-Marc Girardin drew parallels between the land-ownership and tribute-raising systems of the two states, and advocated the Carthaginians' methods. Sismondi, too, in *Les Colonies des anciens comparées à celles des modernes*, argues that the ancient colonies were far preferable to the French ones: 'les colonies des anciens renouvelaient la race humaine, la retrempaient, et lui faisaient commencer l'existence politique avec tous les avantages de la jeunesse...les nôtres, au contraire, naissent vieilles, avec toutes les jalousies, toute l'inquiétude, toutes les misères, tous les vices de la vieille Europe'. He maintained that the ancient colonies benefited the indigenous population by bringing them into contact with civilisation, whereas most European colonisers have had a pernicious effect on foreign cultures: 'ils ont barbarisé les peuples qu'ils nommaient barbares...Ils se sont barbarisés à leur tour.'[42]

Although Flaubert was fascinated by this idea of the mutual influence of civilisation and barbarism, he differs from Saint-Marc Girardin and Sismondi in his criticism of Carthage's colonising methods ('Carthage exténuait ces peuples'). Contact with her decadent civilisation is in no way beneficial. Once again, we must see this as an indirect comment on French policy in North Africa.

Maxime Du Camp visited Algeria in 1848, when the French government was sending out colonisers, hoping to relieve the unemployment problem in Paris by enticing them to North Africa with promises of a new life in a rich agricultural area under a perfect climate – so much so, says Du Camp, that 'les malheureux regardaient du côté "des Iles"'...ils se figurèrent que les cailles rôties y tombaient des nuages, et une quinzaine de milliers d'individus demandèrent à partir'.[43] He vividly evokes their disillusion and the wretchedness of their existence, and must have talked of this to Flaubert with whom he was to set out again for the East only a year later. Flaubert was deeply moved by the miserable conditions of colonies he later saw for himself in North Africa. At Constantine 'cela est d'une pauvreté et d'une malédiction supérieures: ça sent le paria' (II, 707); at Souk-Ahras, 'ville neuve, atroce, froide, boueuse' he meets a particularly unprepossessing group of colonials: 'M. de Serval, sécot, inhospitalier...Table d'hôte: MM. les officiers; ignoble et bête, collet crasseux du directeur des postes; le lendemain, M. Gosse, aliéné' (II, 718–19); and M. le conseiller de préfecture (of Constantine) is an 'homme bien et complètement nul' (II, 719); Millesimo, the 'village atroce', is described as civilisation at its worst, with all the wretch-edness of the suburbs under a blazing African sun (II, 719). And the final paragraph from these notes, written in 1858, leaves one in no doubt as to Flaubert's intention that his impressions of the French colonies should permeate the novel: 'Que toutes les énergies de la nature que j'ai aspirées me pénètrent et qu'elles s'exhalent dans mon livre. A moi, puissances de l'émotion plastique! résurrection du passé, à moi! à moi! Il faut faire, à travers le Beau, vivant et vrai quand même. Pitié pour ma volonté, Dieu des âmes! donne-moi la Force – et l'Espoir!' (II, 720).

It is clear, then, that in writing *Salammbô* Flaubert not only echoed many contemporary preoccupations but also drew inspiration from episodes and details from the Algerian situation and the 1848 revolution. At the same time, he was concerned with representing an acceptably accurate reconstruction of the Mercenary War – his painstaking research leaves no room for doubt on this score. Why, then, did he also include details with no source in ancient history? Why did he consistently select incidents which had parallels in his own period? Why, above all, if he was so concerned with historical documentation, did he overlay his account with the strange, un-historical, unrealistic story of the relationship between Mâtho and Salammbô and their domination by Moloch and Tanit? I believe that the answer lies in the connection between the mythological element and the historical account, and that a closer examination of Flaubert's use of religion and mythology in *Salammbô* will help to explain this unorthodox historical novel.

6 Religion and mythology in 'Salammbô'

Flaubert looked for two qualities in historical writing: first, he wanted rigorous research and scientific accuracy; second, he sought the stimulation of a deeply imaginative account. His greatest admiration was for those writers who managed to combine both techniques, and he worked to bring them together in *Salammbô* where the details gleaned from his careful and extensive research have been selected and ordered according to the nineteenth-century imaginative model already discussed. So on the one hand the modern reader is encouraged to use his understanding of the contemporary situation in order to help him to interpret the social and political structures of Carthage; on the other, he is presented with an ostensibly accurate reconstruction of a strange and distant civilisation which he is invited to consider critically. When these responses combine, the reader's critical response to events in Carthage must carry with it an implied reaction to the analogous situation in nineteenth-century France.

Like his dual approach to history in *Salammbô*, Flaubert's treatment of religion and mythology is both scientific and imaginative. His research was extensive. Writers commenting on the sources of the religious element in the novel have traced his borrowings from many classical authors and have located details provided by more recent commentators – Bochart, Hendreich, Gesenius, Mignot, Movers, Münter and Selden among others. Benedetto in particular has traced many of these sources, and the *Salammbô* dossier provides further evidence of Flaubert's rigorous and wide-ranging research. But the mere accumulation of sources can, in itself, tell us little about Flaubert's method or purpose in making these very disparate borrowings. What is more revealing is to use these sources to discover his principle of selection. Like the historical sources, the curious range of mythological details has been deliberately chosen and ordered with two apparent aims: first, to continue the process of linking Carthage with nineteenth-century France by focusing on analogies between the religious systems of the two states; and second, to direct our responses to the novel, to suggest how we should read it.

'Ce qui m'attire par-dessus tout,' Flaubert once wrote to Mlle Leroyer de Chantepie, '...c'est la religion. Je veux dire toutes les

94

religions, pas plus l'une que l'autre.'[1] Although the remarks he makes about religion in his correspondence are almost as complex in their variety as his reflections on politics, the underlying principle is the same in both cases. He abhorred any kind of restricting force in politics. He detested rigid religious dogma. And he frequently grouped religion and politics together in a condemnatory aside:

Le néocatholicisme d'une part, et le socialisme de l'autre ont abêti la France. Tout se meurt entre l'Immaculée-Conception et les gamelles ouvrières.

C'est parce que je crois à l'évolution perpétuelle de l'humanité et à ses forces incessantes, que je hais tous les cadres où on veut le fourrer de vive force, toutes les formalités dont on la définit, tous les plans que l'on rêve pour elle...Ainsi chercher la meilleure des religions, ou le meilleur des gouvernements, me semble une folie niaise. Le meilleur, pour moi, c'est celui qui agonise, parce qu'il va faire place à un autre.[2]

Just as in politics he tended to consider, discuss or deflate ideas from different parties, adamantly refusing to adopt any one political programme, so, where religious belief was concerned, he rejected the idea of one organised religion. On the other hand, he was convinced that there existed a basic human impulse towards the religious, and he admired the fundamental religious principle that is common to all faiths. 'Que ce soit un besoin de coeur, d'accord', he wrote in 1864. 'C'est ce besoin-là qui est respectable, et non des dogmes éphémères.'[3]

He was particularly interested in man's attraction to the irrational, the supernatural, the inexplicable, and believed that the real and lasting basis of religion was the primitive pull of superstition. Explorations of this emotional need for the irrational and the fantastic find an important place in his work. In the first *Education sentimentale*, for example, he writes of man's impulse towards the supernatural:

N'arrive-t-il pas, à certains moments de la vie de l'humanité et de l'individu, d'inexplicables élans qui se traduisent par des formes étranges?...on a besoin de tout ce qui n'est pas, tout ce qui est devient inutile: tantôt c'est par amour de la vie...tantôt c'est par convoitise de l'infini...on se rue à plaisir dans l'effréné, dans le monstrueux. (I, 357)

But then, in a typical Flaubertian movement, he turns from the spontaneity of the mystical experience to try to rationalise and explain it. In the cold light of day, he says, man will remember his fantasy, be alarmed by it, and attempt to discover what inner compulsion conjured up such unnatural images. By showing 'le fantastique' to be a natural and inevitable part of human experience, Flaubert insists on its artistic importance: 'Compris comme développement de l'essence intime de notre âme, comme surabondance de l'élément moral, le fantastique a sa place dans l'art' (I, 357).

A few years later, in *Par les champs et par les grèves*, he speculates about the strangely beautiful but alien world of ancient mythology, wondering whether our fascination with its fantastic qualities is not really an attempt to go back beyond memory to the very origins of life itself, when matter and spirit were one. Is the fantastic and grotesque world of myth, he wonders, the physical counterpart of some basic mental process (II, 486)?

By the middle of the nineteenth century it had become common practice among French historians to look to mythology for illumination of the darker parts of the mind, and in particular to see it as an oblique record of the mentality of primitive man. Michelet (already deeply influenced by Vico's *Scienza nuova*, which he had translated in 1827) argued in his *Histoire romaine* of 1831 that myths could provide a valuable indication of the way in which primitive man thought and expressed himself, and could reveal historical truths about long-vanished cultures – that they were in fact a primitive means of recording history. 'Les mythes et la poésie des peuples barbares présentent les traditions de ces temps', he wrote; 'elles sont ordinairement la véritable histoire nationale d'un peuple, telle que son génie la lui a fait concevoir. Peu importe qu'elle s'accorde avec les faits.'[4] Flaubert would have met similar ideas in his history lessons at school. In 1835 (the year Flaubert entered his class at the Collège de Rouen) Chéruel published an article entitled 'Du merveilleux dans l'histoire' in which he argued forcefully that mythology provides essential source material for any historian of antiquity who wishes to give more than a straight factual record of battles and conquests: to neglect its resources is to ignore some of the most vital and powerful material ever offered to a historian.[5] So by the time that Flaubert was considering writing *Salammbô*, it was generally felt that the study of mythology was a necessary adjunct to the dry facts of history: in Ernest Renan's words, 'la fable nous donne, comme dans l'empreinte d'un sceau, l'image fidèle de la manière de sentir et de penser propre à [une] nation, son portrait moral tracé par elle-même'.[6]

If Flaubert has used mythology to reflect an authentic 'moral portrait' of Carthaginian mentality in *Salammbô*, he has again selected aspects which seem particularly relevant to certain preoccupations in nineteenth-century France, taking care to maintain a balance between the mystical and the rational. For example, he describes how religion and politics are inextricably bound together: a manuscript note refers to the 'influence de la théocratie. Elle primait tout. Peut-être parce que c'était les prêtres des conquérants, les dieux vainqueurs' (folio 227*). And it is clear that Schahabarim and the priests of Moloch are as important as the military leaders in manipulating the war. The four pontiffs of Eschmoun, Khamon, Moloch and Tanit preside over the *séance de nuit*; and it is due to the influence of Schahabarim that Salammbô takes the vital step of recovering the veil. As Schahabarim rightly calculated, this action marks a turning-point in the course of the war, since the power of the priesthood is such that the Carthaginians fight with renewed conviction once their talisman has been restored. Similarly, when the priests of Moloch engineer the sacrifice to their god, this act of faith is a determining factor in the outcome of the political conflict.

While I do not wish to suggest that these details of the novel have their source in nineteenth-century France, they nevertheless raise questions about the relationship between Church and State which occupied the minds of many Frenchmen as Flaubert was preparing his novel. The problem of the Church's involvement in political affairs had been discussed frequently since the Revolution of 1789. In his lectures to the Collège de France in 1844 and 1845 Quinet had denounced the growing opposition between the Catholic Church and modern society: the true Christian spirit had degenerated in the Church, he said, and instead had found its expression in the revolutionary and democratic movement. By 1861 Michelet was writing to Flaubert of 'ce *corps* du clergé qui était soutenu par un fil...le pouvoir – On voit par les journaux et tribunaux que les juges les abandonnent – cela veut dire que le fil a *cassé*.'[7] All around there were signs that the Church was relinquishing its hold on the country. In literature, for instance, the great impetus given by *Le Génie du Christianisme* was spent, and the real aesthetes of the Second Empire were unenthusiastic about or even hostile to dogma of any kind. When Benjamin Constant discussed the problem of the dissociation of Church from State in *De la Religion* (1824–31) he saw 'la lutte du pouvoir politique et militaire contre le pouvoir sacerdotal' as a struggle that was 'dans la nature des choses et par conséquent inévitable',[8] and he traced what he believed to be a general pattern of events – that a priesthood, which at the outset holds all the power within the state, must gradually relinquish part of its authority until it finally finds itself in open conflict with the new power-holders. What Flaubert shows in *Salammbô* is a society at an early stage in this progression: political and religious power still run together, but there are signs that the supremacy of the priesthood is beginning to weaken. Hamilcar defies Moloch by refusing to sacrifice his son; Schahabarim is tormented by doubts about the power of Tanit; and a kind of syncretism develops among the mercenaries.

Having seen so many cults and religions being practised, they come to lose their former belief in one particular faith, substituting a personal religion composed of elements borrowed from many different sources. In early manuscripts Flaubert notes that: 'ils avaient tant vu de Dieux qu'ils ne devaient plus croire à aucun. tout cela devait faire une confusion dans leur tête. ils se fabriquaient une religion à eux. /amulettes personnelles/ si jamais l'individualisme a régné, c'est là'(folio 197v). And, of course, a similarly eclectic syncretism was common in France as the growing rejection of the established religion coincided with increased interest in ancient religions and the view that Christianity was only one branch of a complex and interrelated network of mythologies.

In 1848 demands for the separation of Church and State were one of the major issues at the elections. Louis Bouilhet, standing as a candidate, took the secularisation of education and the dissociation of the clergy from any kind of political activity as the main points of his platform. 'Pas de congrégations religieuses enseignantes, sous quelque habit, sous quelque nom qu'elles se cachent', he declared. 'Je respecte le prêtre – le prêtre à l'autel – le prêtre dans sa fonction naturelle – le prêtre qui ne fait pas un drapeau de sa soutane et un prospectus de l'Evangile.'[9] Although Schahabarim is a complex figure, full of doubts and uncertainties, one can see in his combined rôles of priest, teacher and politician precisely the kind of anomaly that Bouilhet is criticising. Schahabarim's influence over Salammbô is immense. Flaubert shows how unquestioningly she follows his teaching, accepting symbols as given truths and taking literally the mystical turns of phrase used by the priest. Furthermore it is made clear that Schahabarim himself is uncertain as to where reality ends and fantasy begins; but his relationship with Salammbô is such that his doubts must remain hidden from her. The tendency to present speculation as fact was another of the criticisms commonly levelled against Catholic teaching clergy. Quinet, for example, inveighed against the Catholic education system for being uncritical, unscientific, and quenching any spirit of enquiry among its pupils. 'S'en remettre à la science sacerdotale, croire le prêtre, lui obéir, c'est l'esprit de sa loi.'[10]

A manuscript note suggests a further identification of Schahabarim with the confused religious situation in mid nineteenth-century France: 'confesseur. magnétiseur. pr. la calmer il lui fait des passes' (folio 201). As confessor and teacher his position has obvious connotations of Catholicism; yet as 'magnétiseur', making mysterious passes over Salammbô, he is more akin to the growing number of nineteenth-century devotees of hypnotism and magnetism.

Mesmer's famous doctrine of animal magnetism postulated the existence of a subtle fluid which pervaded all bodies and manifested itself in the motions of the planets and in tidal and atmospheric changes. When the ebb and flow of this fluid within the human body was out of harmony with the universal rhythm, nervous or mental disorders were thought to result. This idea interested Flaubert. 'Ne sommes-nous pas faits avec les émanations de l'Univers?' he wrote to Louise Colet. 'Et si les atomes sont infinis et qu'ils passent ainsi dans les Formes comme un fleuve perpétuel...qui donc les retient, qui les lie?'[11] Although the references to magnetism in his other novels indicate that Flaubert maintained a healthy scepticism, Salammbô's hysterical condition is described in terms which closely correspond to Mesmer's views on the interaction between human and heavenly bodies. She is said to be under the influence of the moon – weak and lethargic by day, she revives at night; her energy fades as the moon wanes; and an eclipse of the moon brings her close to death.

Not only is the religion of Carthage depicted as being involved with politics and education, but it is also shown to be an important economic interest in the state. The priests exact large offerings; a manuscript jotting notes the 'importance du ⟨temple⟩ /pèlerinage/ d'Ammon comme marché',[12] and the temple of Moloch is used by private individuals as a place of safe-keeping for their wealth, as well as serving as the State treasure-house.[13] This is yet another example of the way in which Flaubert uses an institution to highlight certain aspects of the mentality of the society with which he is concerned. In a letter to Mme Roger des Genettes in 1864, he wrote that man's gods have always been a reflexion of himself, and drew comparisons between the way in which human characteristics are attributed to gods of East and West: 'Le *bon* Dieu oriental, qui n'est pas bon, fait payer aux petits enfants les fautes de leur père, comme un pacha qui réclame à un fils les dettes de son aïeul. Nous en sommes encore là, quand nous disons la justice, la colère ou la miséricorde de Dieu, toutes qualités humaines, relatives, finies et partant incompatibles avec l'absolu.'[14] In *Salammbô* the religions are likewise shown to be very much the creation of the Carthaginians themselves, and the framework within which these religions are set reflects the materialistic, commercial and essentially conservative mentality of the state. As he wrote to George Sand later, 'Nous faisons toujours Dieu à notre image.'[15]

By using the Carthaginian religions as a vehicle for his unfolding of the main preoccupations of the people, Flaubert is able to hint at very complex motives, beliefs and aspirations. What was later to be diffused throughout the novel has been schematised in the scenarios, where he notes three aspects of mysticism: 'Taanach naïve (deux faces du mysticisme, l'un ardent & orageux, l'autre calme, populaire, ne va pas plus loin: Schahabarime qui s'élève & progresse en est le troisième terme.)' (folio 201). And again, comparing Taanach and Salammbô: 'l'esclave ne comprend pas ce qui lui manque. différence de manière de croire. l'une calme & l'autre troublée' (folio 198v). These three facets – the naïve, uncomprehending but implicit popular belief; the hysterical, fanatical faith; and the illumination of the priesthood – correspond to the distinction made by many of the nineteenth-century writers on religion and mythology between the superficial, outer meaning of religion which is shown to the populace, and the deep, inner meaning, protected by the initiate.[16] These three types of faith have their counterparts in Flaubert's other novels, so he clearly did not consider them to be characteristics peculiar to the Carthaginians. The first, the 'ardent & orageux' side, manifest as much in Salammbô's hysteria as in the dervishes who rave at Carthaginian street corners, is also seen in *L'Education sentimentale* when a religious fanatic climbs on to the platform at a political meeting and combines religion and politics in a fiery outburst of visionary eloquence. The second, the calm, unquestioning attitude of the populace, exemplified by Taanach in the quotation above, and epitomised by Félicité in *Un Coeur simple* and Catherine Leroux in *Madame Bovary*, represents the undiscriminating acceptance by the majority, but an acceptance which can, at times of stress, be stirred into violent fervour. And the third, the serious, reflective and intelligent faith of Schahabarim, tortured by doubts, has its counterpart in saint Antoine. Schahabarim, constantly tormented by questions and uncertainties, is one of the major forces in the action of the novel – he is a manipulator, being himself unable to act; he uses Salammbô, instilling desires into her and pushing her towards the action which will be the final test of Tanit's supremacy. He is to Salammbô what Spendius is to Mâtho, an instigator, a constant adviser, and a manipulator who counsels a course of action which he himself would be unable to pursue.

Most nineteenth-century commentators described the religions of Carthage as having been based on the opposition of the male and female principles, on the struggle between 'Moloch-le-dévorateur' and 'Tanit fécondatrice'. Flaubert has taken this anthropomorphic interpretation and shown how it corresponds to psychological necessities. His emphasis on the relationship between sexual and religious drives is even more explicit in the manuscript plans than in the finished novel, where they have been carefully integrated into the whole.[17] In the manuscripts Flaubert frequently mentions the idea of religious prostitution and the episode in the tent is seen in these terms: 's'allie très bien à l'idée des prostitutions religieuses' (folio 200). Furthermore, in a page of notes about 'Le Culte', we find 'la circoncision a le même sens que la prostitution. c'est le sacrifice de la chair, initiation à la vie'.[18] The priesthood, aware of the nature of the attraction of their religion, exploit it to the full: 'profitant d'un ancien usage religieux ils exigeaient que les matrones vierges vinssent se prostituer dans le temple de Tanith' (folio 200).

For all Salammbô's strange mysticism, she has many of the characteristics of Emma Bovary.[19] Emma, while attending the convent, 's'assoupit doucement à la langueur mystique qui s'exhale des parfums de l'autel' (I, 586); Salammbô, in the scenarios, is described as being in an 'état hystéro-mystique languissant' (folio 187). Emma believed that she had a true religious vocation; Salammbô 'avait voulu être prêtresse' (folio 187). And Emma, newly-married, is surprised not to feel the happiness she had expected, just as Salammbô in the tent is 'surprise de ne pas avoir ce bonheur qu'elle s'imaginait autrefois. Elle restait mélancolique devant son rêve accompli' (I, 760). It is in the character of Salammbô that Flaubert gives most clear expression to his views about the connection between religious aspirations and sexuality. Just as, for Emma, 'Les comparaisons de fiancé, d'époux, d'amant céleste et de mariage éternel qui reviennent dans les sermons lui soulevaient au fond de l'âme des douceurs inattendues' (I, 586), so Salammbô 'recherche comme la lune un époux qu'elle ne voit jamais' (folio 187). Even her name reinforces the link, since Salambo was a Babylonian goddess, akin to Venus, and constantly in a state of agitation, weeping for her lover Adonis.

Flaubert notes in the manuscript: 'influence du nom de Salammbô sur la fille d'Hamilcar. Astarté pleure Adonis, un immense deuil pèse sur elle – elle cherche. elle a un amour vague & funèbre' (folio 198). So Salammbô, the descendant of Melkarth 'dieu des Sidoniens et père de sa famille' (1, 698), is at the same time described in terms of the type of dreamy and frustrated young nineteenth-century woman frequently referred to by Flaubert.[20] She has all the symptoms of the young relative of Mlle Leroyer de Chantepie discussed in a letter of 1859. This girl had apparently become obsessed with religious ideas and had lost her mind – not an uncommon phenomenon among young women, commented Flaubert. 'Ne voyez-vous pas qu'elles sont toutes amoureuses d'Adonis? C'est l'éternel époux qu'elles demandent. Ascétiques ou libidineuses, elles rêvent l'amour, le grand amour; et pour les guérir (momentanément du moins) ce n'est pas une idée qu'il leur faut, mais un fait, un homme, un enfant, un amant.'[21]

Flaubert has emphasised those sides of the Carthaginian religions which reveal aspects of the Carthaginian mentality, and again we see that he has chosen elements which also seemed particularly relevant in nineteenth-century France. To this extent, the religious element fits into what we have already distinguished as Flaubert's pattern of selection of historical detail, strengthening the links between the two cultures. But it also has another, more important function: Flaubert has related it back to ancient myth, and, drawing on his knowledge of developments in mythological studies, lifts his narrative out of its strict temporal context and thereby reveals the existence of the fundamental, primitive, universal impulses behind his story.

Nowhere is this more evident than in his handling of the relationship between Salammbô and Mâtho.[22] Although we know from Polybius' account that Mathos was the name of one of the leaders of the barbarian army and that Amilcar had a daughter whom he gave in marriage to Naravase, the strange love between Mâtho and Salammbô and its bearing on the course of the war has always been thought to be of Flaubert's own invention. Critics have assumed that it belonged entirely to his creative imagination. An exchange of letters, however, dating from the middle of 1857 when Flaubert was planning his Carthaginian novel, suggests that initial inspiration was provided by the myth of Pasiphaë; on a close reading it becomes clear that this myth forms an organising structure which underlies the finished novel.

Reading the newly published first volume of the *Histoire des religions de la Grèce antique* by his friend Alfred Maury, Flaubert was struck by a passage which read: 'Pasiphaë...est aussi une divinité lunaire, à en juger par l'étymologie de son nom, et sur ses rapports avec le taureau, animal emblématique de la lune. Une légende la fait d'ailleurs fille d'Hélios, le soleil.'[23] When Flaubert wrote to Frédéric Baudry in June 1857 for information relating to Carthage he included a query about this passage and asked: 'M. Maury croit-il qu'il y aurait absurdité à dire que: la légende de Pasiphaë est phénicienne? Cette idée m'a été fournie par la page 507–08 de son volume ou du moins semble en ressortir.'[24] Maury evidently believed that Flaubert was planning to write a novel based on the myth of Pasiphaë and set in Carthage, as his reply to Baudry shows:

Quant à Pasiphaë, on la tenait jadis pour dûment phénicienne, j'ai quelque doute sur l'authenticité de son acte de naissance, mais, en la faisant phénicienne, on ne fera que copier le registre de l'Etat civil mythologique encore déposé dans nos académies. Les Crétois passent pour avoir pris cette légende aux Phéniciens.

Adieu mon cher ami, faites bien mon amitié à l'heureux père de Mme Bovary; j'aimerais à lui voir donner le jour à une plus aimable fille; Mme Pasiphaë me fait peur! Si les boeufs lisaient, cela pourrait les intéresser, mais l'informe bourgeois, le vil bourgeois en serait scandalisé.[25]

Maury's alarm was groundless – Pasiphaë is never mentioned in the novel. Yet her myth does inform the meaning of the finished work.

The myth is a familiar one. As Friedrich Creuzer tells it,[26] Pasiphaë, wife of Minos II of Crete, was the daughter of the sun and herself a moon-goddess. Minos had incurred the wrath of Neptune after refusing the finest bull in his herd to him, and in revenge Neptune made Pasiphaë fall in love with a bull. Their offspring was the Minotaur, a monster with the head of a bull and the body of a man, which lived in the labyrinth built for it by Daedalus and devoured the young people brought to it in sacrifice. According to some versions, the bull became savage and devastated the whole of Crete until Hercules captured it and had it killed.

The symbolism of *Salammbô* closely follows this outline. Salammbô, like Pasiphaë, is constantly associated with the moon and for Mâtho she is the moon-goddess herself. Like Pasiphaë, too, she is descended from the sun – the sun-god Melkarth is 'père de sa famille' (1, 698), and Hamilcar, her father, is several times given the attributes of a sun-god (an association which is corroborated by Maury).[27] Hamilcar makes his first appearance at sunrise – the *Annonciateur-des-lunes* shades his eyes from the light and sounds his trumpet to announce the simultaneous arrival of Hamilcar and the sun – he is the *Oeil de Baal* who stands on the highest step of the altar in the temple of Moloch like a sun-god with rays of golden light fanning out behind him, and Salammbô fears her father 'comme un dieu'. Salammbô also possesses Pasiphaë's ability to calm and soothe – when she appears at the feast the enraged and violent barbarians, 'ces bêtes brutes', suddenly fall silent as if calmed by her presence, just as Pasiphaë was able to subdue 'par son charme les taureaux devenus furieux'. Pasiphaë and Salammbô share this attribute of 'la lune subjuguant tous les êtres par l'attrait de la volupté'.[28]

Mâtho, already singled out from the crowd by his 'taille colossale' (I, 698), is described not as an ordinary man but as the embodiment of animality: he is massive, brutal, fierce, single-minded, sensual and possessed of superhuman strength. His voice is a thunderous bellow; he stands 'béant, la tête basse, les prunelles fixes...et râlant comme un taureau blessé' (I, 704). Salammbô is drawn to him as inexorably as Pasiphaë is drawn to her bull, for 'cet amour est une fatalité des dieux' (folio 193).

After the scene in Mâtho's tent the mercenaries' attack on Carthage is redoubled until the dreadful effigy of Moloch, half-man, half-bull, emerges from its labyrinthine temple.[29] Several of the sources consulted by Flaubert assert that the Minotaur and Moloch were simply two representations of the same concept. In the notes to his translation of Creuzer's *Symbolique*, Guigniaut states that 'Le Minotaure dévorant des enfants est encore une autre légende...qui se fond sur le culte du terrible Moloch, répresenté avec une tête de Taureau.' Maury makes the same point: 'La fable du Minotaure doit certainement son origine à une idole de la divinité solaire à laquelle on sacrifiait, comme à Moloch, des victimes humaines, et très probablement des jeunes gens.'[30] Thus the sacrifice of the Carthaginian children to Moloch, an event which is vouched for in all the histories of the period, merges with the story of the mythological Minotaur. The ending of Flaubert's novel is also in keeping with the myth since just as the bull was said to have been captured by Hercules and put to death after having devastated Crete, so Mâtho, after having laid waste the area around Carthage, is conquered by Hamilcar (associated with Hercules), captured in a net like a wild animal ('avec un de ces larges filets à prendre des bêtes farouches', I, 793), and ritually slaughtered.

On the level of simple narrative, Salammbô's debt to the Pasiphaë myth seems clear, yet it would be of minor interest if the connection went no further than this. What is more revealing is the way in which Flaubert has used the myth, developing its associations, applying its accepted interpretations, and assimilating it into the historical context.

As late as 1861 he was still working on the problem, now trying to relate the myth of Proserpine to Tanit.[31] It is significant that Creuzer, who was undoubtedly his chief source here and who devotes one book of his *Symbolique* to 'Cérès et Proserpine et leurs mystères', should not only relate Proserpine to the Carthaginian Venus–Astarté, but also identify both of them with Pasiphaë: 'L'héroine ou la déesse lunaire Pasiphaë est identique à Proserpine et à Vénus à la fois.'[32] Proserpine, like Tanit and Pasiphaë, belongs 'à l'humide élément, à la sphère humide de la lune', and with her mother Ceres is considered to be the mother of creation.[33] Elsewhere, he explains how the goddesses, Proserpine, Ceres and Astarté, came to merge together in the minds of their worshippers, and says that 'Ce culte étranger se nationalisa tout-à-fait à Carthage après la conquête.'[34] So the reference to the priests of Ceres and Proserpine in Carthage in the finished novel, and Flaubert's note in the dossier explaining that '*La prière de Salammbô*, chap. III. est l'imitation de la tournure de la prière de Psyché à Cérés. (Apulée: *Métamorphoses*, liv. VI)' (folio 160), are not only consistent with contemporary mythological scholarship, but, more important, show Flaubert's determination to draw on the combination of attributes of the Pasiphaë – Proserpine – Ceres – Astarté goddess, which, as we shall see, will enrich and pull together the strands of the fictional narrative.

On the one hand, Flaubert's interest in the myth of Pasiphaë can be seen as an attempt to breathe life into the rather dry facts of his historical sources, and on the other, the mythological element is being used as a means of expressing fundamental truths about man and his relation to the natural world: the interpretations which have been suggested for this myth resonate through the novel and enrich its meaning.

At one level, the myth may be seen as expressing the relationship between two apparently opposing forces in man. 'Toujours des oppositions, des actions contraires', writes Creuzer; 'L'opposition tantôt a lieu entre des êtres distincts, tantôt se concentre dans les aspects divers d'un même individu.'[35] Thus the purity and serenity of Pasiphaë is contrasted with the violent animal instincts of the bull, but it gradually becomes evident that this opposition is far from

clear-cut: Pasiphaë and the bull are drawn to each other, and the
contrast is further confused as the bull is shown to be not only fierce
and destructive but also, on occasion, calm and docile. Similarly,
Pasiphaë is described not only as 'une séduisante, une secourable
déesse, qui porte avec elle la fécondité et le salut', but also as 'une
funeste sorcière'.[36]

The idea of the combination of animal and spiritual qualities in
man is, of course, a familiar one in Flaubert's writing, from Djalioh,
the anthropoid monster who combines violence with fine sensibilities,
to saint Antoine, struggling to deny his baser impulses and achieve
spiritual purity. In *Salammbô* the opposition is clearly presented in the
opening chapter where the mercenary army is described in animal
terms: they are 'bêtes brutes' (i, 696), they 'imitent le cri des bêtes
féroces, leurs bonds' (i, 695), and they fall upon their companions
'comme sur des bêtes sauvages' (i, 697). The Carthaginians on the
other hand are at this stage represented only by Giscon, aloof and
controlled, and by Salammbô and the priests of Tanit with their
gentle, mystical chants. Yet the opposition, as one finds so often with
Flaubert, is an illusory one; the stereotyped categories in which one
is tempted to view the world are broken down, and the novel follows
the pattern of the myth. So Salammbô and Mâtho are drawn together
just as Pasiphaë was drawn to the bull; Mâtho, 'cet homme
formidable qui fait trembler Carthage' (i, 760), is shown to be quiet
and subdued under Salammbô's influence, and even dreams of living
with her in the 'Iles fortunées' whose idyllic calm is symbolised in
an early version by 'des boeufs blancs' which 'ruminent des fleurs
sur les prés verts' (folio 200). Salammbô herself reflects Pasiphaë's
malevolent and beneficent duality by being held responsible both for
the misfortunes of the Carthaginians, and for their final victory.[37]
Likewise, the two armies soon destroy the contrast which had been
established between them:[38] the animal-like barbarians turn out to
have an unexpectedly well-ordered and disciplined camp, and the
Carthaginians soon lose their veneer of civilisation and show themselves to be quite as cruel and savage as their enemies. They, too,
come to be described in animal terms, and eventually bring out the
Moloch – Minotaur figure, the ultimate symbol of man's destructive
qualities, to which their children are sacrificed with the ritual cries
of 'Ce ne sont pas des hommes, mais des boeufs!...Des boeufs! des
boeufs!' (i, 781). Their animalism is further confirmed when a group
of them lure the barbarians to their death in the *défilé de la Hache*
by running in the midst of a herd of galloping steer.

But the Pasiphaë myth affords another interpretation to which *Salammbô* remains equally faithful. Creuzer sees the union of Pasiphaë and the bull as an expression of 'le dogme antique de l'hymen du soleil avec la lune au printemps, et de la fécondation de la terre par la lune, qui en est la conséquence'.[39] This seasonal cycle of fertility and sterility is exactly paralleled in the novel,[40] which opens in the lush, fertile garden and shows the mercenaries admiring the 'opulence de la terre' around the city. As the season advances 'la verdure de la campagne disparaissait par endroits sous de longues plaques jaunes'; the long winter period with its mists and cold winds is followed by the drought and excessive heat of the month of Eloul, and the Carthaginians wearily await 'la fête trois fois sainte' marking the 'résurrection de l'année' – at this stage, the moon-goddess is withholding her fertile influence: 'Elle refusait la bienfaisance de ses eaux, elle avait déserté Carthage; c'était une transfuge, une ennemie. Quelques-uns, pour l'outrager, lui jetaient des pierres' (I, 751). Chapter 11, 'Sous la tente', opens with a description of the parched grass and cracked earth, and the fields are as barren as the desert although it is now spring-time, 'l'époque des semailles' (I, 756).

Appropriately, then, it is at 'l'époque des semailles' that Salammbô loses her virginity to Mathô and is 'prise dans la force du soleil' (I, 760). Not until the emergence of the Moloch – Minotaur figure, however, is the union of sun and moon shown to be fertile as the rain begins to fall: 'Elle tomba toute la nuit, abondamment, à flots; la tonnerre grondait; c'était la voix de Moloch; il avait vaincu Tanit; – et, maintenant fécondée, elle ouvrait du haut du ciel son vaste sein' (I, 781). By the end of that chapter Salammbô's garden is overgrown with vegetation, and more than three months later the ceremonial tables are piled high with grapes, lemons, pome- granates, gourds and water-melons, reminding the reader of the feast of the first chapter and showing that the seasons have come full circle.

The ritual killing of Mâtho at this point in the narrative corresponds, too, to Creuzer's interpretation of the myth. He suggests that the bull was a symbol of force, a force which could be harnessed and used: thus Pasiphaë's ability to calm the bull expressed man's ability to dominate and cultivate the earth, and the ox or bull domesticated for agricultural purposes was seen as symbolising the cooperation of the sun and moon and their fertile influences on herds and crops.[41] It was because of this association of the bull with agriculture and fertility, says Creuzer, that bulls were selected as the most propitious

offering to be sacrificed on great public occasions – particularly to
celebrate the end of a war. And since the bull was dominated by the
moon,[42] the moon was considered at these ceremonies to be
'*victorieuse*, ou, ce qui est la même chose, la *Victoire* personnifiée,
présenté originairement avec les mêmes attributs que la lune. Elle
aussi elle dompte le taureau et l'abat.'[43]

As we have seen, the 'taming' of Mâtho by Salammbô and the
subsequent conjunction of sun and moon mark the return of fertility
and plenty, coinciding with the final defeat of the barbarians. So it
is appropriate that Mâtho should be ritually put to death before
Salammbô (when he saw her for the first time he had had a
premonition that he was to be the victim of a holocaust she had
promised the gods); and that she should be acclaimed by her people
as 'ayant sauvé la Patrie' (I, 794) and symbolise for them the
Carthaginian moon-goddess victorious: 'Salammbô resplendissante
se confondait avec Tanit et semblait le génie même de Carthage, son
âme corporifiée' (I, 795). Mâtho's death, on the other hand, is
described in terms which recall the slaughter of the sacrificial bull
to Proserpine[44] – he is described as an animal, 'courbé en deux, avec
l'air effaré des bêtes fauves quand on les rend libres tout à coup...il
n'avait plus, sauf les yeux, d'apparence humaine' (I, 795–6), and his
heart is cut out with the sacrificial knife reserved for cutting up the
sacred meat in the temple.

It seems clear, then, that the story of Pasiphaë and its related myths
underlie the narrative of *Salammbô* and draw together the historical
and invented elements of the plot. The Mercenary War and the part
played in it by Mâtho, Hamilcar and Moloch are historically verifiable,
yet on the imaginative plane they are absorbed into myth: they
are inseparable from Salammbô, and the sun and moon, and the
changing seasons. Their dual rôles, as historical fact and mythological
metaphor, are perfectly fused. The problem that remains to be
considered, however, is what contribution the underlying Pasiphaë
myth makes to the meaning of the novel.

The same question recurs when we turn to the Christian symbolism
in *Salammbô*. It is of course well known that Flaubert borrowed many
details from the Bible and that he acknowledged a debt to the notes
and commentaries of the Cahen translation. Several critics have
discussed his biblical borrowings which served as a source of
historical detail and local colour;[45] but no one has adequately
explained why, if Flaubert was truly in search of authentic details

and accurate local colour, he should have drawn them from a source so far removed in time and place from Carthage. When Sainte-Beuve raised objections on this very point, Flaubert could only make the feeble retort that Hebrews were closer to Carthaginians than the Chinese![46] An equally puzzling point which has so far escaped attention is that many of the details of the novel form a grotesque parody of Christian teaching, a transposition of Christian symbolism into a pagan context.

Salammbô opens with an idyllic description of the gardens of Hamilcar which invites comparison with the Garden of Eden:

> Des figuiers entouraient les cuisines; un bois de sycomores se prolongeait jusqu'à des masses de verdure, où des grenades resplendissaient parmi les touffes blanches des cotonniers; des vignes, chargées de grappes, montaient dans le branchage des pins; un champ de roses s'épanouissait sous des lis; un sable noir, mêlé à de la poudre de corail, parsemait les sentiers, et, au milieu, l'avenue des cyprès faisait d'un bout à l'autre comme une double colonnade d'obélisques verts. (I, 694)

Flaubert has here assembled a list of elements which all figure prominently in Christian iconography and are associated with concepts of harmony and tranquility; their juxtaposition reinforces the original state of grace of the garden. The fig-tree is associated with the Tree of Knowledge in the Garden of Eden; the pomegranate is a symbol of fertility and as such represents hope of resurrection and immortality; the Bible refers to the vineyard as a protected place where the children of God (the vines) flourish under the tender care of the Keeper of the vineyard, while the grape itself symbolises the Blood of Christ. The rose is particularly associated with the Garden of Eden where, according to Christian tradition, it grew without thorns – it was only after the fall of man that it took on its thorns to remind him of his state of sin, while its fragrance and beauty recalled the splendour of Paradise. The plane-tree represents charity and moral superiority, and the lily, of course, is a symbol of purity. The unlikely sounding 'poudre de corail' seems less out of place when one remembers that coral was used as a charm against the evil eye and denoted protection against evil. But the coral here is mixed with black sand and the sinister note is repeated by the final reference in the description – the cypresses which stretch right across the garden in two straight lines are symbols of death and so prefigure the imminent destruction of the paradise garden.[47]

From the resulting chaos emerges Spendius, who is constantly associated with disorder and destruction. He is a manipulator, an instigator of action, yet cowardly, and from the very beginning is portrayed as a satanic figure. He is most clearly seen as such at the end of the first chapter when, having emerged from his prison, he sets about enthralling Mâtho. He describes himself as being like a serpent, and tempts Mâtho with cunning and flattery. They are high up – 'sur la terrasse' – and a wide panorama spreads out beneath them as the city emerges from darkness. Spendius tempts Mâtho: 'viens! il y a dans la Chambre des Ancêtres un lingot d'or sous chaque dalle'. He taunts him: 'Ah! oui...oui...maître! je comprends pourquoi tu dédaignais tout à l'heure le pillage de la maison.' His voice is a 'sifflement'. He perseveres, taking Mâtho right to the edge of the terrace and conjuring up a picture of all the injustices the mercenaries have suffered, and of all the riches and glory that are rightfully his, finishing with the cry, 'ils t'obéiront. Commande-les! Carthage est à nous; jetons-nous-y' (I, 699–700).

The parallel with the temptation of Christ by Satan is striking. Both episodes take place on a height, overlooking a rich country; the satanic figure uses flattery and taunts to suggest that his companion seize the wealth stretched out beneath him; the double association of Spendius with a serpent and his falsely obsequious manner emphasise the analogy; and the final exhortation to take command of the troops and swoop down on Carthage corresponds to Satan's incitement to Christ to throw himself down from the parapet of the temple, down into the city beneath, and the demand that he should call up heavenly forces to come to his aid. At Mâtho's initial refusal, Flaubert alters the viewpoint of his description, the picture of the wealth of Carthage and of the voluptuous pleasures in store fades, and the reader's attention is drawn instead to the sinister wastes behind the pair: 'Les arbres derrière eux fumaient encore; de leurs branches noircies, des carcasses de singes à demi-brulées tombaient de temps à autre au milieu des plats. Les soldats ivres ronflaient la bouche ouverte à côté des cadavres...Le sol piétiné disparaissait sous des flaques rouges' (I, 700). Mâtho, son of Moloch, will be unable to resist the temptation of Spendius, and the scene behind them is a vision of the future.

A similar reference to the Scriptures recurs towards the end of the novel. The manuscript plans make the identification plainer: Mâtho's torture, his 'Passion', arouses the curiosity of the women of Carthage, and Flaubert notes 'le corps de l'ennemi (l'hostie) est une chose religieuse. on s'étonne qu'il ressemble au corps d'un autre homme' (folio 207). The double meaning of the word 'hostie' is made evident – both the archaic one of victim offered in sacrifice ('ennemi') and the Christian one of the Host, linking Mâtho yet again with a Christ figure. The analogy is continued in the earliest plans for his death, which was to have been by crucifixion. The Carthaginian bourgeoisie were later to make themselves amulets from the wood of his cross (folio 195). It is just possible that these analogies were merely the unconscious result of long familarity with the Scriptures; but it is more likely, given Flaubert's exceptional awareness of his artistic process, that they were inserted for a deliberate purpose.

It is when the biblical references are considered together with the parallels with the myths of Pasiphaë and Proserpine and Ceres, and seen in the light of the various functions attributed to mythology in the mid nineteenth century, that a coherent answer to the problem begins to emerge. The growing conviction among historians that mythology was a key to understanding the past was clearly one of the strongest arguments for Flaubert's use of the myth of Pasiphaë as the basis of much of the narrative. But it was not the only reason; and his readiness to consider biblical details and non-Carthaginian myths suggests that his motives were not prompted by a simple desire for Punic accuracy. Rather, they seem to coincide with contemporary interest in the relationship between different mythologies. Scholars had for a long time speculated about the reasons for similarities between myths of different nations,[48] and much of the most important research in the nineteenth century focused on comparative studies. A common link between all myths was postulated by Charles-François Dupuis, whose *Origine de tous les cultes ou religion universelle* of 1795 was reprinted several times in the nineteenth century and re-edited in abridged versions; this work is referred to by Flaubert in the *Salammbô* dossier. Dupuis argued that the adventures of gods were simply 'les phénomènes de la Nature mis en allégories',[49] and in particular he stressed the importance of the rising and setting of the sun and stars as the primitive source around which many different myths have been elaborated. C.-F. Volney, also used by Flaubert, [50] was one of many who adopted Dupuis's ideas: in *Les Ruines* he wrote that Christianity is entirely based on the cult of the sun; and Karl Otfried Müller argued that if, as was thought, pagan deities were primeval man's personification of natural forces, then similar myths could arise independently in different cultures.[51]

The *Salammbô* dossier shows how ready Flaubert was to draw analogies with other cults or to borrow details from distant religions: '*La cuiller de Schahabarim* est un trait emprunté aux religions du Mexique' (folio 160); in connection with the religious castrations he writes 'Rapprocher les prêtres de Tanit des Galles et des Copsi de Russie (Voyage de Haxthausen)' (folio 161v) and, later, 'Les similitudes entre l'Egypte et Carthage m'ont été indiquées par plusieurs inscriptions de Gesenius où Isis et Osiris sont formellement mentionnés' (folio 168).

A further function of the mythological element is to suggest connections and comparisons. It is of course a common device with Flaubert to suggest sharp contrasts which gradually fade to reveal fundamental similarities. In *Salammbô*, however, it is only through the intermediary agency of the mythological element that such ironic similarities become evident. For example, on the surface no two characters could be more different than the beautiful young Salammbô and the grotesque figure of Hannon. But the mythological framework within which the novel is set provides the ironic suggestion that Salammbô, the 'génie de Carthage', has much in common with Hannon. Both are strongly under the influence of Tanit and both feel the insidious persecution of Moloch.[52] Tanit is, like Salammbô, 'blanche, douce, lumineuse, immaculée, auxiliatrice, purifiante, sereine' (I, 708), yet she also has her terrible side, producing 'les monstres, les fantômes effrayants, les songes menteurs' and causing corpses to putrefy – a side which corresponds to the portrait of Hannon. Both he and Salammbô spend time over 'les soins du corps'; both cover themselves with pearls (it is Tanit who forms pearls at the bottom of the sea, I, 708), and both are shown using parasols to protect themselves from the sun. Both suffer from indolence and lethargy, and are totally lacking in the energy which is imparted by Moloch.[53] That Hamilcar and Mâtho should both be associated with the sun is only one other of the many subtle ironies suggested by the mythological structure.

The main function of biblical and mythological references seems, however, to be to point to basic patterns of human behaviour. It is the timeless quality of this interpretation of mythology that makes it so important in *Salammbô*, and explains why Flaubert had no scruples about using the Bible and other non-Carthaginian sources for local colour. For the essential meaning of the novel is not restricted to ancient Carthage, and in basing the story of Salammbô and Mâtho on one of the best-known Greek myths, Flaubert has not only provided a unifying structure for his novel; he has also used it to suggest to us that the historical events described form part of a much larger pattern. If the course of the war is inextricably bound up with the movements of the sun and moon and the cycle of the seasons, then the war itself must be seen as part of a cyclical pattern – it is thus lifted out of the realm of simple historical reconstruction and becomes a reflection of Flaubert's view of the eternal repetitions of history, inevitable because human nature never changes. The irony of the ending is that although 'partout on sentait l'ordre rétabli, une existence nouvelle qui recommençait' (I, 794), the sense of triumph and order is illusory since ephemeral: the cycle must begin again.

Conclusion

I have tried to show that at one important level *Salammbô* must be read as an attempt to come to terms with the trauma of 1848. The unreasoned aspirations, the infectious enthusiasm for revolt, the violence of the repression, the brutality and greed shown by both sides – all are as characteristic of 1848 as of the Carthaginian episode. More specific similarities between the social and political situations of the two nations strengthen the parallels and provide evidence that Flaubert modelled his account of the Mercenary War to a large extent on his response to the revolution of 1848.

But to accept this reading is not to explain the novel, any more than Flaubert could satisfactorily explain 1848 by writing *Salammbô*. In the final analysis, *Salammbô* is a novel of questions. It may have started out as an attempt to answer some of the questions about contemporary society that were troubling Flaubert, but it also raises wider issues about the relationship between past and present, between history and fiction – and, ultimately, about how we make sense of experience.

We have seen that when *Salammbô* first appeared, contemporary reviewers were perplexed, primarily because it did not seem to fit into any recognisable literary category. Their confusion is understandable, for *Salammbô* does constantly elude attempts at classification. One of the ironies of the novel is that it is full of misleading signs which seem to indicate how it should be read, but which turn out merely to undermine and frustrate that approach.

One of the ways in which Flaubert seems to invite us to interpret the novel is as an epic. Certainly as we begin to read, we come across many encouraging signs: the opening sentences explain the situation baldly and without emotion; the subject to be treated is an important one; the fate of a nation hangs in the balance, and gods intervene in the struggles of man. Vast panoramic views of crowd and battle scenes give way to minute close-ups. Passages of extravagant description and highly coloured imagery interrupt the simple narrative. Long lists of nationalities follow upon enumerations of types of physique, detail upon detail of exotic costume, food and drink, genealogies and extended similes. All this seems to suggest that

Flaubert is narrating events according to the conventions of the epic and that we should read the novel accordingly. But if we try to do so we fail, for there is no true hero, no model of probity and sacrifice, no glorious resolution of the situation. Neither side can be said to have won, and when the novel ends we are left with a sense of bleakness and futility. The expectations raised by the epic framework are not sustained.

The same thing happens if we try to read the work as a romance, as the opening passages also invite us to do. All the basic elements are there – indeed, a summary of the first part of the plot makes it sound like a paradigm of the genre. A handsome warrior meets and falls in love with a beautiful, high-born maiden; a feud erupts and separates the two; and a jealous rival, favoured by the girl's father, poses an additional threat to their future happiness. But again the expectations raised by a familiar pattern of events are undermined. The 'lovers' come together only once after their initial meeting, Salammbô raises a dagger to stab the sleeping Mâtho, and the plot veers away from the love-story to follow the course of the war and the struggles of the gods. When the end comes, we have to see it as a parody of the conventional romantic ending when hero and heroine are finally united in death. The intervening episodes and the physical horror of the final scene have removed any vestiges of romance.

The strongest temptation, of course, is to read the work as a conventional historical novel. The opening lines proclaim their reliability by naming names we recognise – Carthage, Hamilcar, the battle of Eryx – and the novel proceeds to flesh out the bare account of the Mercenary War left to us by reliable sources such as Polybius.

To show the reasons behind certain historical impulses, to suggest the causes that determine the course of events, to hint at what might have happened if diverse factors had not come together in the way they did – these are among the main preoccupations we might expect of any historical novelist. But in *Salammbô* these conventions, too, are undermined. Whereas Flaubert had felt that the fundamental flaw in the first *Education sentimentale* stemmed from the fact that the progression linking cause and effect was lacking, although causes and effects were shown, in *Salammbô* he has turned this defect into a virtue. For he is constantly suggesting causes, from the most trivial (Hamilcar decides to enter the war because a stone shot from one of the mercenary machines lands in the grounds of his palace) to the most grandiose (Salammbô's love for Mâtho is a fate imposed by the gods).

Orthodox historical reasons for the conflict between the Carthaginians and the mercenaries are put forward – Polybius saw the whole affair as stemming from the Carthaginians' failure to rid themselves of the mercenaries once the peace with Rome had been concluded, and Flaubert uses this explanation and describes the unfair treatment of the mercenaries, banished with vague promises instead of the payment due to them. To these causes he adds individual ambitions, commercial interests and personal animosities. Similarly, he proposes a variety of rational reasons for Mâtho assuming leadership of the mercenaries: he is influenced by Spendius's ambition; he is envious of Carthage's wealth and power; he is prompted by the dissatisfied and angry barbarian army; he is sexually attracted to Salammbô, and conquering her and conquering Carthage become merged in his mind.

But mystical explanations are equally important: rival deities struggle for supremacy over Carthage and manipulate humans for their own ends. It is common for critics to assimilate this set of mythological explanations into a strictly rational reading of the novel, arguing that every 'supernatural' event has an ordinary physiological or psychological explanation – that the protagonists' strong faith in their gods influences the course of the war because the loss and recovery of what they believe to be the most sacred symbol of Tanit first saps and then strengthens their will to fight. The confidence that they have fulfilled their duties to Moloch totally restores their fierce determination. But such a simplistic purpose would do Flaubert little credit and one might well wonder why he should have bothered to resuscitate Carthage if it were only to show that Carthaginians were prey to religious delusion.[1]

By the time we reach the novel's closing sentence we are quite sure that the offered explanations and motives are not to be trusted. 'Ainsi mourut la fille d'Hamilcar pour avoir touché au manteau de Tanit' is clearly inadequate as a summing-up of the events of the novel, just as the explanations throughout the work have repeatedly proved to be inconsistent and unreliable.

Unlike the conventional historical novel, Flaubert's work challenges our will to understand, and frustrates any desire we might have to reduce the complexity of existence to a simple meaning. This is a familiar theme in his writings, from *La Tentation de saint Antoine* where Satan mocks the saint's wish for absolute certainty and torments him by pointing out the self-referential (and therefore objectively unknowable) nature of all knowledge, to *Bouvard and*

Pécuchet where the clerks are constantly frustrated in their efforts to *know*. They are disconcerted when accounts of what they had assumed to be objective fact turn out to be subjective interpretations which contradict one another and reveal their inherent unreliability. Bouvard and Pécuchet's final decision to give up their quest for knowledge and to return to copying is a gesture of frustration and despair when faced with the impossibility of ever understanding anything with categorical certainty.

We have already seen that after his youthful enthusiasm for the genre, Flaubert had little taste for the kind of historical novel that was being written in France in the first half of the nineteenth century – he was not particularly interested in accuracy of factual detail; he was unimpressed by novels which used history simply as a ready source of excitement and intrigue; and he scoffed at those who used history to give their novels a spurious respectability. If we come to *Salammbô* with expectations generated by such conventions we are bound to be disconcerted. For it is this refusal to perpetuate the traditional historical novel's simplistic view of the past as 'knowable' in some absolute sense that is one of *Salammbô*'s main achievements.

Flaubert openly admitted that what might appear to be a meticulous Carthaginian reconstruction in fact contains details borrowed from other ancient civilisations and from other periods. More important, he undermines our expectation of a narrative which is firmly rooted in fact, and which will fill the gaps in the historical account with invention that seems both rational and probable. Instead, he weaves his fictional strands round the factual framework in such a way that the expected solidity of historical truth fades away into superstition, hallucination, myth. Myth frees the narrative from its Carthaginian context and illuminates the universal, unchanging nature of the fundamental human traits of love, hate, cruelty, greed, jealousy and fear. It shows us that the events which took place in Carthage were not an isolated phenomenon in a safely distant past, but must have their counterparts in any society, at any time.

History, he seems to be saying, is not fixed and finished; it is akin to myth in that both are attempts to find a conceptual system into which to fit a confusion of facts. The facts of the past have a significance for us which changes in relation to the present – we fit them into patterns of understanding which are inevitably coloured by contemporary problems and preoccupations. 'L'histoire n'est que la réflexion du présent sur le passé, et voilà pourquoi elle est toujours à refaire.'[2]

Appendix   *Unpublished manuscript material*

Many of Flaubert's early manuscript plans and notes for *Salammbô* were
published for the first time in volume II of the Club de l'honnête homme
edition of the *Oeuvres complètes*. They come from the Bibliothèque
Nationale collection, nouvelles acquisitions françaises (BN n.a.fr.) 23.662.

The following pages contain three unpublished folios from the
Bibliothèque Municipale, Rouen, Ms. g322, and a transcription of the
notes and fragmentary plans from BN n.a.fr. 23.662 which have
remained unpublished. (See notes 26 and 27, chapter 3.)

In transcribing the manuscripts I have used obliques (/.../) to indicate
Flaubert's interlinear additions, and pointed brackets (⟨...⟩) to indicate his
crossings-out. I have put in accents, but left abbreviations, spellings and
punctuation as they appear in the manuscript.

The letters or marks in bold type reproduce the manuscript marks
occasionally used by Flaubert to show how his additions link into his
main text. Marked additions which appear as marginal notes in the
manuscript have here been inserted in the appropriate marked place in
the text; other marked additions are printed as they occur in the
manuscript. It should be noted, however, that Flaubert's use of these
marks is not always consistent – sometimes he marks only one of the
elements to be linked, or marks both, but with different letters.

Rouen g322A

{ les mercenaires ⟨arrivent par légions⟩ dans la ville & s'amassent
  on leur donne à chacun une pièce d'or, et on leur promet qu'on les
  paiera tous à Sicca
– à Sicca ils calculent.

{ Hannon les prie de consentir à une réduction. révolte. ils viennent près
  de Tunis. députations des bourgeois. exigences graduelles des
  mercenaires.

{ Giscon. Matho & Spendius existent à la discorde. – ils pillent la caisse &
  chargent de fers G. & ses compagnons.

{ Matho envoie des députés à toutes les villes de la Libye. & assiège
  Utique et Hippone.
  révolte générale des villes soumises à Carthage.

.– Hannon battu par les mercenaires.

{ Hamilcar nommé général (238) bat les M.
{ fait lever le siège d'Utique

{ Hamil. resserré dans une position dangereuse est secouru par Naravase.
{ qui lui promet sa fille.

– supplice de Giscon
– défection d'Utique & d'Hippone
– siège de Carth. par les Mercenaires
– terreur – H. délivre Carth. les mercen. reprenn. la campagne.
– Ham. exterm. l'armée de Spendius qui se livre –
  – siège de Tunis, supplice de Spendius.
Annibal est surpris par M. et attaché à une croix.
– réconciliat. d'Ham & d'H. prise & mort de Mathos.

Rouen g322A verso

– mercenaires chez la fille d'Hamilcar
Pyra X/X est du parti des mercenaries qui à la fin vont trop loin/ – indécise.
on les met à la porte –
Sicca. – on s'embête.
vol du manteau.
tout est désespéré
retour d'Hamilcar
lares
séance de nuit
on convient que Pyra doit le reprendre
nuit dans le camp
Naravase & Hamil.
chute.
mort de Math. – mariage
mort de Pyra.

Rouen g322B

I. Description de Carthage. position topographique – vue
d'ensemble – ce qu'elle était au moral – ⟨religion⟩ races diverses.
/commerce monopole proie/ religion politique.

II. état de Carthage après la 1ère guerre punique – les Mercenaires –
/d'abord se refont. ils arrivent amaigris, échinés – dans le temple
d'Eschmoun – puis convoitent/
troublent la ville
logés dans la maison civile d'Hamilcar à Mégara. X

/X les sénateurs détestent Hamilcar. prquoi. isolement de ⟨Mat⟩
Sallambo cependant/
/ce qu'elle était. palais – magasins – communs – parc – métairie.
viviers. animaux. étoiles/
de plus en plus insolents. Sallambo a l'idée de leur donner un
festin.

III. Festin (2) – Dans les jardins (1) /roues hydrauliques, jarres/ grossier
et terrible. Vantardises /– on parle des chasses différentes/ tour de
forces /imitent la voix des bêtes féroces/ – on s'échauffe.
on entend un chant de rameurs – délivrance des esclaves de
l'ergastule
apparition de Spendius avec les fers aux mains brisés. libation
/parallelisme de Matho et de Naravas et contraste Ψ/ /Ψ
éblouissement de l'un, jalousie de l'autre/
– fureurs – tout à coup Sallambo paraît, au fond, escaliers.
Applaudissements.
Chante /voix funèbre/ danse, /verse à boire à Mathos/Giscon
Naravas s'esquive avec lui /1) Fuite de Sall /qui a peur/ aux
environs dans un char mulets. – dais petits nuages roses fond bleu/
2) Soleil levant sur les débris de l'orgie. les pins brulants comme des
torches fumantes
/soldats couchés, éblouis par le jour qui vient/
M. cherche Sallambo X /X la maison est vide – description de sa
chambre/
et ne la trouve pas.

IV. Le lendemain les bourgeois se mêlent aux mercenaires. on leur fait
entendre raison. Ils partent avec Naravas qui a machiné
secrètement. – filles publiques – expansion de Spendius qui a des
armes. il est libre. /se balance sur son chameau ivre de liberté M/
/M C'est pendant la route qu'ils se font des confidences et exposent
leurs antécédents./

V. A Sicca. S'embêtent. /peu de vivres – changement de
régime – regrettent Carth./ Calculent sur le sable. Naravas essaie
plusieurs fois de perdre Matho, n'y parvient pas /tentatives déjouées
par Spendius/ & s'en va.
Mélancolies de Matho. Spendius le réconforte.
/rêves de retraite – pas de nouvelles – rien! rien – on s'impatiente/
/s'aperçoivent qu'on les a joués. – vont à C. les portes sont fermées.
on ne veut jamais les y recevoir./

VI. Arrivée d'Hannon, un soir, /en litière – cheveux rares frisés
couverts d'huile et de poudre d'or/ vue du camp, troupeaux de
chèvres, les filles servant les soldats. /la vue de son luxe les irrite/
Hannon espèce de Vitellius lépreux. propositions. Caractère féroce

de Spendius. discours indirect aux soldats où il expose tous les griefs. – faux interprète. Hannon ne comprend pas ce qui les révolte & leur dit des injures alors on se fâche. Révolte. on renvoie ignominieusement Hannon. fuite sur un âne pendant qu'on lui jette des pierres. les Mercenaires plient les tentes /il fait beau/ & se mettent en marche brusquement. /joie. on reprend de l'air, on va se battre, on rentre dans la vie active./

VII.   On voit revenir les filles échignées /ce qu'elles racontent des projets des merc. fait peur aux bourgeois/
deputation des bourgeois. ils restent plusieurs jours au camp. /à qque. distance (6 lieues) devant Tunis [feux que l'on aperçoit de Carthage bruit de cymbales]/ – s'y mêlent – disputes pr. le prix des vivres. – confusion. intimité ironique. on leur fait porter les armes, etc. – les prétentions deviennent exorbitantes /ils demandent en mariage les filles des patriciens – des places au sénat, etc./ – allées et venues. on se fâche.

VIII.   Giscon. /arrive par le lac-salé R/ /R la caisse militaire portée par plusieurs hommes/ Autharite. on le retient captif. – (il reste plusieurs jours au camp avant que tout ne soit perdu)

IX.   Matho & Spendius X /X sont embarrassés maintenant mais il faut pousser les choses à outrance. s'attendant à des vengeances/ /Sp. a l'idée de couper l'aqueduc/ se jettent dans l'aqueduc – citernes.

X.   Matho chez Sallambo. /c'est une dernière tentative qu'il fait – une proposition avant de se porter aux dernières extrémités./
Elle le repousse, indécise, étonnée, ahurie.
/au petit jour. elle couchée sur un lit suspendu ⟨divan, l'eunuque & deux femmes à ses pieds, endormis⟩/
vol du peplos dans le temple de Tanit.
/dans la journée, on apprend à Carthage le traitement de Giscon – agitation de la ville. Sallambô seule – 2e visite/ horreur du sacrilège. elle refuse. M. traverse la ville. /quand il étale le voile dans la chambre c'est comme un firmament qui se déploie/

XI.   Fureur de Matho. révolte de toute l'Afrique [énumeration des peuples – /ceci à mettre plus tard au siège de Carthage]/ /il assiège Utique & Hippone/ Hannon battu à Utique. joie des mercenaires. /les M. d'abord effrayés par les éléphants. insister sur la revanche & la facilité avec laquelle ils battent Hannon/ épouvante des bourgeois. on rappelle Hamilcar.

XII.   retour d'Hamilcar. – H. dans sa chapelle. Betyles.
Séance du sénat. /systèmes politiques différents tirés de l'hist. carthag. reproches – injures/ H. l'envoie promener. /assis tous sur

des sièges de cèdre larges: manches oiseau. – défense du poignard./
H. dans sa maison se fait rendre ses comptes. le père & la fille.
/comme on lui a dit que M. était sorti de sa maison avec le peplos &
que sa fille avait participé au vol il déclare qu'il n'est pas de sa
dignité de l'interroger là-dessus – & ne l'interroge pas. tout se passe
en regard/
/état maladif & mystique de tout le monde à Carthage. H. se décide
quand il voit l'ergastule brisé/

/passage du Macar de nuit au clair de lune. bataille du Macar.
insister sur la stratégie. Les M. reviennent sur Tunis. Math. est à
Hippone. Hamilcar pris dans une plaine – il baisse dans l'opinion du
sénat. il est question de le crucifier s'il se laisse battre. On attribue
ce malheur au vol du peplos./
résolution de Sallambô.

XIII. Sallambô au camp. B /B elle arrive à cheval, voilée. près du
retranchement, un archer-sentinelle l'empêche. elle demande M. il
arrive. ⟨se dévoile⟩ sorte d'effroi. elle se dévoile. laisse son cheval
au piquet avec l'eunuque. M. la conduit à sa tente./
baisade sous le peplos /S. s'étonne de la faiblesse de M. qui pleure
d'amour. un homme si terrible qui fait trembler Carth. – Elle a
envie de le tuer *illegible word* lui tombe des sueurs de peur. Il se
réveille – la ronde/ apparition de Giscon. la fosse où on l'a jeté est
sur les derrières du camp près la tente de Mathos.

/Math. a fait sa fonction avec Spendius/

Sallambô s'enfuit.
défection de Naravas – consentement de Sallambô.

XIV. Les mercenaires /1)/ sont battus (Spendius & Autarite s'enfuient)
clémence d'Hamilcar /(3)./ les prisonniers rendus à la liberté
passent devant le camp en blaguant leurs anciens
camarades. – tableau du champ de bataille. 2) funérailles diverses
/4)/ – Supplices de Giscon. retour tendre. la corde se relâche.
Autarite & Sp. reviennent le soir. Avantages des mercenaires.
Utique & Hippone abandonnent Carthage.

Rouen g322B verso

XV. Siège de Carthage – on coupe l'aqueduc. – soif de tout un peuple.
/la ville tendue de noir/ – Moloch /H. est obligé de donner un des
enfants. – convulsion d'Annibal. H. le regarde dormir./ revers des
mercenaires. – défilé de la hache. on se mange. les lions. /Mathos
assiégé à Tunis Ψ/
/Ψ Sp. se livre à Hamilcar. hideux de misère – sale. les députés des

mercenaires sous la tente avec des yeux rouges comme des loups
affamés dévorent un plat/ /double croix – action générale &
dernière/
prise de Matho.
délibération. supplice.
Festin de noces – ⟨retombe⟩ mort. M. s'avance. mouvement de S.
M. expire. Elle se reçoit. on la félicite. Naravas élève sa coupe (tous
l'imitent) & boit au génie de Carthage /en lui passant le bras
gauche sous la taille)/ – Sall. lève la sienne. Mais elle retombe,
morte, pr. avoir touché au peplos d'Astarté.

/xv. à Carth. on arme les vieillards, on répare les fortifications/

/influence du nom de Salambo = Astarté sur le caractère de S.
Astarté pleure Adonis. un deuil immense pèse sur elle. Elle cherche.
S. a un amour vague & funèbre./

/1. Quartier des pêcheurs. – amas de coquilles au pied des maisons
/en bois/ mouches. soleil. gd. filets noirs suspensus avec l'eau
visqueuse entre les mailles comme des toiles.
les filles publiques /du dernier rang/ en dehors des fortifications.
l'étang de la Sabtha. huttes en terre, basses, dans les plis des dunes.

Rouen g322C

Le cri de la hyène.

Son mugissement sonore n'a rien de la majesté de la voix du lion ni de la
farouche âpreté du jappement rauque du léopard, c'est un hululement
plaintif & prolongé sur un ton mineur, qui va crescendo pour s'évanouir
en une finale discordante.

Voy. en Abyssinie.
Rattray (94)

instrument de musique dans les églises:
une sorte d'**U** en fer muni d'une poignée à sa base fermé à son ouverture
par une tige où sont enfilées de petites rondelles qui résonnent en se
choquant, quand on agite l'instrument.

(Bos.)

———

en Abyssinie dans chefs de l'église: l'*Aboussa* est l'évêque spirituel,
toujours étranger & l'*Etchéquié* chef temporel indigène.

BN n.a.fr. 23.662

Fol. 185

ch. III

⟨dans la campagne chameaux en liberté prquoi. v. livr sacrés de l'orient.⟩

---

illegible word sort par les flèches.
jouant dans l'eau.
enfants se mettant des pastèques vides sur la tête, turbans.
soleil couchant comme la queue d'un phénix
dans le temple de tanit intérieur colombes tenant des globes à un fil⟩

15	16	250	192
12	12	3	40
30	32		232
15	16		
180	192		

Fol. 186

I Festin
II le lendemain – en route – Matho & Spendius
III A Sicca
IV Hannon
V ⟨Sallambô chez elle⟩
V les bourgeois au camp
VI Giscon

Fol. 189v

Opposition physique – & haine entr'eux – des prêtres de Tanit & des prêtres de Baal-Schamon. les premiers eunuques, /vêtus de/ blancs, gras, faibles, féminins – qques uns d'une graisse monstrueuse – comme des hippopotames enfarinés. Les seconds rouges, /de vêtement & de teint/ colossaux – des gladiateurs pontificaux.

/supplice/ Matho. il descendit les soixante degrés du ⟨temple⟩ /Byrsa/ – & à chacun, un supplice nouveau le relevait – un enfant lui arracha l'oreille...des femmes lui crachèrent au visage.

Fol. 196

⟨La terre flotte comme une barque au milieu des mers⟩
⟨plus calme /& bon/ dans la nature, quand Tanith va apparaître les flots se calment, les feuilles ne remuent plus, les oiseaux chantent
...la lune mange les pierres. elle est dévorante, qqu'elle féconde⟩
⟨...aient que les   *(folio has been cut at this point)*
...seraient très indisciplinés⟩

Fol. 201v

fin du chapitre x
⟨Narr'havas voulait faire révolter toute l'afriq. & se créer un royaume
indépendant. mais voyant H. le plus fort il se rangea de son côté. En
prévision de toute éventualité il n'avait pas voulu (rappeler cela) faire le
siège de Carth. ce qui eût été une folie alors. & il allégua près
d'Hamilcar que c'était grâce à lui qu'on ne l'avait pas fait. il voulait
toujours se ménager une retraite. Il a attaqué les deux villes ⟨voi⟩
Utique & Hippo-Zaryte, voisines de son pays.⟩
(*paragraph joined by face bracket to*) ⟨c'est ce qu'il dit à Ham. en se donnant
à lui dans sa tente⟩
/Hamilcar jeta sur l'Afrique une partie de l'Afrique. la défection de
Narr'havas fut donc pr. lui de la plus haute importance. ⟨en ay⟩ avec
les Numides, l'occident, il combattait les Lybiens, l'Orient,

———

avait promis le droit de cité à ses soldats-lybiens.
Hannon. l'éléphant est consacré au soleil. rapport de l'éléph. & de
l'éphantiasis [*sic*] Bien que ces malades fissent horreur le doigt des
Dieux est sur eux. (Joseph ant. J. 3.2. – honneurs qu'on leur rend. rage
du coït. on se châtre pr. se guérir. on supprime le soleil. on fait une
farce à l'Excès – Moloch et on entre sous Tanit. rapports du soleil & du
cheval. *Javart* des chevaux. la peste épargne les lépreux.
Le sang des lépreux plus noir que d'autres. & coule à peine. les os en
bouillie. on voit cela lorsqu'Hannon est sur la croix.
Moloch ⟨à sa naissance on passait l'enfant dans le feu. c'était le sacrifier
à Mol. & faire qu'il n'eut pas besoin plus tard d'être brûlé – & comme il
était désormais /protégé/ purifié, par le Dieu il devenait plus robuste.
    Cette cérémonie valait de l'argent aux prêtres. mais pendant le siège,
le peuple plus féroce qu'eux exige des sacrifices effectifs.⟩
Hamilcar a un casque à cornes avec des bandelettes
– un cheval qui plie les genoux pr. se laisser monter.

Fol. 212v

(*folio cut at an angle*)
bois d'o
⟨ils /les vivres/ manquaient⟩
enfin ils atteignirent le
vinrent les prendre.
Hannon était si triste, si las, ⟨et [*page cut*] /si/ ⟨tellement⟩ désespéré
⟨d'avoir perdu les machines⟩ /la perte des éléphants & des machines
surtout/ qu'il demanda ⟨plusieurs fois⟩ /du poison/ à Démonades un
poison ⟨doux⟩ pr. ⟨le faire mourir⟩ /en finir/ ⟨D'ailleurs⟩ /D'ailleurs il se
voyait/ il se sentait *déjà* tout étendu sur la croix.
    Mais Carthage n'eut pas la force de s'indigner contre lui. on avait perdu
/⟨tant dans la bataille que dans la retraite⟩/ quatre cent mille neuf cent

soixante douze /cycles d'argent/ shekels d'or, quinze cent mille six cent vingt trois cycles d'argent, dix huit éléphants quatorze membres du Grand Conseil, trois cents Riches huit mille citoyens. du blé pr. trois lunes /⟨tout le⟩/ /un/ /bagage considérable/ & toutes les machines de guerre. ⟨/Puis trahison/⟩ la défection de Narr'havas était certaine. ⟨la peste⟩

Fol. 213

fêtes des Hennula ou Cervula. prostitutions acharnées sous des masques & peaux de bête fauve.

Vestales, vierges de Minerve, d'Apollon, & de Junon Achéenne

⟨pousser des cris pr secourir la lune en travail⟩
⟨ *Moloch*. quatre aspects. ⟨Feu⟩ planète. Feu. créateur suprême – roi.
le Feu coule comme le sang dans les veines ne diffère pas du caloriq., de l'électricité. jamais plus puissant que lors qu'il détruit.
– De là le sang & les cendres qui accompagnent Moloch⟩
⟨"hommage à toi, Soleil, Dieu des deux zones, créateur qui s'engendre lui-même. – Tu es le père & la mère, tu es le père & le fils"⟩
tradition de sept temples élevés à Memphis aux sept planètes. Memphis avait 40 portes de fer /une/ muraille de fer & de cuivre – l'eau, par une machine, coulait ⟨par⟩ /sur/ le sommet de la muraille.
les Mages viennent en pèlerinage sur des chameaux, autour des pyramides, – tenant des flambeaux allumés depuis le fleuve ils rendent hommage aux génies qui sont en dessous & les supportent. – ils en font le tour – font *des prières au Sphinx* Père de la terreur. lui sacrifient un coq blanc & brûlent de la Sandaraque.
   sont purifiants : l'eau, la terre, ⟨le Feu,⟩ le soleil, le Feu.
LA PURIFICATION est la clef de l'oraison.
pr. les lustrations ne pas se servir d'un vase d'or ou d'argent.
Un bouquet d'hysope pr. les frotter les parties honteuses du cadavre.
terre de Byblos – (palets en) apaise les tempêtes si on jette un peu au vent.
"il connaissait les lustrations, les abstensions, les aspertions, celles qu'on doit faire avec de la crotte de gazelle, avec, etc. un os.
Lustrations avec des oeufs, avec du miel.

---

pr. un mort on brouille un oeuf avec du vin & on en oint la tête.

Fol. 214

Jours malheureux & heureux.
mois de juin : Hecatombeon. les Beutiens ont gagné deux gdes. victoires le 5° jour.
   Leuctres & Gesastes.

Août. Boedromion.   le 6ᵉ jour. bataille de Marathon
                    3ᵉ – Platée, Micales.
                    25ᵉ – Arbelles, victoire navale de
                        Naxos, sous Chabrias.
                    20ᵉ – Salamène.
Mai: Targelion. Granique.
    23ᵉ jour – défaite des Carthaginois par Timoléon
        prise de la ville de Troie.
Metageitnion (le 2ᵉ mois de l'année ath., juillet – (août, selon Clavier)
                    le 7ᵉ – Cheronée
                    le 22ᵉ est redouté des Carthaginois, comme
celui qui leur a apporté autrefois le plus de calamités.
                                    Plutarque. Vie de Camille 34

Fol. 215

Jeûner pr. se donner des songes prophétiques.
Mogbed: prêtres chaldéens.
⟨serpent dans l'évocation /ferme les yeux – à la fois horreur & amour &
alors met la tête dans la bouche/ quand elle s'en est enlacée cauda
flagellabat femorem⟩

———

⟨incendie factice à la porte d'une ville pr. arrêter les assiégeants⟩

———

⟨on les punissait pr. leurs désirs⟩
voûtes en pierres ponces de Sicile.

Ch. IV
⟨"n'était point aussi entière que pensaient leurs ennemis"⟩

———

⟨H. manger des baies de myrthe tout en marchant⟩

———

⟨mais comme un flambeau sur lequel on a soufflé, sa colère se ralluma
plus forte.⟩

———

⟨Jetons (*illegible word*) pr. compter dans un (*illegible word*)⟩

———

⟨Monnaies différentes – pierreries – parfums⟩
⟨Lex Rhodia – defacto⟩
⟨prendre pr. gage les armes⟩
⟨qq chose – des cadeaux de noces sur la table au dern. chapitre.⟩

———

⟨étoffes brodées avec des plumes. ouvrag. phrygien.⟩

———

⟨peaux de loutre pr. les gaulois⟩

———

⟨σαραβαλλα: mot chaldéen. St. Jérome – ch. 3 Daniel⟩

⟨Giddeneme – nom de nourrice dans le (*illegible word*)⟩

⟨haine du dieu ennemi qui se nourrit mieux que nous. on y croit, parce qu'il fait peur. Mais on l'exècre. on voudrait le tuer.
    l'Euphrate : Prath.
    la Mer Rouge : la mer de (*illegible word*)⟩
⟨cadavres avec le poing coupé en se défendant
rues tellement encombrées de cadavres qu'il est impossible d'y passer⟩

⟨Derviche (dans le siège de Carth.) sautant de créneau en créneau avec une hache /à deux tranchants dont il fait moulinet/ à la main, écumant, effrayant – au risque de se tuer.⟩

⟨dans la m. de Sallambo *iris* . pierre précieuse.⟩

⟨corps de l'ennemi *religieux* (Matho). on s'étonne de voir qu'il ressemble à un autre.⟩

⟨*horreur* des mines teintes?⟩

⟨Promettre aux vaincus qu'on leur fera grâce, s'ils se tuent, comme des gladiateurs. puis successivement on égorge les vainqueurs.⟩

⟨rêve : ⟨cafés⟩ /thermopoles/ où les pauvres écoutent un homme parler d'argent – ils prennent plaisir par avarice à voir & écouter des comptes.⟩

⟨Pendant le siège. Les Carthaginois reviennent à la coutume (abolie par Darius) de brûler cadavres. Moloch veut tout.⟩

⟨pr. Salambo. émigrat. des pigeons à Eryx Ath. (p. 5)⟩

chev. d'*Hamil* nourri avec de la farine & de la peau de serpent. Chardin

⟨les esclaves au (*illegible word*) chantent⟩

(*in pencil*) ⟨dans le siège. prendre les murs /de bois/ factices que l'on mettait en avant des galères⟩

⟨sesikoth : soie
scherih : coton
petite épeautre pain pr. les pauvres
vin de Caroubier⟩

Fol. 216v

⟨chute d'eau. Sp. court sur la plateforme éperdu d'orgueil & levant les bras comme un conduct. de char /d'un quadrige/ – qui est vainqueur aux jeux olympes – arrivé au terme de sa course⟩

⟨Derviches s'ennivrant de jusquiame.⟩
import. mytholog. du reflux & flux de la mer.

⟨Sultan Hakem (3ᵉ (*illegible word*)) fit lier un rebelle sur un chameau, ayant derrière lui un singe qui lui frappait le haut de la tête avec une pierre⟩
⟨ce supplice est proposé pr. Matho. comme il a attaqué Tanit les singes de Tanit doivent la venger.⟩

Zoharah nom de l'étoile de *Vénus*, signifie la Belle, la Fleurie.
Ouriai – (orus) /ou Ouroio/ nom de Hermès chez les Chaldéens, c'est à dire le gd. Maître. était aussi le nom du serpent *ouro* chez les Egyptiens.
– l'Hermès Babylonien demeurait à Calovaz ville de Chaldée.
Comparaison du serpent qui dans son avidité avale ses dents.
Plus l'abstinence a été longue, plus il y en a.
⟨Schahabarim. origines de sa suspicion envers Tanit il se rappelait /avec horreur le jour où/ le gd. prêtre armé d'une buire pleine d'eau bouillante l'avait étendu sur une table de (*illegible word*) pr. lui enlever ce qui devait être sa virilité.⟩
⟨à cause du zaimph il considère Matho comme le chef c'est à lui qu'il faut s'adresser. d'ailleurs c'est lui qui le détient⟩
Khallatzbâal, nom d'un suffète dans l'inscript. de Marseille.
Galeotes : devins de Sicile
"& il y avait pr. tant une certaine indépendance. le sentiment de la hiérarchie antipathique aux Sémites (Renan)
⟨neque solarium est apud nos neque fenestra nisi (*illegible word*) Plaute Miles II iv 25. Winckelman remarq. sur l'arch. des anciens p. 64 & Maquis⟩
⟨la salive *barath* chasse le diable du corps des possédés chez les Juifs⟩
⟨bois de *Rana* : palissandre⟩
⟨les frondes faites avec le schoenus vigricans; mélancranie⟩
⟨les Nomades mangent sur des peaux de boeuf ou de mouton étendues par terre⟩
⟨ch. IX Salam. hait Schahabarim. elle ne peut s'en passer. & l'exècre.
Haine du confesseur /& du magnétiseur/⟩
⟨Hacam – ancien Docteur⟩
⟨Les gens de la campagne repoussés de Carthage parce qu'on a peur que les vivres manquent. s'en retournent, & s'ajoutent aux Mercenaires.⟩
Les Mules engendrent en Afrique.
Lièvres blancs en Lybie
⟨les étendards comme des mâts de vaisseaux qui sombrent⟩

Dusaris ⎫
Obodas ⎭ divinités des Arabes
Dusaris
Dusarès

ch. VIII ⟨Spendius est resté devant /Utique/ où il prétend trouver des
intelligences. Matho seul au Makar (ce qui le mettra plus en relief)
   Matho envie de combattre le père de Salammbô
   Atrocités de l'armée d'Autharite.⟩
⟨l'armée de Matho impatiente s'est portée en avant⟩

Fol. 217

écriture toujours en rapport avec le reste
Aspect général
les échoppes des pauvres /en dehors/ s'accrochant aux parois de la
ville. – rochers – comme ceux /les misérables/ que l'on jette à la mer,
quand le vaisseau est trop plein.

———

les enceintes /distin/ n'étaient pas contemporaines, villes
différentes = races differentes. Byrsa la plus ancienne & l'on pouvait voir
/présumer/ à la noirceur des pierres l'âge.
Byrsa s'est abaissé, comme le capitole.
à ⟨gauche⟩ droite en continuant vers La Marse, quartier des voiliers etc.
– la canaille du côté de Tunis.
/foulons marteaux/
un phare énorme à Sidi-B.-Saïd (Alexandrie)
⟨ – Quamart plein de tombeaux, stèles avec les mains levées comme pr.
attester – les catacombes casiers /tombeaux où l'on pouvait se cacher.
Asdrubal/⟩
– statues sur des domes.
⟨ – chameaux sur les terrasses, – eau⟩ qui montait dans des colonnes
aspect noir, à cause du bitume, peu de pierres de taille – Maisons de bois,
gourbis.
les colonnes ⟨de Dugga⟩ ayant la base en anneaux.
– dans les rues, des santons couronnés d'herbes se promenant –
changeurs armuriers vendeurs d'herbes & de poissons salés /au miel/
com de change l'argent en arabie valait 10 fois l'or – d'espagne –
⟨principe de la politique civique "n'engraisse pas ton chien, il te
dévorerait. affame-le il te suivra."⟩
(1) Position –
⟨(2) – aspect général /architecture/ fouilles, choses laides, & choses
grandioses – ⟨aqueduc coupant la campagne.⟩
/division par quartiers/
trois races, trois enceintes – murs extérieurs, tours & boucliers suspendus.
Byrsa – monuments de l'Acropole – temples, bois sacrés, voie des
Mappales – tombeaux.

bord de la mer.
canailles au bord du lac, Malquâ – ports.
monnaies : petites barres & cuirs.
Voies mais la vraie voie c'était la mer. commerce – hommes rouges.⟩
⟨coqs pr. indiquer les heures. défense de les manger. colombes, musc.⟩
Le lac plein d'immondices & de poissons.
⟨1ᵉʳ les Assyriens se mêlant aux Lybiens devinrent les Numides
2ᵉ invasion phénicienne⟩

———

⟨les mangeurs de sauterelles très agiles des pieds mais meurent de
vermine⟩

———

⟨chevelures artificielles
école des esclaves à Syracuse⟩
⟨esprit commercial – haine de la tyrannie. les républiques plus favorables
que les monarchies au commerce. les richesses des compagnies de la
nature des richesses publiques. pays de commerce peu hospitaliers.⟩

Fol. 217v

Marginal note, linked to paragraph 1 Politique. développer à la
séance du sénat.

Carth. avait gardé des relations avec la Perse. elle l'aide dans la
guerre médique. ⟨le génie politique manque à Carthage quelle différence
avec Rome⟩
esprit mercantile étroit.
influence de la théocratie.
corruption & intrigues. la théocratie primant tout
⟨l'etat ne s'alimentait que des tributs frappés sur les territoires conquis,
car les citoyens ne payaient pas d'impôts & ne contribuaient pas même en
cas de besoin, comme à Rome, aux charges de l'Etat par des avances
remboursables.
Les Communes voisines étaient intéressés à la chute de Carth.⟩
La Poésie qui devait être nulle (littérature utilitaire devait se reporter sur la
religion.

———

Mercenaires. lien moral entre les peuples.
⟨ils avaient tant vu de Dieux qu'ils ne devaient plus croire à aucun.
confusion – se faisaient une religion – égoïsme furieux.
Mirage des conquérants. Pyrrhus, Alexandre, Agathocles, idée
d'Hercule – gd. mépris pr. les moeurs civiles de Carth. – admiration &
mépris mêlés. retour sur eux-mêmes. envie. haine.⟩

(*written upside down at foot of folio*) ⟨Je l'ai attrapée pr. avoir eu (*illegible
words*)⟩

Singes aveugles à la nouvelle lune
   ne mangent pas de poissons.
oignon de mer guérit l'hydrop. causée par les marais /voir Eneth./
(Carthagène : Oenyssa)
influence mythol du flux & reflux de la mer.
"tu iras au marché des odeurs suaves."
Sistre : Remken
Les 4 branch les 4 élém
cône tronqué : trou dans le mur, symb. de lumière & la procure.
Dusarès ⎫
Obodas ⎭ divinités solaires des Arabes .

_____

Khallatzbaal nom d'un suffète dans l'inscription de Marseille
Galeotes : divins de Sicile
Zoharah Vénus : la belle la Fleurie
Ouriai, orus : Hermès chez les Chaldeens : gd. maître. ouroio nom du
serpent chez les Egyptiens.
l'Hermès Babylonien demeurait à Calovaz ville de Chaldée

_____

⟨hte. aigrette des Ligures, boucl. de cuir des Espagnols les Cantabres se
serv. de hache⟩

_____

"...& il y avait pr. tant une certaine indépendance...le sentim. de la
hiérarchie antipathique aux Sémites.
⟨Mogbed : prêtres de Chaldée⟩
urine de bouc en guise de flacon de sel anglais.
Rêve : thermopoles où les pauvres prennent plaisir à écouter un homme
parler d'argent – faire des calculs – ils voient & écoutent des chiffres & des
comptes par avarice.
Hamilcar a un casque à cornes avec des bandelettes, comme Ammon.
⟨cheval d'Hamilcar nourri avec de la farine & de la peau de serpent il plie
les genoux pr. se laisser monter⟩
⟨xi. Schahabarim lui avait donné le moyen d'aller jusqu'au Camp. – la
montrer dans la campagne – à cheval – empaquetée dans ses voiles – Elle
arrive –
voile sur la bouche – enroulée comme une momie yeux seulement qu'on
voit. et une de ses torsades sur le bras comme la bandelette de la tiare
pontificale.
ses cheveux noirs semés de poudre d'or comme une nuit d'été toute
couverte d'étoiles.⟩
⟨les prêtres de Tanit compt. par années lunaires
——————de Moloch———————solaires.
L'année solaire commence au mois de 7bre automne, pluvieuse, orageuse.⟩
⟨on prit les murailles de bois que l'on mettait devant les galères⟩

_____

⟨analyser *l'idee du Sacrifice*
la mort des enfants était aussi pr. purifier la ville – purifier par le feu⟩
⟨plume d'autruche emblème de justice & de vertu.
éventail————————du repos & du bonheur céleste.⟩

⟨noms des serpents gardant chacun des 12 h. du jour
à Thèbes /d'Egypte/
rek-Ko : serpent à face étincelante.
Setempefbal : serp. dont l'oeil lance la flamme.
Tapenthô : la corne du Monde.⟩

Fol. 221

Elyma nom de chef africain.
Molouya. limite de la Numidie & de la Mauritanie.
Automolax. limite de la Cyrénaïque.
Le silphium arrive /de (*illegible word*)/ par le compt. de *Charax.*
Battos (en lybien roi). effray les lions du bruit de sa voix.
⟨bouclier qu'on promène contre les murs, pour reconn. les mines.⟩
⟨effrayer les enfants par le nom de la reine Lamia, ogresse⟩
⟨à Balacrès près de Cyrène, une école de médecine⟩
⟨Magara vainq. de la Lybie pr. les (*illegible word*) périt d'obésité.
Apton Knos dieu lybien⟩
Eugamion de Cyrène, auteur de la télégonie : dern. avent. d'Ulysse.
son arrivée chez les Thesprotes et sa mort sous les coups de Télégone.
⟨Les Juifs établis à Cyrène dev. être pr. Carthage⟩
⟨Ptol. – Philad. voulait ⟨pr.⟩ march. contre Magas. Mais se defiant de ses
mil. gaul. il les laissa périr de faim dans une île du Nil.⟩
Himilcon (3 ou 5 av JC) avait abandonné à Syrac. les auxil. lybiens.
200 m. sold prir Tunis. Carth achet des traits
Denys profita de l'épuisem pr. recomm. les hostilités. Les Merc. av.
complété de livr Lylibée aux Rom., défend par Imilcar
⟨eaux corrompues avec de l'ellébore⟩
beau terme militaire – eruptio : sortie d'une place assiégée.
⟨Hecatompyle : Qatssah
Malchus avait assiégé Carth avec ses sold. 530 crucifié.
Magas de Cyrène mort d'obésité⟩

———————

Catapulte employée par Denys au siège de Motye. les C. l'ignor.
auparavant
Les auxiliaires /gros/ de Magon se mêlèr aux sold. de Timoléon
Hamilcar se brûla, à Palèrme le jour de la bat. de Salam.
Imilcon rentre. à C avec une tunique d'escl et se tua
un autre Imilcon se laissa mourir de faim. Magon /vainc par Timoléon/se
tue à Carth.
Agathocl. n'av emporté que 50 tel. il affranch les esclav & les encorp dans
ses troupes

———————

à mesure que le cadavre se refroidit la vermine (les morpions)
abandonnent le corps, filent de tous côtés.
Dans le territ de Carth châteaux dans la plaine, ouverts de tous côtés
⟨les sold d'Annibal battu par Scipion qui ven de prend Alexia. le
crucifient (*two or three illegible words*)⟩

———

G. Coepio & Caius Semp. Blâmés après la vict de Xantippe avaient fait une
descente en Afriq.

———

⟨Ptolem. Philad – a refusé un prêt de 2 mil talents⟩

———

⟨la défect. des /mercs/ Gaulois à Eryx venait des retards de solde. Hamilc
le rappelle dans le conseil⟩

———

⟨Les chevaux numid peuv soutenir l'odeur des éléph.⟩

———

⟨Marques ineff. sur la main des enrôlés, de sorte que si un Mercen a servi
plus. états il a plusieurs marques indélébiles. c'est à cela qu'on les
distingue (cadavres) des volontaires africains⟩

———

⟨faire couper les cheveux de devant pr. éviter d'être pris dans le combat:
thébaïde.⟩
⟨les pourceaux font peur aux éléph. – enduits de poix. ruse des (*illegible
word*) contre les éléph. d'*illegible word*⟩

———

Mons Ferratus : jurjura dev fournir du fer.
à trois journées SE de Const une mine d'argent. Plomb à 7 journées au
SSO de Sétif.

———

⟨Les libyens ont les veines du ht. de la tête brûlées avec de la laine
brute.⟩
⟨les Africains ont des chars de guerre : /ils/à la suite d'Agathocles⟩

———

le fer durci trempé par des paroles magiques

———

⟨javelots en bois de cornouiller⟩
⟨anciennes villes: Lebda, Zoucla, Barca.⟩
Eléphants bons à Tunis, funestes à Palerme (les Mercs. gaulois s'ét.
d'ailleurs ennivrés)
⟨conducteurs : indiens /ou nègres/ – habillés comme des indiens par
coutume & pensant que ça plairait même aux éléph.⟩

Fol. 222v

"l'odeur de l'animal mort répugne à qui ne l'a pas tué."
les éléph. dans les lances comme des sangliers dans les herbes.

———

frotter de sa sueur leur trompe pr. les adoucir.

———

toutes les palissades du camp couchées dans le même sens

————

petits dards empoisonnés dans la chevelure la pointe entrant & dont la couleur disparaît sous le poison qui les couvre.

Les oiseaux entament les charognes par les yeux & les chiens par le ventre ou l'anus.

————

⟨bruit caverneux des intestins de l'éléphant.
ils se jett. du sable mouillé⟩ ————

⟨apporter à manger (aux temples) de la part de sa maîtresse qui est malade⟩

⟨l'éléph. adore le soleil – encore le matin⟩

⟨rafraîchir les chevaux & leur donner de l'ardeur en leur frottant les naseaux de sang frais⟩

& le poussant du pied, rouge de sang fumant, comme on écrase un tison qui fume encore.

⟨(*illegible word*) : Melkarth : celui qui coupe avec le glaive le jarret des chevaux (*illegible word*)⟩

les Mercen. prenn les ongles des cadavres pr. s'en faire des cuirasses.

⟨Hamilcar a un casque à cornes avec bandelettes⟩

⟨Cariens d'origine cananéenne représentations sur leurs boucliers⟩

⟨Le rhinocéros piétine sa fiente odeur poivrée de l'excrément des éléphants⟩

⟨H. a un cheval (espagnol) qui plie les genoux⟩

/ ————

⟨quand on a faim comprimer l'estomac par des courroies⟩

Sitarah : rideau

Cantabres : haches

Les Ligures bouclier long – tunique à ceinturon

⟨Espa⟩ibériens, épée longue, pointue, affilée des deux côtés, inflexible se porte sur la cuisse droite.

– d'autres 2 épées plus petites, une sur chaque cuisse.

Sammites, la jambe gauche seulement couvert d'un jambart.

espagnols & Maures – boucliers de cuir – /citra/ en peau d'onces.

Lusitaniens boucliers en nerfs tressés – les frapp en cadence & en dansant lorsqu'ils s'avancent au combat.

Les Campaniens javelots de cornouillers & *Aclydes* v. Silius Italicus.

/épées de Salerne, massue du Buxentum/

les Ibères montent à deux sur le même cheval.

⟨(vers la fin) dans les hallucinat. forte.

chaleurs. la pointe /en fer/ des flèches sur l'arc.

paraît comme une petite torche allumée agitée par le vent. flambe exhaussée, insaisissable.⟩ ————

⟨les ailes d'une armée s'étendant comme deux bras noirs pr. envelopper.⟩

————

⟨le feu dans les tours des éléphants, – les éléph. comme des volcans qui courent⟩

Fol. 223

⟨arbres sacrés auxquels on append des morceaux d'étoffes ou des crins⟩
Dans la campagne, *chameaux en liberté*, pr. quoi. (V. liv. sacrés de l'Orient)
enfants qui jouent dans l'eau avec des pastèques vides sur la tête – comme
des turbans.
Pins du Peloponèse & cyprès de Caudie pr. les construct. navales

---

Mouches dans les temples à cause des viandes –

La poix adoucit les vins & épile les hommes.

Le soleil nourri des vapeurs de l'océan. il fait embaumer la terre dans les
endroits où l'extrémité d'un arc en ciel a posé.

---

la noix symbole de modestie.

---

se frappèr sur la hanche en signe d'indignation.

---

on frottait *d'huile les boucliers* pr. faire glisser les flèches.

⟨*suspendre le vin* à la fumée pr. le faire vieillir⟩

Lancer des pierres dans un champ, symbole de prise de possession.

---

il est défendu de faire *des libations avec du vin foulé par un pied malade.*

Pour garder le froment on y mêle de la coriandre qui pue. les feuilles
sentent la punaise. les graines ont une odeur aromatique.

---

charriot punique pr. battre le blé: rouleau hérissé de dents terminé par des
boules de fer.
boeufs dont le sabot est frotté avec de la poix.

La naissance des filles considérée comme un malheur. H. a maudit Salam. à
sa naissance.
Sall. est *gnouth???*

---

	se frotter de raifort *contre les scorpions*
	garum fait avec des scombres de Mauritanie
nourriture	artich. de Carth. confits dans du vinaigre où l'on délaye du
	miel avec de la racine de laser & de cumin

---

escargots engraissés avec de la farine & du vin cuit cuit *sic*
dans des pots – grillés pris avec du vin & du garum
truffes blanches de la Cyrénaïque.

Araboth : fenêtres
une branche de palmier à la main /pr. prier/

Fol. 223v

dans le temple de /Moloch/ arbre qui empoisonne le vent (Chardin 3. 296)
besoars.
⟨morts restés la bouche ouverte comme pr. crier.⟩

———————

⟨beurre sur les moustaches⟩

———————

⟨enfants jouant avec les squelettes⟩

———————

⟨battre les malades pr. les faire fuir du pays; par peur des maladies
contagieuses.⟩

———————

⟨frotter les jarres avec des amandes⟩
⟨ – "par l'oeil" juron fréquent⟩

———————

⟨vêtements posés sur une corde dans les petits logemens?⟩
Dans les incantations de Salambô Tanaach chantait trois mots : toujours
les mêmes – & ces trois mots (comme des coups) tantôt faibles tantôt
forts – d'abord faibles puis par gradation & ça redescend.
Elle tape sur un disque – accroupie, se balançant la tête – ça fait dresser le
serpent.
/la tête du/ le serpent coule comme une grosse goutte d'eau.
⟨geste de /jambe droit de/ cheval grattant la terre /un peu cabré/ semblait
dire "elle est à moi" comme pr. la prendre⟩
⟨tas de mains coupées, avec bagues. différences de forme & d'expression.⟩
une épée qui a des vertèbres pr. dire pliante.

Fol. 224

:Achtoret : Acht-thé
Astarté fut la terre & l'eau & cette flamme immortelle qui se sert d'un lit
pr. aller au ciel –
Anahed à Babylone
Addirdaga à Ascalon
– à Paphos, c'était aux entrailles des chevaux qu'on avait le plus de
confiance.
⟨dans les villes⟩ en Pamphylie on sacrifiait à Vénus des porcs & peut-être
des sangliers. χοῖρος : le cochon, le con.

———————

/à Cyprès/ – ceux qui se faisaient initier offraient une piece de monnaie &
recevaient en revanche du sel (indiquant la mer berceau de la déesse) &
un phallus –

(voy. Lachan, attributs de Vénus)
Chabar & non Schebar planète de Vénus.

⟨Plus tard quand les Mercen. ont des tumeurs c'est pr. avoir mangé des poissons sacrés⟩

Laisse-moi dormir que j'aie un songe

⟨Harokel : marchand
Courtiers : Schadchanim⟩
"Maoul en fut irrité & cria à l'Eternel toute la nuit"
Debhir : sanctuaire. Saint de Saints

Les planètes de Vénus & de Mars sont au dessus du soleil

"comme l'escargot qui agite sa semence dans une boule de fumier."
la bathe mesure de capacité : 29 pintes, chop demi setir & un peu plus.
600 coudees 1,620 pieds
la coudée hebr. de 20 pouces et demi

Le térébinthe brûle quand on l'allume. Mais le feu éteint, il se retrouve sain & entier comme auparavant.

⟨ch. IV. que S. engage M. plus fort⟩
Dieu circule dans le monde comme le miel court dans les cellules d'un rayon.

chaque période du monde est comprise entre un déluge & une conflagration.
l'homme "une âme qui traîne un mort" Epictete

Fol. 225

– Narr'havas & Mâtho se rencontrent dans la bataille face à face – Narr'havas cale.
et le poussant du pied rouge de sang comme un tison qui fume encore

soleil couchant comme la queue d'un phénix

Les Lybiens dont les agneaux naissent avec des cornes.

Fers durcis trempés par des paroles magiques.
⟨Les ongles regardés comme l'image de la fécondité & l'image de la force.⟩
Le jour des noces fixé dans la nouvelle lune.

Reko : dont la face est étincelante	⎫	serpents,
Setempefbal : dont l'oeil lance la flamme	⎬	gardiens des 12h.
Tapentho : corne du monde	⎭	du jour à Thèbes

comme des sangliers

_____

pas plus de bruit que si ses pieds eussent été garnis d'un feutre épais

_____

si épuisés qu'ils sonnaient moins fort dans les trompettes

_____

⟨Matho reconn. la tête. 103. voit plus loin Narr'havas
1 Les marchands relevaient les auvents de leur boutiq.⟩

_____

on casse les pots lorsque les parties ont réglé la dot & le douaire.
– nouer les deux extrémités des manteaux des conjoints.
on répand des cendres sur la tête des mariés.
L'époux a une couronne composée de sel & de soufre. le sel transparent
comme le cristal & l'on y /avait/ tracé avec le soufre diverses figures. La
couronne de la mariée, est d'or faite en forme de tour crénelée.
l'épouse tourne 3 fois autour de l'homme. Le mari 2 fois autour de la
femme.

_____

Le vase dans lequel les époux ont bu deux fois est jeté à terre.
(*four illegible words*)

Fol. 226

(*this folio is a fragment of paper cut from fol. 194*)

Jardin

*cèdres, sycamores, figuiers, ifs, cyprès, orangers, citronniers, genèvriers,
bananiers, dattiers, arbousiers, jujubiers* (arbrisseau noueux chargé d'épines)
Cactus opuntia (fleurs jaunes, aux feuilles aplaties & charnues recouvertes
d'un faisceau d'épines)
tamarisc (*illegible word*) plante bulbeuse dont l'oignon sort de terre.
grenadier Paneficier (feuilles ailées délicates d'un vert tendre fleurs d'un
jaune doré, gousses d'un mêtre de longueur : bâtons bruns à travers le
feuillage.)
/aspergés du (*illegible*) avec du silphium cinq espèces./
Cotonnier : vaste calice double, corolle rose, /ou jaune tendre/ fruits
ressemblant à de gros globes remplis d'une laine blanche.
hybiscus fruits /allongées & anguleuses./
Autour de l'étang: le lis blanc du Nil: nénuphar.
⟨Nebal⟩ Nelumbo: lotus roses. les feuilles semblables à d'immenses
entonnoirs.
papyrus
cannes de Provence
Narcisses, anemones, lis, violette, iris sur le gazon.
un champ de roses, jasmin.
lis pourpre en jetant dans la fosse de la lie de vin.

Fol. 227

1° les Assyriens se mêlant aux Lybiens devinrent les Numides
2° invasion phénicienne

———————

pays de commerce. peu hospitaliers.
les richesses des compagnies de la nature des richesses publiques
Les républiques plus favorables que les monarchies au commerce.
haine de la tyrannie.
Carthage avait gardé des relations avec la Perse – (guerre médique)
————————————————————————la Phénicie. le tribut à Tyr,
tous les ans.
influence de la théocratie. Elle primait tout. Peut-être parce que c'était les
prêtres des conquérants, les dieux vainqueurs
La Poésie (nulle, utilitaire, comme art) devait comme sentiment se
reporter sur la religion.

———————

coqs pr. indiquer les heures
colonnes, ayant la ⟨terre⟩ /base/ en anneaux.
———————— creuses, dans lesquelles l'eau monte.

———————

Les enceintes n'étaient pas contemporaines, villes différentes, races
différentes. à la noirceur des pierres on devinait l'antiquité des habitants.

———————

sur les enceintes intérieures, cabanes comme des ruches d'abeilles.

———————

Le Lac plein d'immondices & de poissons

———————

Les Africains ont des chars de guerre à la suite d'Agathocles.
Les Libyens ont les veines du ht. de la tête brûlées avec de la laine brute.

———————

Dans le territoire de Carth. châteaux dans la plaine, ouverts de tous côtés.

Fol. 228

une épée qui a des vertèbres pr. dire pliante
soleil couchant comme la queue d'un phénix

———————

les flammes s'échappant des maisons comparées aux jets de sang qui
jaillissent des artères.

———————

au milieu à qque. distance du champ de bataille, monté sur une butte les
lignes des hommes allant & venant comme des courants contraires dans
un torrent. la butte est le roc – immobile au milieu.
sur le champ de bataille : *tas de mains coupées* avec des bagues, différentes
de forme & d'expression.

———————

par l'oeil : juron fréquent
morts restés la bouche ouverte comme pr. crier
enfants jouant avec des squelettes – dans l'eau, avec des pastèques vides sur la tête, comme des turbans.
battre les malades pr. les faire s'aller du pays, de peur des maladies contagieuses, des épidémies.
Dans les petits logemens, *vêtemens posés sur une corde.*
beurre sur les moustaches.
Le soleil nourri des vapeurs de l'océan
Le Feu artiste de l'univers
Mouches dans les temples, à cause des viandes.
La Noix symbole de modestie.
Chameaux en liberté dans la campagne. (liv. sacrés de l'Orient)
suspendre le vin à la fumée pr. le faire vieillir
frotter les jarres avec des amandes.
pins du Peloponèse & de Caudie pr. les constr. navales.
la poix adoucit les vins & épile les hommes.
⟨la noix⟩
frotter d'huile les boucliers pr. faire glisser les flèches.
Lancer des pierres dans un champ, symbole de prise de possession.
ne pas faire des libations avec du vin foulé par un pied malade.
pr. garder le froment y mêler de la coriandre qui pue. Les feuilles sentent la punaise. les graines ont une odeur aromatique.
Charriot punique pr. battre le blé : rouleau hérissé de dents terminé par des boules de fer.
boeufs dont le sabot est frotté avec de la poix.
se frotter de raifort contre les scorpions.
nourriture. – garum fait avec des scombres de Mauritanie. artich. de
        Carthag. confits dans du vinaigre où l'on délaye du miel avec
        de la racine de laser & du cumin. escargots engraissés avec
        de la farine et du vin cuit. Grillés pris avec du vin & du
        garum. truffes blanches de la Cyrénaïque.

Fol. 228v

———

un souvenir où l'on s'accroche comme à un débris dans un naufrage.

———

L'amour fait plaisir & mal comme la menthe qui fait froid & chaud.
les gdes. passions disparaissent par teintes successives comme les ecchymoses
"J'aime à prendre les femmes comme les amphores par les deux oreilles pr. les baiser."

———

plus lent qu'une gabarre par un calme plat

———

classicus horror, le froid du métal semble entrer dans les chairs.

———

L'ivresse du courage.

———————

La sagesse sort du malheur comme l'huile du pressoir.
"là où le sang a couché, l'herbe est toujours épaisse."

noms | Zebina, nom d'esclave
propres | Croum : suie nom de nègre
        | Cothon : gobelet de Sparte. en effet le port était un vase.
        | Aschpenay : homme dont le visage est triste.
        | /Apton Knos, dieu Lybien/

———————

Les oreilles comme les deux plateaux d'une balance qui pèsent le pr. & le contre.

———————

statues qui jettent dans un état de rage comme l'Opir de Sparte.
"mon courage se détend sous les pleurs comme la corde d'un arc sous les pluies."

———————

"n'engraisse pas ton chien. il te dévorerait – affam le il te suivra.
Principe de politique.
/à Hannon/ "la nourriture que tu as fourrée dans ton ventre l'a élargi & grossi comme un sac."
les Espagnols dans les délibérations sur la manière de combattre,
proposent des ⟨statues⟩ charriots à torche.
tirer le sort par les flèches.

———————

nègres comme des mûr. roulées dans la poussière.

———————

les Lybiens dont les agneaux naissent avec des cornes.
geste de la jambe du cheval grattant la terre semble dire "elle est à moi"
/comme pr. la manger avec ses pieds./
Fer durci, trempé par des paroles magiques.

Fol. 229

mer de Souf : mer Rouge
Prath. : Euphrate
Sitarah : rideau
Harokel : marchands
Schadchanim : courtiers
Araboth : fenêtres

Serikoth : soie
Schesch : coton
Chamnatsasach dans la
    montagne d'Ephraïm
Hacam : ancien, Docteur.

Debhir : sanctuaire, saint des saints
Makkar (est nom de Melkarth & d'un des 7 cabires) : celui qui coupe avec le glaive le jarret des chevaux.
les Carthag. avaient donné ce nom au fleuve qui pénètre dans, qui coupe l'Afrique.
– chez les Libyens ⟨dont⟩ les agneaux naissent avec des cornes
– en Afrique les mulets engendrent

– lièvres blancs en Lybie
une branche de palmier à la main pr. prier.
gnouth.

———

tournure liturgique " – qui me dira les 40 prophéties pr. entrer dans le
paradis
" – tu y entreras si" etc.
Pabadia : Java, indigo, ébène, bétel, noix de coco, noix d'arec.
al mugghim : bois de palissandre ou bois de Rana.
Achtoret : acht- pté
Anahir à Babylone
Addirdaga à Ascalon.
le talisman se fait pendant l'exercice de la constellation qui doit avoir de
l'influence sur lui.
– les frondes faites avec le Schoenus vigricans : mélancranie
– les Nomades mangent sur des peaux de boeuf ou de mouton étendues
par terre.
le bathe : 29 pintes etc.
600 coudées : 1.600 pieds
la coudée hébraïque : 20 pouces et demi

———

Astarté fut la Terre & l'Eau etc. & cette flamme immortelle qui se sert d'un
lit pr. aller au ciel.

———

à Paphos c'était aux entrailles des chevaux qu'on avait le plus de
confiance.
en Pamphylie on sacrifiait à Vénus des porcs & peut-être des sangliers
χοῖρος le cochon : le con.
à Chypre ceux qui se faisaient initier, offraient une pièce de monnaie &
recevaient en revanche du sel indiquant la mer (berceau de la Déesse) &
un phallus. (voir Lachan, Attributs de Vénus)

———

Les planètes de Vénus & de Mars sont au dessus du soleil.

———

⟨L'argent en Arabie valait dix fois l'or d'Espagne⟩

———

Les mangeurs de sauterelles agiles des pieds. Mais meurent de vermine. La
vermine (les morpions) abandonne les cadavres à mesure qu'ils se
refroidissent.

———

Les oiseaux entament les charognes par les yeux & les chiens par le ventre
ou l'anus.
Anciennes villes : Lebda, Zoucla, Barca.
Molouya limite de la Numidie & de la Mauritanie
Automolax limite de la Cyrénaïque. Le silphium arrive
par le comptoir de Charax
Elyma nom de chef africain
Magas, vainqueur de Cyrène pr. les Lagides périt d'obésité

Apton Knos, dieu Lybien
à Balacrès, près Cyrène, une école de Médecine.
Lamia, ogresse (effrayer les enfants par son nom.)
Hecatompyle : Qatssah
du plomb à 7 journées S.S.O. de Setif.
à 3 journées S.E. de Constantine, une mine d'argent.
Mons Ferratus : jurjura devant fournir du fer.
Leinth : divinité des Etrusques.

Fol. 229v

"comme l'escargot qui agite sa semence dans une boule de fumier.

———

"Shaoul en fut irrité & cria à l'Eternel toute la nuit."

———

Le térébinthe brûle quand on l'allume mais le feu éteint il se retrouve sain
& entier comme auparavant.

———

Dieu circule dans le monde comme le miel coule dans les cellules d'un
rayon.

———

Chaque période du monde est comprise entre un déluge & une
conflagration.

———

L'homme "une âme qui traîne un mort" – Epictete.
"n'engraisse pas ton chien. il te dévorerait. affame-le. il te suivra."

———

"l'odeur de l'animal mort ne répugne pas à qui l'a tué.

———

éléphants. odeur poivrée de leurs excréments. Les chevaux numides
peuvent soutenir leur odeur.
/il coule/ /d'un petit trou derrière/ /de leur oreille, un liquide infecte à
l'(*illegible word*)
les éléphants dans les lances, comme des sangliers dans des touffes
d'herbe. – les éléph. bons à Tunis, funestes à Palèrme. /les Mercs. gaulois
s'étaient d'ailleurs ennivrés./
bruit caverneux des intestins
il se jette du sable mouillé.
frotter de sa sueur leur trompe les attire.
– adore le soleil, encense avec sa trompe, le matin.

———

Le Feu dans les tours des éléphants
les éléphants comme des volcans qui courent.
toutes les palissades du camp couchées dans le même sens quand ils ont
passé.
⟨pr. refraîchir les chevaux & leur donner de l'ardeur leur frotter les
naseaux avec du sang frais.⟩

———

quand on a faim comprimer l'estomac par des courroies.

———————

Les ailes d'une armée s'étendant comme deux bras noirs pr. envelopper.
Dans les hallucinations (vers la fin) & par une forte lumière, la pointe en
fer des flèches appuyée sur l'arc paraît comme une petite torche allumée,
agitée par le vent, flamme exhaussée, insaisissable.

———————

⟨Les oise⟩ ⟨Petits dards empoisonnés dans la chevelure, la pointe en haut,
et dont la couleur disparaît sous le poison qui la couvre.⟩

———————

belle expression: eruptio: sortie d'une place assiégée.
"& le poussant du pied, rouge de sang, comme on écrase un tison qui
fume encore."

Fol. 230

Hannon. l'éléphant est consacré au soleil. rapport de l'éléph. &
   de l'éléphantiasis – malgré l'horr. qu'elle inspire cette
maladie est chose sainte. Honneurs qu'on lui rend. (Joseph Antiq. Jud. 32)
rage du coït, on se châtre pr. se guérir. on supprime le soleil, Moloch, on
⟨fait⟩ bat ainsi l'Excès, le principe fécondateur. & on entre sous la
domination immédiate de Tanit.
la peste épargne les lépreux.
le sang des lépreux plus noir que d'autres & il coule à peine. les os sont en
bouillie. on voit cela lorsqu'Hannon est sur la croix.
rapports du soleil & du cheval. *javart* des chevaux –

———————

Haine du Dieu ennemi on y croit parce qu'il fait peur. on le cultive mais on
l'exècre. on voudrait l'anéantir. Jalousie…il se nourrit mieux que nous.
/xii retranchem. de cadavres/

Synchronismes

en Egypte : Ptolémie iii (*illegible word*) 246–221 – guerres contr. Seleucus ii
– conquêtes en Asie, jusqu'en Bactriane – dans l'intérieur de l'Ethiopie
/Abyssinie Darfour/ & sur les côtes occidentales de l'Arabie.
en Syrie : Seleucus ii Callinicus ou Pogon : le Barbu 242–227.
assassinat de Bérénice – par Laodice. ⟨/hommes substitués dans le (*illegible
word*) du roi Antioc./⟩ /Les femmes de Bérénice dissem. sa mort/ jalousie de
son frère Antiochus Hierax gouvern. de l'Asie antérieure. /les gaulois
secondent Hierax. ils sont 120 mille/ Antiochus est vaincu 240
Eumène roi de Pergame s'agrandit aux dépens de la Syrie 242.
– expédition contre les Parthes 238. Seleucus est battu & fait prisonnier.
En Grèce, Antigone Gonatas ✚ en 233 chassé par Pyrrhus à son retour
d'Italie 274. revient à sa mort. effort pr. dissoudre la ligue Athen. – s'allie
avec les Etoliens /brigands/
Aratus délivre Sicyon 251 Corinthe 243 – Athènes accède à la ligne en
229. L'invasion des Gaulois à Delphos en 278. les tectosages, les

tolistobii, les tocmi s'étaient enfoncés dans l'asie mineure & avaient reçu des terres de Nicomède roi de Bithynie 277.
De là, ils s'employaient comme mercenaires.
à Sparte extermination d'Agis & de sa famille 241.
Rome en 238 incursion des gaulois cisalpins; peut-être suscitée par Carthage?
les gesates : gaulois des bords du Rhône : mercenaires.
xiv. retranchem. de cadavres/

Fol. 231

(*fragment cut from large page*)
constellation de
rahab: crocodile à côté de la constell. du dragon.
Vénus : Astorit Naama
      Naama : (*illegible word*)
constellation d'Hercule : constell. du chameau.
Mars ou *Azir* feu destructeur.

Saturne *Kyn* ou *Keivan*	
Bel : Jupiter /ou Cocab-Baal/	mâles
Merodach : Mars	
Nebo : Mercure	
(*illegible word*) la lune	femelles
Mylitta ou Baaltis	

Vénus /Noga/ & Mars /Cochab/ étaient croyait-on, au dessus du soleil.
Baal – tsephou – (*illegible word*) placé près du pôle boréal gardant le Nord représenté par un chien.
Orion : nipha ou Miphleseth placé à côté du taureau dont il annonce le retour au printemps par son coucher héliaque.
Nesra ou Nesroch : constellation du vautour près de la const. du cygne.

Fol. 232v

Sabins, boliques, – lames de frène, de myrthe, de cornouiller.
Marses gds. boucliers
Jucaniens petits boucliers en osier recouv. de cuir.
Gques, Herniques casque de peaux d'ours ou d'écorce de chêne liège
Arabes assis par couples dos à dos sur les dromadaires hache à 2 tranchants.
⟨Lien moral entre Carthage & les peuples⟩
Etrusques : bouclier rond de métal. cottes de mailles – *hasta* trompette d'airain.
Cariens – d'origine cananéenne, représentations /peintes/ sur leurs boucliers. v. Herodote liv. 7.
Cantabres : haches
Ethiopiens : boucliers ronds. une moitié du corps frottée avec du vermillon, l'autre avec du plâtre.

Ligures. bouclier long, tunique à ceinturon. htes aigrettes.

Espagnols & Mores boucliers de cuir (*citra*) en peaux d'onces.

Sammites	⎧ casques à aigrettes. bouclier pointu en bas, large en ht.
	⎪ tuniques peintes /armes dorées ou argentées/ la jambe gauche
	⎨ seulement couverte d'un jambart /de cuir – ou de bronze
	⎪ élastique/
	⎪ *les Herniques* le porte. sur la droite.
	⎩ lance – épée. /courte/ fronde.
Lusitaniens	boucliers en nerfs tressés, ils les frappent en cadence & en dansant lorsqu'ils s'avancent.
Campaniens	javelots de cournouiller. & *Aclydes* (v. Silius Italicus) épées de Salèrne massue du Buxentum.
ibériens	montent à deux sur le même cheval.
	épée longue, pointue, affilée des deux côtés, inflexible, se porte sur la cuisse droite.
	d'autres ont deux épées plus petites, une sur chaque cuisse.
Lydiens	longues piques. bons lanceurs de javelots.
les Maures	boucliers ay. la forme du coeur d'un homme.
Gaulois	peaux de loutres sur la tête.

Les mercenaires prennent les ongles des cadavres pr. s'en faire des cuirasses.

/Les merc. gaulois ayant pris un convoi de vin font perdre la bataille de Palerm. 251 av. J.C./

Les auxiliaires de Magon se mêlèrent aux soldats de timoléon

Malchus avait assiégé Carthage avec ses soldats crucifié 530 av. J.C.

Ptolem. Philad. se défiant de 4 mille gaulois les laissa périr de faim dans une île du Nil.

Les Mercen. avaient comploté de livrer Lilybée aux romains.

Himilcon abandonne à Syracuse les aux. libyens. 200 mille sold. prir.

Tunis – Denys profita de l'épuisement.

Chefs qui se tuent : Hamilcar se brûle à Palerme. le jour de la bataille de Salamène.

Imilcon rentre à Carth. avec une tunique d'esclave & se tue.

un autre Imilcon se laissa mourir de faim.

Magon, vaincu par Timoléon, se tue à Carth.

les soldats d'Annibal battus par Scipion qui venait de prendre Alexia le crucifient 1^{er}g. p. 259

Agathocles n'avait emporté que 50 talens. il affranch les esclav & les incorpora dans ses troupes.

Catapulte employée par Denys au siège de Motye. Les Carthaginois ignoraient cette machine.

bouclier qu'on promène contre les murs pr. reconnaître les mines

/et/ eaux corrompues avec de l'ellébore.
⟨marques ineffaçables sur les mains des enrôlés. s'il y a servi plusieurs
gouvernem il en a plusieurs. on distingue à cela leur cadavres.⟩
(*illegible word*) : cheveux coupés devant pr. éviter d'être empoignés.
retrancher partout les orangers

Fol. 233

(*this folio is all in pencil, and clearly dates from the final stages of composition*)

167. continuation
     continuer
298 *repouss* les ouvertures
301 manière *infranchissable*
303 Spendius...
316 *Carthaginois* (souvent répété –
321 /*avait* ou *possédait?*/
    bandelettes...trop long.
325 ...*boule verdâtre?*
ibid. *sous le* souffle
     sous le gen.
329 défilé de la hache

106 où où
    où vas-tu /étendu – il avait/
107 *vêtement?*
    Si déjà empl. à la pag
    précédente
    & est plus bas "*si* vraisembl. &
    à la p. suivan *s'ils* avaient.
110 "*ils seraient au contr.*" à
    enlever.
⟨ibid.⟩ iii. resterait – le reste
112. (c'était le bras)
115. long du jour, longs cheveux.
     jour. jour.
117 "Puis il lui *semblait*" (déjà dit)
    enlever tout jusqu'à qqfois
    il sortait
    il y a 2 *puis*

Fol. 234

Carthagène : oenyssa
influence mythologique du flux & reflux de la mer.
singes aveugles à la nouvelle lune. ne mangent pas de poisson.
oignon de mer guérit l'hydropsie causée par les marais.
Sistre: Rem. Ken. ses 4 branches ; les 4 éléments.
cônes tronqués : trous dans le mur, symbole de la lumière & la procurent.
Zoharah : Vénus : la Belle, la Fleurie.
Duzares ⎫
Obodos ⎭ divinités /solaires/ des Arabes
Galeotes, devins de Sicile.
Khallatzbaal (inscript. de Marseille)
Ouriaï, Orus : Hermès chez les Chaldéens : gd. maître. Ouroio nom du
serpent chez les Egypt.
l'Hermès Babylonien demeurait à Calvaz ville de Chaldée

———

Le sentiment de la Hiérarchie antipathique aux Sémites
Hamilcar a un casque à cornes avec des bandelettes comme Ammon.
(*marginal note*) rêve : thermopoles où les pauvres prenn. plaisir à écouter

un homme parler d'argent. Par avarice ils aiment à voir & à ecouter des chiffres.

Urine de bouc en guise de flacon de sel anglais.

"Des⟨yeux⟩ /ongles/ sur les dents, il⟨entrefermait⟩ /restait/ les paupières /entrefermées/ & ses pupilles jaunes s'allongeaient comme au gd. jour celles des léopards."

ses pupilles minces /et luisantes/ comme la lame d'un poignard.

xiii...les vivres manquent aux B. /les/ nom. venus les accaparent.

on se bat. Du haut de Carth. agitation de la terre...& à côté la mer calme "qui avait pr. eux des tempêtes moins terribles."

Fol. 236

corriger les *mois*
Caton
continuellement trop répété dans le IXe ch.
Anahid mieux qu'Anaitis
tanos et non tianos
Palibotza – et non *na*
taprobane : tamzapani ontambapanni
Haroudsch – noir   collop : colle
Daritienne : Daritite
Tunis : Tunès
Icosium & non Iconium
XII à Narr'H d'aller chercher du renfort & de revenir.
(*six or seven illegible words written in pencil*)

Fol. 237v

(*this part of the folio consists of scored-out notes, in pencil, from late stage*)
surveiller partout. *immobile*
faire comme │
                    │ fréquent
semble comme │
x259 qui (*two or three illegible words*) continuellement
x149 marchaient autour de
          continuellement : perpétuellement
x38   & il en survenait d'autres continuellement
x37   arrivaient par derrière continuellement
⟨149 march.⟩
x239 soufflaient avec force continuellement. une pitié l'(*illegible word*)
38   Ham avec l'esclave
404   une sorte de pitié l'(*illegible word*)
96   (*illegible phrase*)
436   en plein ciel bleu
460   en plein ciel bleu
118   en plein azur

125   en plein azur
374   en plein ciel bleu
404   luisant en plein azur (*illegible word*)
⟨massacre⟩
XII fin *couvert*
(*remainder of folio written other way up, in ink*)
symbole de richesse – fils d'araignée en or.
plissés comme les palmiers meilleurs.
pr. le mariage voir Cant des Juifs.
⟨Narr'havas porte en bracelet la chainette de Salam.⟩
⟨les buffles prennent tant d'eau à demi couchés dans les marais qu'ils la revomissent⟩
IV. (*illegible word*) de Carth recrutait des soldats.
⟨Leur faire porter de la nourriture par une tribu qui se tient à l'écart.
– elle est exterminée /peu de temps avant/⟨après⟩ la mort Mathô?
ou peut-êt. les trois mille de la Hache⟩
Ptolemé envoya 12 talens (*two illegible words*)
effrayé par (*two illegible words*) terr. /à présent/ restait silencieux.

Notes

All quotations from Flaubert's published works other than his correspondence are indicated in brackets in the text. References are to the two-volume *Oeuvres complètes*, ed. B. Masson, Editions du Seuil (Paris, 1964). Correspondence references are to Flaubert, *Correspondance (Corr.)*, ed. L. Conard (9 vols., Paris, 1926–33), and to *Correspondance. Supplément (Corr. Supp.)*, ed. R. Dumesnil, J. Pommier and C. Digeon (4 vols., Paris, 1954).

Introduction

1 G. H. Lewes, 'Historical romance', *Westminster Review*, XLV (March 1846), p. 35.
2 Georg Lukács, *The historical novel*, trans. H. and S. Mitchell (Harmondsworth, 1969) p. 402.
3 Armand de Pontmartin, 'M. Gustave Flaubert – Salammbô', *La Gazette de France*, 21 Dec. 1862, p. 1.
4 See Ernest Bernbaum, 'The views of the great critics on the historical novel', *PLMA*, XLI (June 1926), p. 429.

1 Flaubert and historical fiction

1 *Corr.* I, 16–17 (18 June 1835); *Corr.* I, 19 (12 July 1835); *Corr.* I, 20 (23 July 1835); and see *Correspondance*, ed. J. Bruneau (vols. I- , Paris, 1973–), I, 845, n.3. See also the theatre news in Flaubert's own *Art et progrès* (1835), I, 42–3.
2 *Corr.* I, 16 (18 June 1835) and *Corr.* I, 21 (14 Aug. 1835) where he adds, 'J'ai un autre drame dans la tête'. See also J. Bruneau, *Les Débuts littéraires de Gustave Flaubert, 1831–1845* (Paris, 1962). There is considerable discussion of historical drama in the first *Education sentimentale*, where Jules writes his own play, '*Le Chevalier de Calatrava*'.
3 *The Journal of Sir Walter Scott*, ed. J. G. Tait and W. M. Parker (Edinburgh, 1950), p. 462 (28 Dec. 1827).
4 Sir Walter Scott, 'Dedicatory Epistle' to *Ivanhoe*, vol. IX of the *Waverley Novels*, ed. A. Lang (25 vols., London, 1923–32), p. xlvii.
5 Scott, *Journal*, p. 230 (15 Sept. 1826).
6 See *Corr.* I, 20 (23 July 1835) and Bruneau, *Correspondance* I, 848, n.2; *Corr.* I, 21 (14 Aug. 1835); *Corr.* V, 271–2 (23–4 Jan. 1857); *Corr. Supp.* I, 184 (7 Aug. 1854). Bouilhet was also an admirer of Scott – in a letter to Flaubert in 1858 he wrote enthusiastically about *Le Monastère* and *Les Eaux de St. Ronan*, Bibliothèque de l'Institut de France, collection

Spoelberch de Lovenjoul, Chantilly (hereafter Lovenjoul), H1367 (CI), fol. 85 verso.

7 Lewes, 'Historical romance', pp. 34–5.

8 Anonymous review of Horace Smith's *Tales of the early ages* in *The Athenaeum*, no. 234 (21 April 1832), p. 251; and the preface to first edition of *La Peau de chagrin*, reprinted in Honoré de Balzac, *Oeuvres complètes* (28 vols., Paris, 1956–63), XVIII, p. 576.

9 See Alfred de Vigny, 'Réflexions sur la vérité dans l'art', first published as a preface to the fourth edition (1829) of *Cinq-Mars*. Cf. Vigny, *Le Journal d'un poète, Oeuvres complètes*, ed. F. Baldensperger (2 vols., Paris, 1948), II, 888: 'Dans l'art la vérité n'est rien, c'est la probabilité qui est tout; de mauvais romans historiques ont été faits où l'on copiait les chroniques et les dialogues des inconnus. Tout était vrai, l'on n'y croyait pas.'

10 Quoted by Fernande Bartfeld, *Sainte-Beuve et Alfred de Vigny*, Archives des lettres modernes, no. 115 (Paris, 1970), p. 24. For Vigny's reaction to Sainte-Beuve's criticism see *Le Journal d'un poète*, p. 1028.

11 *Corr.* IV, 53 (7 Apr. 1854); *Corr.* I, 417–18 (11 Nov. 1846).

12 Victor Marie Hugo, *La Muse française* (July 1823), quoted by M.-F. Guyard, ed. in *Notre-Dame de Paris* (Paris, 1959), p. iv.

13 Quoted by L. Maigron, *Le Roman historique à l'époque romantique* (Paris, 1912), p. 176.

14 *Corr.* V, 34–5 (July 1862); *Corr.* V, 309 (15 June 1867); *Corr.* VII, 137 (1 May 1874).

15 *Corr.* VIII, 281 (Dec. 1875). Cf. Edmond and Jules de Goncourt, *Journal. Mémoires de la vie littéraire*, ed. R. Ricatte (22 vols., Monaco, 1956–8), IV, 166–7: 'Flaubert nous dit: "L'histoire, l'aventure d'un roman, ça m'est bien égal. J'ai l'idée, quand je fais un roman, de rendre une couleur, un ton. Par exemple, dans mon roman de CARTHAGE, je veux faire quelque chose de pourpre. Maintenant, le reste, les personnages, l'intrigue, c'est un détail"' (17 Mar. 1861).

16 Balzac, 'Avant-propos' to *La Comédie humaine*, *Oeuvres complètes* (28 vols., 1959–63), I, 79–80.

17 A. G. P. Brugière de Barante, *Histoire des ducs de Bourgogne de la maison de Valois. 1364–1477*, 3rd edn (13 vols., Paris, 1825–6), I, pp. 33–4.

18 Vigny, *Le Journal d'un poète*, p. 886.

19 Scott, *Journal*, pp. 248–9 (18 Oct. 1826).

20 Vigny, *Le Journal d'un poète*, pp. 1064 and 942.

21 *Corr.* V, 363 (14 Mar. 1868).

22 Maxime Du Camp, *Souvenirs littéraires* (2 vols., Paris, 1882–3), II, 208. But cf. *Corr.* IV, 239 (Nov.–Dec. 1857).

23 Quoted in 'Mingle-Mangle by Monkswood. Of novels, historical and didactic', *Bentley's Miscellany*, XLVI (July 1859), p. 51.

24 Prosper Mérimée, *Romans et nouvelles*, ed. M. Parturier (2 vols., Paris, 1967), I, 85–8.

25 *Corr.* V, 253 (5–6 Dec. 1866); cf. also *Corr.* V, 227–8 (20 Aug. 1866).

26 *Corr.* IV, 297–8 (Dec. 1858).

27 Scott, 'Introductory' to *The Fair Maid of Perth*, vol. xxii of the *Waverley Novels*, p. 14.
28 *Corr.* iv, 239 (Nov.–Dec. 1857).
29 Goncourt, *Journal*, iii, 167 (16 Nov. 1859); *Corr.* iv, 379 (3 July 1860).
30 *Corr.* v. 59 (23–4 Dec. 1862); *Corr.* iv. 215 (Aug. 1857).
31 Unfortunately we cannot know for certain which historical novels Flaubert read. His letters show that in addition to the authors discussed here, he was also familiar with several minor writers whose works included historical novels: Frédéric Soulié (1800–47); Ludovic Vitet (1802–73); Roger de Beauvoir (1809–66); Eugène de Mirecourt (1812–80); Amédée Achard (1814–75); Paul Féval (1817–87); Octave Feuillet (1821–90); Emile Erckmann (1822–99) and his co-author Alexandre Chatrian (1826–90); and Pierre Alexis Ponson du Terrail (1829–71). Most of the references to these writers date from after the publication of *Salammbô*; all (apart from a comment about Soulié) are uncomplimentary; and none specifically mentions these authors' historical fiction.
32 *Corr. Supp.* ii, 19 (Nov. 1864).

2 Flaubert and the historians

1   See 'Voltaire jugé par Flaubert', *Travaux sur Voltaire et le dix-huitième siècle*, ed. T. Besterman, i (1955), pp. 133–58.
2   Ibid. pp. 155, 151, 145.
3   *Corr.* v, 412 (17 Oct. 1868).
4   *Corr.* vi, 283 (8 Sept. 1871).
5   François-René de Chateaubriand, *Etudes ou discours historiques sur la chute de l'Empire romain. La naissance et les progrès du Christianisme, et l'invasion des barbares*, vols. iv–vi of *Oeuvres complètes* (22 vols., Paris, 1833–5), iv, 38.
6   Ibid. i, 66. Chateaubriand also distinguishes a third grouping, 'les grands réformateurs', Sismondi, Guizot and Augustin Thierry. With hindsight, however, Guizot and Sismondi seem to belong to the 'fatalistes' and Thierry to the 'école descriptive', and I shall discuss them in these categories.
7   Louis Adolphe Thiers, *Histoire du consulat et de l'empire, faisant suite à l'histoire de la révolution française* (21 vols., Paris, 1845–69), i, iii.
8   C. A. Sainte-Beuve, '*Histoire de l'Empire*, par M. Thiers' and '*Discours sur l'histoire de la Révolution d'Angleterre* par M. Guizot' in *Causeries du lundi*, 3rd edn (15 vols., Paris, 1857–76), i.
9   *Corr.* i, 38 (26 Dec. 1838); *Corr.* v, 346 (18–19 Dec. 1867).
10 *Corr.* iv, 248 (23 Jan. 1858). Bouvard and Pécuchet turn to Sismondi's history because 'L'histoire ancienne est obscure par le défaut de documents, ils abondent dans le moderne' (ii, 240).
11 J. C. L. Simonde de Sismondi, *Précis de l'histoire des Français* (2 vols., Paris, 1839), i, 11; *Histoire de la chute de l'Empire romain et du déclin de la civilisation de l'an 250 à l'an 1000* (2 vols., Paris, 1835), i, iv.

12 François Pierre Guillaume Guizot, 'Lettre aux éditeurs', *Histoire de France depuis les temps les plus reculés jusqu'en 1789 racontée à mes petits-enfants* (5 vols., Paris, 1870–6), I, iii.

13 Cf. *Corr.* I, 417 (11 Dec. 1846): 'La vérité est tout autant dans les demi-teintes que dans les tons tranchés.' Jules's method, in the *Education sentimentale* of 1845, is in sharp contrast to these historians': 'Chaque époque perdit pour lui quelque chose de la couleur tranchée sous laquelle on a coûtume de l'envisager... il perdit, en fait d'histoire et de critique, beaucoup d'opinions toutes faites, d'adages commodes et de convictions communes' (I, 356).

14 *Corr.* I, 168 (1 May 1845).

15 *Corr.* IV, 181 (18 May 1857). Cf. II, 75.

16 F.-A. Mignet, *Histoire de la révolution française depuis 1789 jusqu'en 1814* (Paris, 1824), p. 4; Sismondi, *Précis de l'histoire des Français*, I, 3.

17 Barante, *Histoire des ducs de Bourgogne*, I, 13 and I, 40–1.

18 *Voltaire's correspondence*, ed. T. Besterman (107 vols., Geneva, 1953–65), x, 26 (26 Jan. 1740).

19 Jacques Nicolas Augustin Thierry, *Dix ans d'études historiques*, *Oeuvres complètes* (5 vols., Paris, 1851–3), III, 284–95.

20 Thierry, *Récits des temps mérovingiens* (2 vols., Paris, 1840), I, pp. xviii-xx.

21 *Corr.* I, 19 (12 July 1835).

22 Quoted by Daniel Mornet, 'La Méthode historique de Salammbô et la méthode historique d'Ernest Feydeau', *RHLF*, XXXIII (1926), p. 209.

23 *Corr.* IV, 416 (26 Jan. 1861).

24 Jules Michelet, *Histoire de France*, new edn (17 vols., Paris, 1871–4), x, 444; I, viii; I, iii.

25 *Corr.* I, 171 (13 May 1845); *Corr.* I, 206 (April 1846); *Corr.* III, 210 (26–7 May 1853).

26 Barante, *Histoire des ducs de Bourgogne*, I, 36. See also ibid. I, 41.

27 *Corr.* III, 37 (8 October 1852).

28 Victor Cousin, *Cours de l'histoire de la philosophie moderne*, new edn (3 vols., Paris, 1847), I, 180.

29 Emile Zola, 'Les Droits du romancier', *Le Figaro*, 6 June 1896. (In *Nouvelle Campagne*, *Oeuvres complètes*, ed. H. Mitterand (15 vols., Lausanne, 1966–70), XIV, 800.)

30 See Michelet's analysis of Vico's method in 'Discours sur le système et la vie de Vico', in Vico, *Principes de la philosophie de l'histoire* (Paris, 1827).

31 Michelet, 'Préface' (1869) to *Histoire de France*, I, vii.

32 Thierry, *Histoire de la conquête de l'Angleterre par les Normands* (3 vols., Paris, 1825), I, xiii-xiv; and I, v.

33 Thierry, *Récits des temps mérovingiens*, I, xi-xii.

34 Ms. carnet 2, fol. 5v (Bibliothèque historique de la ville de Paris). Flaubert was still writing about this idea in 1877 – see *Corr.* VIII, 94 (10 Nov. 1877).

35 *Corr.* IV, 314 (18 Feb. 1859). Cf. *Corr.* III, 271 (7–8 July 1853): 'Qu'est-ce qui a, jusqu'à présent, fait de l'histoire en naturaliste?'

3 The genesis and development of 'Salammbô'

1   Partially reprinted in appendix 4 to the Club de l'Honnête Homme edition of *Salammbô* (15 vols., Paris, 1971–5), vol. II. This version of the dossier contains many misreadings and should be read in conjunction with Isabelle Strong, 'Deciphering the *Salammbô* dossier: appendix 4 of the Club de l'Honnête Homme edition', *Modern Language Review*, LXXII (July 1977), pp. 538–54.
2   *Corr.* IV, 164.
3   Louvenjoul ms. 1361 B1 (fol. 396–7); Lovenjoul ms. 1361 B (fol. 97–8).
4   Hugo, *Oeuvres poétiques*, ed. P. Albouy (3 vols., Paris, 1964-74), I, 580.
5   See Jean Seznec, 'Les Lectures antiques de Flaubert entre 1840 et 1850', *Revue d'histoire de la philosophie et d'histoire générale de la civilisation*, fasc. 27–8 (July–Dec. 1939), pp. 274–82, and the chronological list of his reading between 1845 and 1849 in Jean Bruneau, *Le 'Conte oriental' de Gustave Flaubert* (Paris, 1973), pp. 64–8.
6   *Corr.* IV, 175–6 (April 1857).
7   *Corr.* IV, 176–8 (10–11 May 1857).
8   *Corr.* IV, 189 (end May 1857).
9   *Corr.* IV, 191 (beg. June 1857).
10 *Corr.* IV, 199 (June–July 1857); *Corr.* IV, 208 (22 July 1857).
11 *Corr.* IV, 209 (July–Aug. 1857).
12 *Corr. Supp.* I, 244 (26 Dec. 1858); *Corr. Supp.* I, 226 (24 June 1857); *Corr.* IV, 176 (beg. May 1857).
13 *Corr.* IV, 178–9 (14 May 1857).
14 *Corr.* IV, 266 (20 May 1858).
15 *Corr.* IV, 175 (April 1857); *Corr.* IV, 189–90 (end May 1857); *Corr. Supp.* I, 229 (28 June 1857).
16 *Corr.* IV, 209 (22 July 1857).
17 *Corr.* IV, 212 (July–Aug. 1857).
18 *Corr.* IV, 240–3 (12 Dec. 1857).
19 *Corr.* IV, 226 (Sept. 1857); *Corr.* IV, 239 (Nov.–Dec. 1857).
20 *Corr.* IV, 279 (Oct. 1858); *Corr.* IV, 287 (19 Dec. 1858).
21 *Corr.* IV, 379 (3 July 1860); *Corr.* IV, 383 (4 July 1860).
22 *Corr.* IV, 238 (24? Nov. 1857); *Corr.* IV, 272 (11 July 1858).
23 *Corr.* IV, 384 (July 1860); *Corr.* IV, 406 (21 Oct. 1860); *Corr.* IV, 441 (15 July 1861); *Corr.* IV, 445 (24 Aug. 1861); *Corr.* IV, 447 (1 Sept. 1861).
24 *Corr.* IV, 449–50 (Oct. 1861); *Corr. Supp.* I, 274 (25 Sept. 1861); Goncourt, *Journal*, V, 17 (3 Nov. 1861).
25 *Corr. Supp.* I, 289 (5 July 1862).
26 N. a. fr. 23.656 (Flaubert's autograph version); N. a. fr. 23.657 (publisher's copy); N. a. fr. 23.658–662 (brouillons, notes and plans). At the time of writing, the June 1980 acquisition has not yet been catalogued.

The scenarios and early notes are in n. a. fr. 23.662. Unless otherwise stated, all folio references are to this volume. Some of these scenarios and notes were published for the first time in the Club de l'Honnête Homme edition of *Salammbô* – unfortunately the published version is strewn with misreadings and should be read in conjunction with the emendations given in Alison Fairlie and Anne Green, 'Deciphering Flaubert's manuscripts. The "Club de l'Honnête Homme" edition', *French Studies*, xxvii (July 1973), pp. 287–315. The remaining notes and plans are published for the first time in the appendix to this book. References to folios reproduced in the appendix are marked with an asterisk.

27   Rouen Ms. g322. At the time of writing, the individual folios have not yet been numbered. I propose to refer to them as fols. g322A-G. Fols. g322A* and g322B* are plans of the novel from beginning to end; fol. g322C* contains three background notes (fols. A*, B* and C* are published for the first time in the appendix). Fols. g322D-G are all fragments of 'brouillon': D recto is a description of Salammbô asleep, watched by Mâtho; D verso describes the slaughter of the bull and sheep for Mâtho and Narr'Havas; E recto is an account of Mâtho's escape with the veil; E verso describes Spendius contemplating the aqueduct; F recto deals with Mâtho's feelings for Salammbô – a mixture of hatred and desire; F verso describes a sunset and dust storm, as does G recto, while G verso depicts Autharite's army encampment.

     For a discussion of the variant spellings of characters' names, see p. 34.

28   See Léon Cellier, *Etudes de structure*, Archives des lettres modernes, no. 56 (Paris, 1964), pp. 2–10.

29   Cf. 'insister sur La Peur de se compromettre' (in notes for Second Empire novel, carnet 20, fol. 12 verso); 'La peur de se compromettre' (in notes for *Sous Napoléon III*, carnet 17, fol. 4); 'Je suis effrayé, épouvanté, scandalisé par la couillonnade transcendante qui règne sur les humains. A-t-on peur de se compromettre!!!' (*Corr.* iv, 317–18, June 1859); and 'Madame Tuvache...déclara devant sa servante que Madame Bovary se compromettait" (i, 605).

30   *Corr.* iii, 396 (14 Dec. 1853).

31   Many of the problems of woman's place in society are discussed at the Club des Femmes in *L'Education sentimentale*.

32   Charles Baudelaire, *Oeuvres complètes*, ed. M. Ruff (Paris, 1968), p. 452.

33   The unexpected arrival of Giscon '/comme un serpent qui rampe/ – maigre – hideux – méconnaissable. il la force à partir', is an embodiment of the grotesque, and may be compared to the appearances of the blind beggar in Madame Bovary and the dog in the first *Education sentimentale*.

34   *Corr.* iv, 287 (19 Dec. 1858).

35   Cf. Théophile Gautier's *Le Roman de la momie* (1858), ed. A. Boschot (Paris, 1955), which also includes passages describing 'des échantillons divers de races exotiques' (p. 205), and differentiating between the

characteristics of 'les nègres du haut Nil...les Ethiopiens bronzés...les Asiatiques au teint jaune clair...les Pélasges vêtus de peaux de bêtes', etc. (pp. 205–6). Flaubert's main source for the 'funérailles diverses' was Ernest Feydeau's *Histoire des usages funèbres et des sépultures chez les peuples anciens*; this was also used extensively by Gautier, who dedicated *Le Roman de la momie* to Feydeau.

36   *Corr.* III, 317 (23 Aug. 1853).
37   Claudine Gothot-Mersch, *La Genèse de Madame Bovary* (Paris, 1966), pp. 124 and 147.
38   *Corr. Supp.* I, 266 (24? June 1857).
39   A note in fol. 229* runs: 'Astarté fut la Terre & l'Eau etc. & cette flamme immortelle qui se sert d'un lit pr. aller au ciel.
40   Cf. fol. 213*: '⟨*Moloch* quatre aspects. ⟨Feu⟩ planète. Feu. créateur suprême – roi. *le Feu* coule comme le sang dans les veines ne diffère pas du caloriq., de l'électricité. jamais plus puissant que lors qu'il détruit. – De là le sang & les cendres qui accompagnent Moloch⟩.'
41   L. F. Benedetto, *Le Origini di 'Salammbô'* (Florence, 1920), p. 328.
42   Polybius, *Histoire*, trans. Dom Vincent Thuillier (6 vols., Paris, 1727–30), II, 56.
43   There are of course many parallels between the war between the Carthaginians and barbarians, and the relationship between Salammbô and Mâtho. Folard, in his commentary on Polybius' account of the battle of Utica (where Hannon's downfall is caused by his over-confidence in believing he has won) notes that: 'tout comme fit Hannon, qui la [sa victoire] vit pourtant disparoître sans avoir pensé ni même prévu qu'il pût en être abandonné, comme si la victoire n'étoit pas une femme'. *Histoire*, II, 27. This is in fact what happens to Mâtho in the chapter 'Sous la tente', where he finds that Salammbô has disappeared after he believed she was finally his. Like Hannon, he too had not 'pensé ni même prévu qu'il pût en être abandonné'.
44   Ibid. II, 65–6.
45   Ibid. II, 66–7.
46   *Corr.* V, 69 (23–4 Dec. 1862).
47   Polybius, *Histoire*, II, 71.

4   *'Salammbô and nineteenth-century French society*

1   Lukács, *The historical novel*, p. 220; Victor Brombert, *Flaubert par lui-même* (Paris, 1971), p. 76; Dennis Porter, 'Aestheticism versus the novel: the example of *Salammbô*', *Novel* IV (1971), pp. 101–6; Albert Thibaudet, *Gustave Flaubert*, new edn (Paris, 1935), p. 135; Jean-Paul Sartre, *L'Idiot de la famille: Gustave Flaubert de 1821 à 1857* (3 vols., Paris, 1971–2), III, 450.
2   Lukács, *The historical novel*, pp. 223–8.
3   'Du Progrès dans les siècles de décadence', *Correspondant* XXX (1852), p. 257. Quoted in Koenraad W. Swart, *The sense of decadence in nineteenth-century France* (The Hague, 1964), p. 86. Cf. Homais, who,

on seeing the blind beggar, comments: 'Le Progrès, ma parole d'honneur, marche à pas de tortue! Nous pataugeons en pleine barbarie!' (I, 675).

4   Pierre Citron, *La Poésie de Paris dans la littérature française de Rousseau à Baudelaire* (2 vols., Paris, 1961), I, 111, 122, 125, 332; II, 28, 29, 31.

5   Pierre Leroux, *La France sous Louis-Philippe* (1842), *Oeuvres* (2 vols., Paris, 1850–1), I, 414–15.

6   Michelet, *Histoire de la révolution française* (7 vols., Paris, 1847–53), I, vi. Compare the orgies and atrocities of *Salammbô* with the imagery of these nineteenth-century views of Paris:

La grande cité court dans les flots d'une orgie,
Ne respirant que feu de ses poumons ardents,
Cheveux collés de vin, lambeaux de chair aux dents.

J.-F. Destigny, 'Mascarade politique', quoted by Citron, *La Poésie de Paris*, I, 359.

Je ne te voyais pas, Babylone frivole...
Je ne te voyais pas, dans la fange et le sang,
Pousser de crime en crime un peuple incandescent,
Phare des nations, brûlant plus qu'il n'éclaire,
Enflammer et trahir la fureur populaire,
Et montrer pour exemple aux vassales cités
Les horribles tableaux de tes atrocités.

Louise Colet, 'Paris', *Poésies complètes* (Paris, 1844), p. 32.

7   Michelet, 'A. M. Edgar Quinet' (1846), *Le Peuple*, ed. R. Casanova (Paris, 1965), pp. 70–1. Cf. Guizot, *Histoire de la civilisation en France depuis la chute de l'Empire romain*, new edn (4 vols., Paris, 1846), I, 25: 'On dit...que...le dévouement et l'énergie, les deux grandes puissances comme les deux grandes vertus de l'homme, et qui ont brillé dans les temps que nous appelons barbares, manquent et manqueront de plus en plus aux temps que nous appelons civilisés, et particulièrement au nôtre.' While believing that there is some truth in this, Guizot had faith in man's ability to find other sources of energy.

8   Dossier of *L'Education sentimentale*, Rouen ms. IV, 138 and 139, quoted by A. Cento, *Il realismo documentario nell'Education sentimentale* (Naples, 1967), p. 273.

9   *Corr.* III, 10–11 (1 Sept. 1852).

10   Du Camp, *Souvenirs littéraires*, I, appendix: 'Pièces justificatives no. 1'.

11   N.a.fr. 23.659 fol. 31v.

12   Ibid. fol. 74v.

13   Ibid. fol. 73: 'comme par les temps de peste les maisons étaient fermées'.

14   T. Gautier, 'Premières poésies', *Poésies complètes* (2 vols., Paris, 1884), I, 109 ('Paris' was written in 1831).

15   See Citron, *La Poésie de Paris*, II, 443.

16   Sénard, *Banquet réformiste de Rouen, 25 décembre 1847: Discours de M. Sénard, président du banquet* (extrait du Journal de Rouen); Duvergier de

Hauranne, *Discours prononcé à Rouen par M. Duvergier de Hauranne au banquet de la réforme électorale et parlementaire* (Paris, 1847), (25 Dec. 1847).

17   *Corr.* III, 40 (8 Oct. 1852).

18   A. Moreau de Jonnès, *Eléments de statistique* (Paris, 1856), p. 300.

19   1857, the year in which Flaubert began to write *Salammbô*, was one of extreme drought in Paris. The water in the Seine dropped to the lowest level since records of river stages were first kept in 1719, and caused a severe water shortage in the city. See David Henry Pinkney, *Napoleon III and the rebuilding of Paris* (Princeton, 1958), p. 112, and chapter 5, 'A Battle for Water', *passim*.

20   *Corr.* V, 70 (23–4 Dec. 1862).

21   Is there not here an analogy with the superficial, physical order which Haussmann and his colleagues imposed on Paris, a replanning which many claimed was motivated by strategic considerations? Haussmann himself said quite openly that 'la destruction des vieux quartiers enlèverait un camp à l'émeute'. See J. M. and B. Chapman, *The life and times of Baron Haussmann: Paris in the Second Empire* (London, 1957), p. 184.

22   Saint-Marc Girardin, 'De la Domination des Carthaginois et des Romains en Afrique comparée avec la domination française', *Revue des Deux Mondes* (1 May 1841), pp. 413–14.

23   *Corr.* IV, 302 (10 Jan. 1859); cf. similar comments in *Corr.* II, 414 (15–16 May 1852), and *Corr.* III, 58 (9 Dec. 1852).

24   Cf. Goncourt, *Journal*, V, 228 (14 Dec 1862): 'Flaubert regrette une grosse barbarie, un âge de force, de déploiement de nudité, une ère primitive et sadique, l'âge sanguin du monde; des batailles, des grands coups; des temps héroïques, sauvages, tatoués de couleurs crues, chargés de verroteries.'

25   C.-M.-R. Leconte de Lisle. *Poèmes barbares* (Paris, 1947), p. 356. See also B. H. Morel. *Traité des dégénérescences physiques, intellectuelles et morales de l'espèce humaine* (Paris, 1857).

26   *Corr.* III, 150 (31 Mar. 1853).

27   A. Esquiros, 'Des études contemporaines sur l'histoire des races', *Revue des Deux Mondes*, new series XXI (1848), pp. 982–1003. See also a lecture on race by Serres in A. Esquiros (ed.), *Paris ou les sciences, les institutions et les moeurs au XIXe siècle* (Paris, 1847); and Michel Lémonon, 'L'Idée de race et les écrivains français de la première moitié du XIXe siècle', *Die neueren Sprachen*, LXIX (June 1970), pp. 283–92.

28   See, for example, Guizot's *Histoire de la civilisation*, I, 32–3, where he describes how a combination of Roman and Germanic elements have produced 'le caractère de la civilisation française'; and Michelet, *Le Peuple*, pp. 251–8.

29   Thierry, *Dix ans d'études historiques*, III, 292. See also above, pp. 25–6.

30   Joseph-Arthur de Gobineau, *Essai sur l'inégalité des races humaines* (4 vols., Paris, 1853–5), I, v.

31   Ibid, I, 50 and 56. Other commentators held similar ideas. Cf. Auguste Romieu, *Le Spectre rouge de 1852*, 3rd edn (Paris, 1851): 'La nation

française n'existe plus. Il y a, sur le vieux sol de Gaule, des riches inquiets et des pauvres avides; il n'y a que cela.' And Flaubert himself lamented that in France 'le sang aristocratique est épuisé', *Corr.* III, 129 (25–6 Mar. 1853).

32 Hippolyte Taine, introduction to *Histoire de la littérature anglaise* (5 vols., Paris, 1863), vol. I.
33 *Corr.* III, 129 (25–6 Mar. 1853).
34 *Corr.* IV, 164 (18 Mar. 1857).

5   Political and economic parallels

1 Flaubert, *Lettres inédites à la Princesse Mathilde*, ed. Conard (Paris, 1927), p. xxii.
2 Du Camp, *Souvenirs littéraires*, I, 396 and 416.
3 *Corr.* VI, 279 (6 Sept. 1871); *Corr.* VI, 283 (8 Sept. 1871).
4 Sartre, *L'Idiot de la famille*, III, 447–9.
5 *Corr.* IV, 170 (30 Mar. 1857); *Corr.* IV, 184 (18 May 1857); *Corr.* IV, 377 (May 1860); *Corr.* VI, 228 (29 Apr. 1871) etc.
6 *Corr.* III, 337 (7 Sept. 1853).
7 *Corr.* V, 149 (Summer 1864); *Corr.* V, 146 (July 1864); *Corr.* VI, 33 (June–July 1869).
8 *Corr.* II, 87 (6 May 1849).
9 *Corr.* III, 146 (31 Mar. 1853). The most obvious examples of this characteristic are the travel notes, which begin as jottings made on the spot, are then expanded and reworked for publication, and reappear out of context and after undergoing various transformations as descriptive fragments in later novels.
10 Benedetto, *Le origini di 'Salammbô'*, pp. 52–4.
11 *Corr.* II, 78 (Dec. 1847). The banquet is also described by M. Du Camp, *Souvenirs de l'année 1848*, 2nd edn (Paris, 1892), p. 42. The organising committee included a certain M. Homais.
12 Daniel Stern, Eugène Pelletan, Jules Lecomte, and in particular *Le Constitutionnel* of 23 Feb. 1848. See Cento, *Il realismo documentario*, pp. 183–4.
13 As early as 1839 Flaubert had noted in his essay 'Les Arts et le commerce' that commercial interests dominated all else in Carthage. Because of her government's ruthlessness in furthering these interests, he wrote, we now think of Carthage with horror (I, 185).
14 Edgar Quinet, 'Avertissement au pays' (1841), *Oeuvres complètes* (10 vols., Paris, 1857–8), X, 34.
15 Chateaubriand, *Essai historique, politique et moral sur les révolutions anciennes et modernes, Oeuvres complètes*. Chapters 30–3 of vol. I concern Carthage; see especially chapter 32 which deals with the period about which Flaubert was to write in *Salammbô*. J. Michelet, *Histoire romaine*, 2nd edn (2 vols., Paris, 1833), I, 259.
16 N.a.fr. 23.659 fol. 178v; see also 23.659 fol. 206v.
17 Quinet, 'Avertissement au pays', p. 33.

18 When peace was concluded between France and Morocco in September 1844 the widespread relief was reflected in the Stock Exchange – 'la rente est augmentée de 50 centimes' – *Journal des débats* (23 Sept. 1844).

19 Polybius, *Histoire*, II, 3–4.

20 See Charles Schmidt, *Des Ateliers nationaux aux barricades de juin* (Paris, 1948), p. 24.

21 Ibid. p. 32; and Alexandre-Thomas Marie, Minister of Works in the provisional government, had addressed them on 26 March with the words: 'Ah! vous êtes bien dignes de cette liberté que vous avez conquise, bien dignes de vivre sous cette République que vous avez fondée; cette République, on ne vous l'escamotera pas cette fois'. Georges Duveau, *1848* (Paris, 1965), p. 146.

22 Schmidt, *Des Ateliers nationaux*, p. 32. On June 22 Marie told them, 'Vous ne voulez pas partir pour la province? Nous vous y contraindrons par la force, vous entendez bien, par la force'. Duveau, *1848*, p. 146.

23 Moreau de Jonnès, *Statistique des céréales de la France. Le blé, sa culture, sa production, sa consommation, son commerce*. (Paris, 1843), p. 47. This deficit in corn production may be compared with Salammbô's lament for the days when Carthage was able to export corn in abundance (I, 697–98).

24 N. a. fr. 23.659 fol. 40.

25 Polybius, *Histoire*, II, 18.

26 N. a. fr. 23.659 fol. 196.

27 N. a. fr. 23.659 fol. 191v.

28 Du Camp, *Souvenirs littéraires*, II, 30–1.

29 Jean-Jacques Mayoux, 'Flaubert et le réel', *Mercure de France*, CCL (15 Feb. 1934), p. 43, n. 5.

30 'Notice de Salammbô' (anon.), in *Salammbô*, Edition du Club de l'Honnête Homme, p. 24.

31 *Corr. Supp.* I, 253 (Nov. 1859).

32 Carnet de lecture, 12, fol. 33v.

33 Du Camp, *Souvenirs de l'année 1848*, p. 42.

34 N. a. fr. 23.659 fol. 187.

35 *Corr.* IV, 339 (8 Oct. 1859).

36 Charles Augustin Sainte-Beuve, 'De la littérature industrielle' (1839) in *Portraits contemporains* (5 vols., Paris, 1869), II, 444–71; Pelletan, *La Nouvelle Babylone* (Paris, 1862), pp. 165–8.

37 Du Camp, *Souvenirs littéraires*, II, 542.

38 Chateaubriand, *Essai sur les révolutions*, Oeuvres complètes, I, 141.

39 Du Camp, *Souvenirs littéraires*, II, 209; Goncourt, *Journal*, IV, 190 (1887 addition to entry of 6 May 1861).

40 Louise Colet, '*Le Marabout de Sidi-Brahim*', *poème dédié à l'armée, suivi de la 'Chanson des soldats d'Afrique'* (Musique de Hte. Colet, *professeur au Conservatoire*) (Paris, 1845).

41 A. J. Tudesq, *Les Grands Notables en France (1840–49): étude historique d'une psychologie sociale* (2 vols., Bordeaux, 1964), II, 829.

42 J. C. L. Simonde de Sismondi, *Les Colonies des anciens comparées à celles des modernes, sous le rapport de leur influence sur le bonheur du genre humain* (Geneva, 1837), pp. 7–8.
43 Du Camp, *Souvenirs littéraires*, I, 389.

6 Religion and mythology in 'Salammbô'

1 *Corr.* IV, 170 (30 Mar. 1857). Much later he boasted to Princess Mathilde that he was something of an expert in religious matters – *Corr.* VIII, 320 (5 Nov. 1879).
2 *Corr.* V, 407 (1868); *Corr.* IV, 184 (18 May 1857).
3 See *Corr. Supp.* I, 264 (1860) and *Corr.* IV, 358 (18 Dec. 1859); *Corr.* III, 16–17 (4 Sept. 1852); *Corr.* IV, 170 (30 Mar. 1857); *Corr.* II, 433 (1852); *Corr.* V, 148 (Summer 1864).
4 Michelet, *Histoire romaine*, I, 57.
5 A. Chéruel, 'Du Merveilleux dans l'histoire', *Revue de Rouen*, n.s. VI (1835), pp. 57–69.
6 Ernest Renan, 'Des Religions de l'antiquité et de leurs derniers historiens', *Revue des Deux Mondes* (15 May 1853), p. 822.
7 Ms. letter dated 3 May 1861. Lovenjoul 1365 (BV) fols. 5–6.
8 Benjamin Constant, *De la Religion considérée dans sa source, ses formes et ses développements* (5 vols., Paris, 1824–31), II, 175.
9 André Dubuc, 'Une Déclaration politique de Bouilhet en 1848', *Bulletin des Amis de Flaubert*, no. 35 (Dec. 1969), pp. 14–17.
10 E. Quinet, *L'Enseignement du peuple*, 7th edn (Paris, 1876), p. 106.
11 *Corr.* III, 210 (26–7 May 1853). See the whole of this letter for Flaubert's reactions to various aspects of the occult. Flaubert claimed that a phrenologist once told him that he ought to practise magnetism – *Corr.* III, 218 (1 June 1853) and in 1860, while he was writing 'La Bataille du Macar', he wrote to Feydeau, 'Je viens de lire un livre sur le magnétisme.' *Corr.* IV, 382 (4 June 1860). There are several references to magnetism in his other novels. At the *comices agricoles* in *Madame Bovary*, 'Rodolphe, avec Madame Bovary, causait rêves, pressentiments, magnétisme' (I, 624); Homais, too, is interested in magnetism, and after Emma's death Charles 'se rappelait des histoires de catalepsie, les miracles du magnétisme; et il se disait qu'en le voulant extrêmement, il parviendrait peut-être à la réussite' (I, 686). Most of chapter 8 of *Bouvard et Pécuchet* is devoted to accounts of the clerks' experiments with table-turning, magnetism, passes, hypnotism, etc., largely based on their reading of Montacabère's *Guide du magnétiseur* (II, 262–77).
12 N. a. fr. 23.659 fol. 79v.
13 'Dans le temple de M. fortunes des particuliers en dépôt.
      – trésors de l'état.
      – étalons des poids et mesures' fol. 203v.
14 *Corr.* V, 148 (Summer 1864).
15 *Corr.* V, 271 (23–4 Jan. 1867).

16 The long tradition of esoteric beliefs is discussed by P. G. Castex, *Le Conte fantastique en France de Nodier à Maupassant* (Paris, 1951), pp. 13–24, and by C. McIntosh, *Eliphas Levi and the French occult revival*. The most important influences were Swedenborg, Martines de Pasqually and Claude de Saint-Martin; Antoine-Joseph Pernety, a disciple of Swedenborg and founder of the 'Illuminés d'Avignon' was convinced that all ancient myths were hermetic allegories, and expounded this idea in his very widely read *Fables égyptiennes et grecques dévoilées et réduites au même principe avec une explication des hiéroglyphes de la guerre de Troie* (1758), and in his later *Dictionnaire mytho-hermétique*. Renan is deeply scathing about writers who claim that mythology is the guardian of sacred truths – see 'Des Religions de l'antiquité', p. 825.

17 N. a. fr. 32.661 fol. 348: 'Elle (i.e. Salammbô) allait dormir sur les tombeaux dans les Mappales afin d'avoir des songes /qui l'éclaircissent sur l'avenir/ Une fois elle l'avait vu. Il ⟨était⟩ debout au milieu ⟨?⟩ /de Carthage/ & ses épaules dépassaient le fronton des temples. Elle avait /ensuite/ allumé du feu par terre entre ses jambes. alors il ⟨était devenu⟩ /s'était changé/ en airain ⟨comme la statue puis⟩ il l'avait pris dans ses bras et sans qu'elle éprouvat aucune douleur /peu à peu/ ils s'étaient fondus ensemble.'

18 N. a. fr. 23.658 fol. 59v.

19 See *Corr.* V, 57–8 (23–4 Dec. 1862) where Flaubert rejects Sainte-Beuve's accusation that Salammbô resembles Emma.

20 Cf. especially the passage in *Novembre* where Marie describes her religious experience: 'A l'église, je regardais l'Homme nu étalé sur la croix, et je redressais sa tête, je remplissais ses flancs; je colorais tous ses membres, je levais ses paupières; je me faisais devant moi un homme beau, avec un regard de feu; je le détachais de la croix et je le faisais descendre vers moi, sur l'autel; l'encens l'entourait, il s'avançait dans la fumée, et de sensuels frémissements me couraient sur la peau' (I, 265).

21 *Corr.* IV. 313 (18 Feb. 1859).

22 The material which follows is also discussed in my article, '*Salammbô* and the myth of Pasiphaë', *French Studies*, XXXII (April 1978), pp. 170–8.

23 Alfred Maury, *Histoire des religions de la Grèce antique* (3 vols., Paris, 1857–9), I, 507–8.

24 *Corr. Supp.* I, 227 (24 Jun. 1857).

25 Lovenjoul ms. 1366 (BVI) fol. 428, and partly reproduced in *Corr. Supp.* I, 227, n. 2.

26 Friedrich Creuzer, *Religions de l'antiquité considérées principalement dans leurs formes symboliques et mythologiques*. trans. J. D. Guigniaut (4 vols, Paris, 1825–51), III, 8, 482. Creuzer wrote his *Symbolik* in 1810–12, but although Benjamin Constant, the Baron d'Eckstein and Edgar Quinet were among those who brought his ideas to France, it was not until 1825–51, as Guigniaut published his annotated translation and elaboration of Creuzer's work with additional notes by Maury, that the full influence of the *Symbolik* reached a French audience. Flaubert

owned a copy of Guigniaut's version of Creuzer, and used it extensively for *Salammbô*. He first mentions reading it in 1848 while keeping vigil after the death of Alfred Le Poittevin (*Corr.* II, 81 – 7 Apr. 1848) and it also served as an important source for *La Tentation de saint Antoine*.

27   Maury notes in Creuzer, *Symbolique*, II, 4, 1040: 'Hercule est le même que Baâl-Khamon...lequel est identique au Baâl-Moloch et au Melkarth de Tyr. Ce dernier nom se retrouve chez les Carthaginois dans celui d'Amilcar. Athénagore nous dit positivement qu'Amilcar était un dieu phénicien.'

28   Creuzer, *Symbolique*, III, 8, 489–90.

29   In his notes to Creuzer's *Symbolique*, Maury points to similarities between Eschmoun, one of the greater Carthaginian deities, and Daedalus, constructor of the labyrinth (II, 4, 1041).

30   Creuzer, *Symbolique*, II, 4, 833; III, 8, 1075.

31   *Corr.* IV, 452 (Sept.–Oct. 1861).

32   Creuzer, *Symbolique*, III, 8, 481. Cf. Guigniaut's notes, ibid. pp. 1068–73, where he puts forward linguistic reasons for identifying Pasiphaë with Proserpine.

33   Ibid., III, 8, 554 and 416.

34   Ibid., II, 4, 247.

35   Ibid., III, 8, 489.

36   Ibid., III, 8, 488–9.

37   Pasiphaë's attribute of creating both fertility and sterility is reflected more clearly in the name which Flaubert originally gave his heroine – Pyrrha. The mythological Pyrrha, sole survivor of the Great Flood together with Deucalion, was mother of the human race; but she is associated also with the idea of sterility since her 'children' were stones which she cast behind her.

38   The contrast is firmly maintained in Polybius' account. In his view, the barbarians 'passent toutes bornes: ce ne sont plus des hommes, ce sont des bêtes féroces, il n'est pas de violence qu'on n'en doive attendre'. *Histoire*, II, 5. The Carthaginians, although occasionally behaving badly, are shown as winning a glorious victory over the rebels.

39   Creuzer, *Symbolique*, III, 8, 489.

40   Flaubert has contrived to remain faithful both to historical fact and to the mythological metaphor. A year passes between the return of Hamilcar (February) and the battle of Macar (January), and the war lasts for a full three years. Yet in the text of *Salammbô* the length of the war is stylised and condensed. Events are described in relation to the time of year, and these form one complete seasonal cycle.

41   Creuzer, *Symbolique*, III, 8, 506–11 and 567. Cf. the dying barbarians in the *défilé de la Hache* who dream of 'des campagnes au coucher du soleil, quand les blés jaunes ondulent et que les grands boeufs remontent les collines avec le soc des charrues sur le cou' (I, 785).

42   When Mâtho makes his first appearance in the novel he is wearing a silver moon-symbol on his chest (I, 698).

43   Creuzer, *Symbolique*, III, 8, 567.

44 See Ibid. III, 8, 665: he believes that the sacrifice of bulls to Proserpine 'fut un adoucissement et une substitution d'un sacrifice plus ancien dont l'homme était la victime'.

45 E.g. Benedetto, *Le origini di 'Salammbô'*, pp. 115–258; A. Hamilton, *Sources of the religious element in Flaubert's 'Salammbô'* (Baltimore–Paris, 1917); A. Coleman, '"Salammbô" and the Bible', *Sources and structure of Flaubert's 'Salammbô'* (Baltimore–Paris, 1914), pp. 37–55. Coleman seriously underestimates Flaubert's use of the Bible.

46 *Corr.* V, 61 (23–4 Dec. 1862).

47 See George Ferguson, *Signs and symbols in Christian art* (New York, 1966), pp. 31–41.

48 Pierre-Daniel Huet, for example, had studied pagan mythology and its relation to certain Bible stories, and had concluded, in his *Demonstratio evangelica* (1679) that the Bible was the source of all myths and that mythology is little more than a vast plagiarism of the Bible; Voltaire had taken an opposing view in *La Bible enfin expliquée*, seeing Old Testament stories as imitations of ancient pagan legends; Fontenelle noted parallels between Greek and Italian mythology in *De l'Origine des fables*; Joseph-François Lafiteau saw similarities between primitive American legends, Homer's mythology and certain Bible stories, and so tried to prove that most of the inhabitants of America were of Greek descent, in his *Moeurs des sauvages américains comparées aux moeurs des premiers temps* (1723). See Jan de Vries, *Forschungsgeschichte der Mythologie* (Fribourg–Munich, 1961), pp. 76–9; and Pierre Albouy, *La Création mythologique chez Victor Hugo* (Paris, 1963), p. 36. (Albouy confuses Pierre Lafitau with Joseph-François Lafitau.)

49 Charles-François Dupuis, *Origine de tous les cultes ou religion universelle* (Paris, An III), I, p. x. Cf. the earlier work of Nicolas Boulanger and Antoine Court de Gébelin. Boulanger, in *L'Antiquité dévoilée par ses usages, ou Examen critique des principales opinions, cérémonies et institutions religieuses et politiques des différens peuples de la terre* (Amsterdam, 1776) saw myths as figurative representations of geological catastrophes – of the Flood in particular. Boulanger concludes: 'nous avons fait voir que sous le voile de l'allégorie elle n'est tantôt qu'une cosmogonie, tantôt une histoire des révolutions de la nature, tantôt un emblème de sa destruction finale; elle nous peint le désordre des élémens lors de la ruine et du renouvellement du monde' (p. 409). Cf. fol. 224*; 'Chaque période du monde est comprise entre un déluge et une conflagration.' Court de Gébelin claimed that all myths could be interpreted as agricultural symbols or allegories: see *Le Monde primitif analysé et comparé avec le monde moderne, considéré dans son génie allégorique et dans les allégories auxquelles conduisit ce génie* (9 vols., Paris, 1773–82), especially I, 68–9.

50 He used C.-F. Volney's *Voyage en Syrie* for ethnographical details. See fol. 149.

51 Flaubert was familiar with Müller's work – cf. *Corr.* III, 198 (17 May 1853).

52 Cf. fol. 201v*: 'Hannon. l'éléphant est consacré au soleil. rapport de l'éléph & de l'éléphantiasis.'
53 See, for example, the description of the coming of daylight to Carthage. The landscape comes to life as the sun rises; horses paw the ground; temple doors swing open; shops raise their shutters as the sun seems to kindle the potential energy of the city (1, 699).

Conclusion

1 See Jonathan Culler, *Flaubert. The uses of uncertainty* (London, 1974), p. 217.
2 *Corr. Supp.* II, 19 (Nov. 1864).

Select bibliography

(i) Manuscript sources

(a) Bibliothèque Nationale, Paris

Nouvelles acquisitions françaises:
23.656: *Salammbô* (autograph version)
23.657: *Salammbô* (copy)
23.658–61: *Salammbô* (drafts)
23.662: *Salammbô* (drafts, notes, plans and sources)
23.824–45: documents and notes on Flaubert
14.135: *A Maman pour sa fête*
14.152: *Les Sept fils du derviche*
14.153: *Pierrot au sérail*
14.155: *Parisina*
14.278: *Mythologie – autograph notes*

(b) Bibliothèque historique de la ville de Paris

Ms. Flaubert, carnets de notes de lecture

(c) Bibliothèque de l'Institut de France. Collection Spoelberch de Lovenjoul

Série A, I-VI (Letters from Flaubert)
Série B, I-VI (Letters to Flaubert)

(d) Taylor Institution, Oxford

Ms. Flaubert, 'De finibus Bonorum et Malorum' (notes from Cicero)

(e) Bibliothèque Municipale, Rouen

Ms. g322: plans, notes and drafts for *Salammbô*

(ii) Primary sources

(*Note*. Unless otherwise stated, all books are published in Paris.)

Balzac, Honoré de. *Oeuvres complètes*. 28 vols. 1959–63.
Baudelaire, Charles. *Oeuvres complètes*. Ed. M. Ruff. 1968.
Le Bonhomme Richard, nos. 1–2. 1848.
Boulanger, Nicolas Antoine. *L'Antiquité dévoilée par ses usages, ou Examen*

critique des principales opinions, cérémonies et institutions religieuses et politiques des différens peuples de la terre. Amsterdam, 1776.

Brugière de Barante, Amable Guillaume Prosper. *Etudes historiques et biographiques.* 4 vols. 1857.

Histoire des ducs de Bourgogne de la maison de Valois. 1364–1477. 13 vols. 3rd edn, 1825.

Caro, E. 'L'Auteur de *Madame Bovary* à Carthage'. *La France*, 9 Dec. 1862, p. 3.

Chasles, Philarète. *Etudes sur l'antiquité, précédées d'un essai sur les phases de l'histoire littéraire et sur les influences intellectuelles des races.* 1847.

Chateaubriand, Francois-René de. *Mémoires d'outre-tombe.* Ed. M. Levaillant. 4 vols. 1948.

Oeuvres complètes. 22 vols. 1833–5.

Chéruel, A. 'Du Merveilleux dans l'histoire'. *Revue de Rouen*, n.s. VI (1835), pp. 57–69.

'Progrès de l'histoire du XIXe siècle'. *Revue de Rouen*, n.s. II (1833), pp. 153–67.

Colet, Louise. '*Le Marabout de Sidi-Brahim*', poème dédié à l'armée, suivi de la '*Chanson des soldats d'Afrique*'. *Musique d'Hte. Colet, professeur au Conservatoire.* 1845.

Poésies complètes. 1844.

Constant, Benjamin. *De la Religion considérée dans sa source, ses formes et ses développements.* 5 vols. 1824–31.

Court de Gébelin, Antoine. *Le Monde primitif analysé et comparé avec le monde moderne, considéré dans son génie allégorique et dans les allégories auxquelles conduisit ce génie.* 9 vols. 1773–82.

Cousin, Victor. *Cours de l'histoire de la philosophie moderne.* 3 vols. New edn, 1847.

Creuzer, Friedrich. *Religions de l'antiquité considérées principalement dans leurs formes symboliques et mythologiques.* Trans. J. D. Guigniaut. 4 vols. 1825–51.

Dargez, E. 'Le Quinzaine d'un liseur'. *Le Figaro*, 4 Dec. 1862, p. 4.

Du Camp, Maxime. *Souvenirs de l'année 1848.* 2nd edn, 1892.

Souvenirs littéraires. 2 vols. 1882–3.

Dumas Davy de la Pailleterie, Alexandre. *Alexandre Dumas, illustré. Oeuvres complètes.* 25 vols. 1907.

Dumesnil, Alexis. *Considérations sur les causes et les progrès de la corruption en France.* 1824.

Dupuis, Charles-François. *Origine de tous les cultes ou religion universelle.* An III (1795).

Duvergier de Hauranne. *Discours prononcé à Rouen par M. Duvergier de Hauranne au banquet de la réforme electorale et parlementaire.* 1847.

Escudier, M. 'Salammbô'. *Le Pays*, 2 Dec. 1862, p. 2.

Esquiros, A. 'Des Etudes contemporaines sur l'histoire des races'. *Revue des Deux Mondes* n.s. XXI (1848), pp. 982–1003.

Flaubert, Gustave. 'Une Composition d'histoire et de géographie (classe de troisième)'. *Trois Normands: P. Corneille, G. Flaubert, G. de Maupassant: études documentaires.* Ed. G. Dubosc. Rouen, 1917. pp. 110–22.

Correspondance. Ed. J. Bruneau. vols. 1– . 1973– .

Correspondance. Ed. Conard. 9 vols. 1926–33.

Correspondance. Supplement. Ed. R. Dumesnil, J. Pommier and C. Digeon. 4 vols. 1954.

'Influence des Arabes d'Espagne sur la civilisation française du moyen âge'. Ed. E. Vinaver. *French Studies*, I (1947), pp. 37–43.

Lettres inédites à la Princesse Mathilde. Ed. Conard. 1927.

'Lettres inédites de Flaubert à Sainte-Beuve'. Ed. B. F. Bart. *Revue d'histoire littéraire de la France*, LXVI (1964), pp. 427–35.

Madame Bovary. Nouvelle version précédée des scénarios inédits. Ed. J. Pommier and G. Leleu. 1949.

Oeuvres complètes. Club de l'honnête homme edn. 15 vols. 1971–5.

Oeuvres complètes. Ed. B. Masson. 2 vols. 1964.

Poésies de jeunesse inédites. Ed. George M. Reeves. University of South Carolina Bibliographical Series no. 3. 1968.

Souvenirs, notes et pensées intimes. Ed. Lucie Chevalley-Sabatier. 1965.

'Le Théâtre de Voltaire'. Ed. T. Besterman. *Travaux sur Voltaire et le dix-huitième siècle*, L-LI (1967).

'Voltaire jugé par Flaubert'. Ed. T. Besterman. *Travaux sur Voltaire et le dix-huitième siècle*, I (1955), pp. 133–58.

Frœhner, Guillaume. 'Le Roman archéologique en France. G. Flaubert, *Salammbô*'. *La Revue contemporaine*, 31 Dec. 1862, pp. 1–2.

Gautier, Léon. '*Salammbô* par Gustave Flaubert'. *Le Monde*, 5 Dec. 1862, pp. 3–4.

Gautier, Théophile. *Le Capitaine Fracasse.* Ed. A. Boschot. 1955.

Poésies complètes. 2 vols. 1884.

Le Roman de la momie. Ed. A. Boschot. 1955.

'*Salammbô* par Gustave Flaubert'. *Le Moniteur universel*, 22 Dec. 1862, pp. 2–3.

Gobineau, Joseph-Arthur de. *Essai sur l'inégalité des races humaines.* 4 vols. 1853–5.

Goncourt, Edmond and Jules de. *Journal. Mémoires de la vie littéraire.* Ed. Robert Ricatte. 22 vols. Monaco, 1956–8.

Pages retrouvées. 1886.

Guigniaut, J. D. 'Notice historique sur la vie et les travaux de George-Frédéric Creuzer'. *Académie des Inscriptions et Belles-Lettres*, 1863, pp. 39–85.

Guizot, François Pierre Guillaume. *Cours d'histoire moderne: histoire générale de la civilisation en Europe depuis la chute de l'Empire romain jusqu'à la révolution française.* 1828.

Histoire de la civilisation en France depuis la chute de l'Empire romain. 4 vols. New edn, 1846.

L'Histoire de France depuis les temps les plus reculés jusqu'en 1789 racontée à mes petits-enfants. 5 vols. 1870–6.

Herder, Johann Gottfried. *Ideen zur Philosophie der Geschichte der Menschheit. Sämmtliche Werke*, XII-XIII. Berlin, 1877–1913.

Idées sur la philosophie de l'histoire de l'humanité. Trans. E. Quinet. 3 vols. 1827.

Horeau, H., Buquet, J. and Luce, E. *De l'Organisation des ateliers nationaux et de leur application à divers travaux d'utilité publique et à la colonisation de l'Algérie.* Algiers, 1848.

Hugo, Victor Marie. *Choses vues, 1847–8.* Ed. H. Juin. 1972.

Notre-Dame de Paris. Ed. M-F. Guyard. 1959.

Oeuvres poétiques. Ed. P. Albouy. 3 vols. 1964–74.

Quatre-vingt-treize. 1874.

Théâtre complet. Eds. J. J. Thierry and J. Mélèze. 2 vols. 1963.

Jouvin, B. 'M. Gustave Flaubert. Salammbô.' *Le Figaro,* 28 Dec. 1862, pp. 1–3.

Lamartine, Alphonse de. *Histoire de la révolution de 1848.* 2 vols. Brussels, 1849.

Leconte de Lisle, Charles-Marie-René. *Articles, préfaces, discours.* Ed. E. Pich. 1971.

Poèmes barbares. 1947.

Leroux, Pierre. *La France sous Louis-Philippe.* (1842). *Appendice aux trois discours sur la situation actuelle de la société et de l'esprit humain. Oeuvres.* 2 vols. 1850–1.

Levallois, Jules. 'Salammbô par M. Gustave Flaubert'. *L'Opinion nationale,* 14 Dec. 1862, pp. 1–2.

Lucas, Hippolyte. 'Bibliographie'. *Le Siècle,* 26 Dec. 1862, p. 2.

Lytton, Edward Bulwer. *The Last Days of Pompeii.* London, 1834: rpt. 1897.

Malot, Hector. 'Salammbô par M. Gustave Flaubert'. *L'Opinion nationale,* 29 Nov. 1862, p. 3.

Manzoni, Alessandro. *The Betrothed.* Trans. A. Colquhoun. London, 1968.

Marchangy. L.-A.-F. de. *La Gaule poétique, ou l'histoire de France considérée dans ses rapports avec la poésie, l'éloquence et les beaux-arts.* 8 vols. 1813–19.

Marsay, Léon de. 'Lettre parisienne'. *Revue de la semaine,* 9 Dec. 1862, p. 2.

Maury, Alfred. *Croyances et légendes de l'antiquité, essais de critique appliquée à quelques points d'histoire et de mythologie.* 1863.

Fragment d'un mémoire sur l'histoire de l'astrologie et de la magie dans l'antiquité et au moyen age. 1859.

Histoire des religions de la Grèce antique. 3 vols. 1857–9.

La Magie et l'astrologie dans l'antiquité et au moyen âge, ou étude sur les superstitions païennes, qui se sont perpétuées jusqu'à nos jours. 1860.

Recherches sur la religion et le culte des populations primitives de la Grèce. 1855.

Mérimée, Prosper. *Chronique du règne de Charles IX.* Ed. M. Rat. 1949.

Romans et nouvelles. Ed. M. Parturier. 2 vols. 1967.

Michelet, Jules. *Bible de l'humanité.* 1864.

'Discours sur le système et la vie de Vico'. In G. B. Vico. *Principes de la philosophie de l'histoire.* Trans. J. Michelet. 1827.

Histoire de France. 17 vols. New edn, 1871–4.

Histoire de la révolution française. 7 vols. 1847–53.

Histoire romaine. 2 vols. 2nd edn, 1833.

Le Peuple. Ed. R. Casanova. 1965.

Précis de l'histoire moderne. 5th edn, 1835.

Migne, Abbé. *Dictionnaire universel de mythologie ancienne et moderne*. 1855.

Mignet, F. A. *Histoire de la révolution française depuis 1789 jusqu'en 1814*. 1824.

Montesquieu, Charles de Secondat, Baron de. *Considérations sur les causes de la grandeur des Romains et de leur décadence*. Ed. Jean Ehrard. 1968.

Moreau de Jonnès, A. *Eléments de statistique*. 1856.

Statistique des céréales de la France. Le blé, sa culture, sa production, sa consommation, son commerce. 1843.

Morel, B. H. *Traité des dégénérescences physiques, intellectuelles et morales de l'espèce humaine*. 1857.

Musset, Alfred de. *La Confession d'un enfant du siècle*. 2 vols. 1836.

Nouvelle biographie générale, depuis les temps les plus reculés jusqu'à nos jours. Ed. Firmin Didot Frères. 46 vols. 1852–66.

Paris ou les sciences, les institutions et les moeurs au XIX siècle. Ed. A. Esquiros. 1847.

Pelletan, Eugène. *La Nouvelle Babylone*. 1862.

Polybius. *Histoire*. Trans. Dom Vincent Thuillier. 6 vols. 1727–30.

Pontmartin, Armand de. 'M. Gustave Flaubert – Salammbô'. *La Gazette de France*, 21 Dec. 1862, pp. 1–2.

Preller, Ludwig. *Griechische Mythologie*. 2 vols. Leipzig, 1854.

Proth, Mario. '*Salammbô* par Gustave Flaubert'. *Le Courrier du dimanche*, 7 Dec. 1862, pp. 5–6.

Quinet, Edgar. *L'Enseignement du peuple*. 7th edn, 1876.

Le Génie des religions. 2nd edn, 1851.

Histoire de mes idées. 10th edn, n.d. (1923).

Oeuvres complètes. 10 vols. 1857–8.

Renan, Ernest. 'Des Religions de l'antiquité et de leurs derniers historiens'. *Revue des Deux Mondes*, 15 May 1853, pp. 821–48.

Sade, Donatien Alphonse François. *Histoire secrète d'Isabelle de Bavière, reine de France*. Ed. Gilbert Lely. 1953.

Sainte-Beuve, Charles Augustin. *Causeries du lundi*. 15 vols. 3rd edn, 1857–76.

Nouveaux lundis. 13 vols. 1863–72.

Portraits contemporains. 5 vols. New edn, 1869.

Saint-Marc Girardin. 'De la Domination des Carthaginois et des Romains en Afrique comparée avec la domination française'. *Revue des Deux Mondes*, 1 May 1841, pp. 408–45.

Saint-Victor, Paul de. '*Salammbô* par M. Gustave Flaubert'. *La Presse*, 15 Dec. 1862, pp. 1–2.

Scherer, E. 'Variétés. M. Gustave Flaubert'. *Le Temps*, 16 Dec. 1862, p. 2.

Scott, Sir Walter. *Waverley Novels*. Ed. A. Lang. 25 vols. London, 1923–32.

Sénard. *Banquet réformiste de Rouen. 25 décembre 1847. Discours de M. Sénard, président du banquet*. 1847.

Sismondi, J. C. L. Simonde de. *Les Colonies des anciens comparées à celles des modernes, sous le rapport de leur influence sur le bonheur du genre humain*. Geneva, 1837.

Histoire de la chute de l'Empire romain et du déclin de la civilisation de l'an 250 à l'an 1000. 2 vols. 1835.

Julia Sévéra ou l'an 492. 1822.
Précis de l'histoire des Français. 2 vols. 1839.
Stern, Daniel. *Histoire de la révolution de 1848.* 3 vols. 1850–3.
Taillandier, Saint-René. 'Le Réalisme épique dans le roman'. *Revue des Deux Mondes,* 15 Feb. 1863.
Taine, Hippolyte. *Histoire de la littérature anglaise.* 5 vols. 4th edn, 1877–8.
Thierry, Jacques Nicolas Augustin. *Dix ans d'études historiques.* III, *Oeuvres complètes.* 5 vols. 1851–3.
   Histoire de la conquête de l'Angleterre par les Normands, de ses causes, et de ses suites jusqu'a nos jours, en Angleterre, en Ecosse, en Irlande et sur le continent. 3 vols. 1825.
   Lettres sur l'histoire de France. 5th edn, Brussels, 1840.
   Récits des temps mérovingiens, précédés de considérations sur l'histoire de la France. 2 vols. 1840.
Thiers, Louis Adolphe, and Bodin, Félix. *Histoire de la révolution française, accompagnée d'une histoire de la révolution de 1355 ou des Etats-Généraux sous le roi Jean.* 10 vols. 1823–7.
Thiers, Louis Adolphe. *Histoire du consulat et de l'Empire, faisant suite à l'Histoire de la révolution française.* 21 vols. 1845–69.
Vico, G. B. *Principes de la philosophie de l'histoire traduits de la Scienza nuova.* Trans. J. Michelet. 1827.
Vigny, Alfred de. *Oeuvres complètes.* Ed. F. Baldensperger. 2 vols. 1948.
Volney, C. F. *Voyage en Syrie et en Egypte pendant les années 1783, 1784 et 1785.* 2 vols. 1787.
   Les Ruines, ou méditation sur les révolutions des empires, suivies de la loi naturelle. Brussels, 1830.
Voltaire, François Marie Arouet de. *Voltaire's Correspondence.* Ed. T. Besterman. 107 vols. Geneva, 1953–65.
   Oeuvres historiques. Ed. R. Pomeau. 1957.
   Oeuvres complètes. Ed. T. Besterman. 135 vols. Geneva and Toronto, 1968–77.
Zola, Emile. *Oeuvres complètes.* Ed. H. Mitterand. 15 vols. Lausanne, 1966–70.

(iii) Secondary sources

Albouy, Pierre. *La Création mythologique chez Victor Hugo.* 1963.
   Mythes et mythologies dans la littérature française. 1969.
Allem, Maurice. *La Vie quotidienne sous le Second Empire.* 1952.
Baker, E. A. *A guide to historical fiction.* New York, 1914.
Baldensperger, F. *L'Appel de la fiction orientale chez Honoré de Balzac.* Oxford, 1927.
Bardèche, Maurice. *Balzac, romancier.* 1940.
Barron, J. D. 'La Première *Education sentimentale* de Flaubert'. *Bulletin des Amis de Flaubert,* no. 12 (1958), pp. 3–18.
Bart, Benjamin F. *Flaubert.* Syracuse, 1967.
Bartfeld, Fernande. *Sainte-Beuve and Alfred de Vigny.* Archives des lettres modernes, no. 115 (1970).

Barthes, Roland. *Le Degré zéro de l'écriture, suivi de nouveaux essais critiques.* 1972.

'Flaubert et la phrase'. *Word*, XXIV (1968), pp. 48–54.

Bem, Jeanne. *Désir et savoir dans l'oeuvre de Flaubert. Etude de 'La Tentation de saint Antoine'.* 1979

Benedetto, L. F. *Le Origini di 'Salammbô'. Studio sul realismo storico di G. Flaubert.* Florence, 1920.

'L'Interpretazione filologica di Polibio in *Salammbô*'. *Atene e Roma*, XXII (1919), pp. 128–37.

Bernbaum, Ernest. 'The views of the great critics on the historical novel'. *PMLA*, XLI (1926), pp. 424–41.

Bersani, Léo. *Balzac to Beckett.* New York, 1970.

'The narrator and the bourgeois community in *Madame Bovary*'. *The French Review*, XXXII (1958), pp. 527–33.

Bertrand, Louis. *Gustave Flaubert.* 2nd edn, 1912.

Bevernis, Christa. 'Vergangenheitdarstellung und Gegenwartbezug in Gustave Flauberts Roman *Salammbô*'. *Beitrage zur Romanischen Philologie*, XI (1972), pp. 22–38.

Bidney, David. 'Vico's new science of myth'. *Giambattista Vico: an International Symposium.* Ed. Giorgio Tagliacozzo and Hayden V. White. Baltimore, 1969, pp. 259–77.

Bollème, Geneviève. *La Leçon de Flaubert.* 1964.

Bolster, R. 'Flaubert et "le défaut" du genre historique'. *Bulletin des Amis de Flaubert*, no. 52 (1978), pp. 8–12.

Bonaccorso, G. 'Sulla cronologia del viaggio in Oriente di Flaubert e Du Camp'. *Studi Francesi*, VII (1963), pp. 495–9.

Bonnefis, Philippe. 'Flaubert: un déplacement du discours critique'. *Littérature*, no. 2 (1971), pp. 63–70.

Bosse, M. and Stoll, A. 'Die Agonie des archaischen Orients. Eine verschlüsselte Vision des Revolutionszeitalters'. *Salammbô.* Trans. G. Brustgi, pp. 401–48. Frankfurt, 1979.

Bourgeois, Nicolas. *Balzac, historien français et écrivian régionaliste.* 1925.

Bourget, Paul. *Essais de psychologie contemporaine. Baudelaire. M. Renan. Flaubert. M. Taine. Stendhal*, 2 vols. New edn, 1916.

Bouvier, E. 'L'Original de Salammbô'. *Revue d'histoire littéraire de la France*, XXXVII (1930), pp. 602–9.

Brogan, D. W. *The French nation from Napoleon to Pétain.* London, 1957.

Brombert, Victor. *Flaubert par lui-même.* 1971.

The novels of Flaubert: a study of themes and techniques. Princeton, 1966.

'La première *Education sentimentale*'. *Europe*, XLVII (1969), pp. 22–31.

Bruneau, Jean. *Le 'Conte oriental' de Gustave Flaubert.* 1973.

Les Débuts littéraires de Gustave Flaubert, 1831–1845. 1962.

'*Salammbô*, roman de la lumière'. *Bulletin des Amis de Flaubert*, no. 23 (1963), pp. 4–8.

Buck, Stratton, 'Sources historiques et technique romanesque dans l'*Education sentimentale*'. *Revue d'histoire littéraire de la France*, LXIII (1963), pp. 619–34.

Burguet, Frantz André. 'Tristesse sanguine'. *Cahiers Renaud-Barrault*, LIX (1967), pp. 106–12.

Bury, J. P. T. *France 1814–1940*. 4th edn, London, 1969.

Butterfield, Sir Herbert. *The historical novel*. Cambridge, 1924.

Cahm, Eric. *Politics and society in contemporary France (1789–1971). A documentary history*. London, 1972.

Calmy, Christophe. 'Flaubert et le nihilisme de gauche'. *Esprit*, II (1963), pp. 251–60.

Cannon, J. H. 'Flaubert's documentation for *Herodias*'. *French Studies*, XIV (1960), pp. 325–39.

Carlut, Charles. *La Correspondance de Flaubert, étude et répertoire critique*. 1968.

Carlut, Charles (ed.). *Essais sur Flaubert en l'honneur du professeur Don Demorest*. 1979.

Carter, A. E. *The idea of decadence in French literature, 1830–1900*. Toronto, 1958.

Cassirer, Ernst. *Language and myth*. Trans. Susanne K. Langer. New York, 1946.

Castex, P. G. *Le Conte fantastique en France de Nodier à Maupassant*. 1951.

'Flaubert et l'Education sentimentale'. *Bulletin des Amis de Flaubert*, no. 18 (1961), pp. 3–17.

Cellier, Leon. *L'Epopée humanitaire et les grands mythes romantiques*. 1971.

Etudes de structure. Archives des lettres modernes, no. 56 (1964).

Cento, A. 'Flaubert e la rivoluzione di febbraio'. *Rivista di letterature moderne e comparate*, XV (Dec. 1962), pp. 270–85 and XVI (Mar. 1963), pp. 20–49.

Il realismo documentario nell'Education sentimentale. Naples, 1967.

Chapman, J. M. and B. *The life and times of Baron Haussmann: Paris in the Second Empire*. London, 1957.

Charlton, D. G. *Secular religions in France, 1815–1870*. London, 1963.

'Victor Cousin and the French Romantics'. *French Studies*, XVII (1963), pp. 311–23.

Charpentier, J. *Tours d'horizon*, 1943.

Chiari, Joseph. *Realism and imagination*. London, 1960.

Citron, Pierre. *La Poésie de Paris dans la littérature française de Rousseau à Baudelaire*. 2 vols. 1961.

Cobban, A. *A history of modern France*. 2nd edn, Harmondsworth, 1961.

Coleman, A. *Flaubert's literary development in the light of his 'Mémoires d'un fou', 'Novembre', and 'Education sentimentale' (version of 1845)*. Baltimore–Paris, 1914.

'Some inconsistencies in Flaubert's *Salammbô*'. *Modern Language Notes*, XXVII (1912), pp. 123–5.

'*Le Roman de la momie* and *Salammbô*'. *French Quarterly*, IV (1922), pp. 183–6.

Coleman, A. and Fay, P. B. *Sources and structure of Flaubert's 'Salammbô'*. Baltimore–Paris, 1914.

Cortland, Peter. *The sentimental adventure. An examination of Flaubert's 'Education sentimentale'*. The Hague, 1967.

Croce, Benedetto. *Theory and history of historiography*. Trans. Douglas Ainslie. London, 1921.

Crouzet, Michel. 'Le Style épique dans *Madame Bovary*'. *Europe*, XLVII (1969), pp. 151–72.

Culler, Jonathan. *Flaubert. The uses of uncertainty*. London, 1974.

Danahy, M. 'The Esthetics of Documentation: the Case of l'*Education sentimentale*'. *Romance Notes*, XIV (1972), pp. 61–5.

Dane, Ivo. 'Symbol und Mythos in Flauberts *Salammbô*'. *Zeitschrift für französische Sprache und Literatur*, LIX (1935), pp. 22–45.

Danger, P. *Sensations et objets dans le roman de Flaubert*. 1973.

Daspre, André. 'Le Roman historique et l'histoire'. *Revue d'histoire littéraire de la France*, LXXV (1975), pp. 235–44.

Debray-Genette, Raymonde. 'Flaubert: science et écriture'. *Littérature*, no. 15 (Oct. 1974), pp. 41–51.

Debray-Genette, Raymonde (ed.). *Flaubert à l'oeuvre*. 1980

Delcourt, Marie. *Pyrrhos et Pyrrha: recherches sur les valeurs du feu dans les légendes helléniques*. 1965.

Demorest, D. L. *L'Expression figurée et symbolique dans l'oeuvre de Gustave Flaubert*. 1931.

Démoris, René. 'De l'Usage du nom propre: le roman historique au XVIIIe siècle'. *Revue d'historie littéraire de la France*, LXXV (1975), pp. 268–88.

Descharmes, René and Dumesnil, René. *Autour de Flaubert. Etude historique et documentaire*. 2 vols. 1912.

Flaubert, sa vie, son caractère et ses idées avant 1857. 1909.

Digeon, Claude. 'Un Discours inconnu de Flaubert'. *Revue d'histoire littéraire de la France*, L (1950), pp. 420–34.

Flaubert. 1970.

Dillingham, L. B. 'A Source of *Salammbô*'. *Modern Language Notes*, XV (1925), pp. 71–6.

Dimoff, P. 'Autour d'un projet de roman de Flaubert'. *Revue d'histoire littéraire de la France*, XLVIII (1948), pp. 309–35.

Dubuc, André. 'Une Déclaration politique de Bouilhet en 1848'. *Bulletin des Amis de Flaubert*, no. 35 (1969), pp. 14–17.

'L'*Education sentimentale* dans les carnets de notes de Flaubert'. *Bulletin des Amis de Flaubert*, no. 34 (1969), pp. 21–44.

Duchet, Claude. 'L'Illusion historique. L'enseignement des préfaces (1815–1832)'. *Revue d'histoire littéraire de la France*, LXXV (1975), pp. 245–67.

Dugan, J. R. 'Flaubert's *Salammbô*, a study in immobility'. *Zeitschrift für französische Sprache und Literatur*, LXXIX (1969), pp. 193–206.

Dumesnil, René. *Flaubert, son hérédité, son milieu, sa méthode*. New edn, 1906.

Gustave Flaubert, l'homme et l'oeuvre. 1932.

'Introduction'. *Salammbô*. 1944. I, ix–clxiii.

'Les Sources de *Salammbô*'. *Revue des Deux Mondes*, LXXIV (1943), pp. 414–30.

Dupee, F. W. 'Flaubert and the *Sentimental Education*'. *New York Review of Books*, 22 April 1971, pp. 42–51.

Dupuy, Aimé. *En Marge de 'Salammbô'*. 1954.

Duquette, Jean-Pierre. 'Flaubert, l'histoire et le roman historique'. *Revue d'histoire littéraire de la France*, LXXV (1975), pp. 344–52.

Durry, Marie-Jeanne. *Flaubert et ses projets inédits*. 1950.

Gérard de Nerval et le mythe. 1956.

Duveau, Georges. *1848*. 1965.

Eliade, Mircea. *Aspects du mythe*. 1963.

El Nouty, Hassan, *Le Proche-Orient dans la littérature française de Nerval à Barrès*. 1958.

Fairlie, Alison. 'Flaubert et la conscience du réel.' *Essays in French Literature* (Nov. 1967), pp. 1–12.

Flaubert: 'Madame Bovary'. London, 1962.

Fairlie, Alison and Green, Anne. 'Deciphering Flaubert's manuscripts. The "Club de l'honnête homme" edition'. *French Studies*, XXVII (1973), pp. 287–315.

Fay, P. B. and Coleman, A. *Sources and structure of Flaubert's 'Salammbô'*. Baltimore–Paris, 1914.

Ferguson, George. *Signs and symbols in Christian art*. New York, 1966.

Fischer, E. W. *Etudes sur Flaubert inédit*. Leipzig, 1908.

Forrest-Thomson, Veronica. 'The Ritual of Reading *Salammbô*'. *Modern Language Review*, LXVII (1972), pp. 787–98.

François, A. 'Gustave Flaubert, Maxime Du Camp et la révolution de 1848'. *Revue d'histoire littéraire de la France*, LIII (1953), pp. 44–56.

Frier-Wantiez, Martine. *Sémiotique du fantastique. Analyse textuelle de 'Salammbô'*. Berne, 1979.

Gans, E. L. *The discovery of illusion. Flaubert's early works, 1835–1837*. Berkeley, Los Angeles and London, 1971.

Gaultier, J. de. 'Le Bovarysme de Salammbô'. *Mercure de France*, CIII (1913), pp. 31–40.

Genette, Gérard. 'Silences de Flaubert'. *Nouvelle Revue Française*, XXVII (1966), pp. 473–83.

Giorgi, Giorgetto. 'Un progetto "Flaubertiano": La Spirale'. *Belfagor*, XXIV (1969), pp. 19–40.

'Salammbô tra esotismo e storia contemporanea'. *Belfagor*, XXV (1970), pp. 371–94.

Girard, René. *Mensonge romantique et vérité romanesque*. 1961.

Gooch, G. P. *History and historians in the nineteenth century*. London, 1913.

Gothot-Mersch, Claudine. 'Le Dialogue dans l'oeuvre de Flaubert'. *Europe*, XLVII (1969), pp. 112–21.

La Genèse de Madame Bovary. 1966.

Gothot-Mersch, Claudine (ed.). *La Production du sens chez Flaubert*. 1975.

Green, Anne. '*Salammbô* and the myth of Pasiphaë'. *French Studies*, XXXII (1978), pp. 170–8.

Guisan, Gilbert. 'Flaubert et la révolution de 1848'. *Revue d'histoire littéraire de la France*, LVIII (1958), pp. 183–204.

Haas, Eugen. *Flaubert und die Politik*. Biella, 1933.

Haggis, D. K. 'Scott, Balzac and the historical novel as social and political analysis: *Waverley* and *Les Chouans*'. *Modern Language Review*, LXVIII (1973), pp. 51–68.

Hamilton, A. *Sources of the religious element in Flaubert's 'Salammbô'.* Baltimore–Paris, 1917.

Hankiss, Jean. 'Problèmes du roman historique'. *Zagadnienia rodzajow literackich*, II (1960), pp. 5–34.

Hardy, Georges. *Histoire de la colonisation française.* 5th edn, 1947.
Histoire sociale de la colonisation française. 1953.

Hemmings, F. W. J. *Culture and society in France. 1848–1898.* London, 1971.

Herval, René. *Les Véritables Origines de Madame Bovary.* 1957.

Hill, Leslie. 'Flaubert and the rhetoric of stupidity'. *Critical Inquiry*, Winter 1976, pp. 333–44.

Hunt, H. J. *The epic in nineteenth-century France.* Oxford, 1941.

James, Henry. *Selected literary criticism.* Ed. M. Shapira. London, 1968.

Jay, B. L. 'Anti-history and the Method of *Salammbô*'. *Romanic Review*, LXIII (1972), pp. 20–33.

Jolas, P. 'Remarques sur le style de *Salammbô*'. *Bulletin des Amis de Flaubert*, no. 38 (1971).

Jourda, P. *L'Exotisme dans la littérature française depuis Chateaubriand.* 2 vols. Paris–Montpellier, 1938–56.

Jullian, C. *Extraits des historiens français du XIXe siècle, publiés, annotés et précédés d'une introduction sur l'histoire en France.* 1897.

Jung, C. and Kerenyi, C. *Introduction à l'essence de la mythologie.* 1953.

Kenner, Hugh W. *Flaubert, Joyce and Beckett, the Stoic comedians.* 1964.

Landelle, F. 'Roman et histoire: *L'Education sentimentale*'. *Bulletin des Amis de Flaubert*, no. 52 (1978), pp. 5–7.

Leal, R. B. '*Salammbô*: an Aspect of Structure'. *French Studies*, XXVII.

Lefebvre, Georges. *La Naissance de l'historiographie moderne.* 1971.

Lémonon, Michel. 'L'idée de race et les écrivans français de la première moitié du XIXe siècle'. *Die neueren Sprachen*, LXIX (1970), pp. 283–92.

Lewes, G. H. 'Historical romance', *Westminster Review*, XLV (1846), pp. 34–55.

Lukács, Georg. *The historical novel.* Trans. H. and S. Mitchell. Harmondsworth, 1969.

Maigron, Louis. *Le Roman historique à l'époque romantique. Essai sur l'influence de Walter Scott.* 1912.

McIntosh, Christopher. *Eliphas Levi and the French occult revival.* London, 1972.

Maranini, Lorenza. *Il '48 nella struttura della 'Education sentimentale' e altri studi francesi.* Pisa, 1963.

Martin, Gaston. *Histoire de l'esclavage dans les colonies françaises.* 1948.

Mason, Germaine. *Les Ecrits de jeunesse de Flaubert.* 1961.

Matignon, Renaud. 'Flaubert et la sensibilité moderne'. *Tel Quel*, I (1960), pp. 83–9.

May, Georges. 'L'Histoire a-t-elle engendré le roman? Aspects français de la question au seuil du siècle des lumières'. *Revue d'histoire littéraire de la France*, LV (1955), pp. 155–76.

Maynial, Edouard. 'Flaubert orientaliste et le *Livre Posthume* de Maxime Du Camp'. *Revue de littérature comparée*, III (1923), pp. 78–108.

Mayoux, Jean-Jacques. 'Flaubert et le réel'. *Mercure de France*, 15 Feb. 1934, pp. 33–52.

178   *Select bibliography*

Molino, J. 'Qu'est-ce que le roman historique?' *Revue d'histoire littéraire de la France*, LXXV (1975), pp. 195–234.

Monod, Gabriel. 'Du Progrès des études historiques en France depuis le XVIe siècle'. *Revue historique*, 1 (1876), pp. 5–38.

Mornet, Daniel. 'La Méthode historique de *Salammbô* et la méthode historique d'Ernest Feydeau'. *Revue d'histoire littéraire de la France*, XXXIII (1926), pp. 201–12.

Naaman, Antoine. *Les Débuts de Gustave Flaubert et sa technique descriptive.* 1962.

Nadeau, Maurice. *Gustave Flaubert écrivain.* 1969.

Neefs, Jacques. '*Salammbô*, textes critiques'. *Littérature*, no. 15 (Oct. 1974), pp. 52–64.

Nélod, Gilles. *Panorama du roman historique.* Paris–Brussels, 1969.

Pézard, M. '*Salammbô* et l'archéologie punique'. *Mercure de France*, 16 Feb. 1908, pp. 622–38.

Picard, G. C. 'Flaubert, Carthage et l'archéologie contemporaine'. *Revue de Paris*, LXIII (1956), pp. 105–13.

Pinkney, David Henry. *Napoleon III and the rebuilding of Paris.* Princeton, 1958.

Piquet, V. *La Colonisation française dans l'Afrique du Nord.* 1912.

Pochon, J. 'Edgar Quinet et les luttes du Collège de France, 1843–1847'. *Revue d'histoire littéraire de la France*, LXX (1970), pp. 619–27.

Pommier, Jean. *Les Ecrivains devant la révolution de 1848.* 1948.

Ponteil, Félix. *1848.* 3rd edn, 1955.

Porter, Dennis. 'Aestheticism versus the Novel: the example of *Salammbô*'. *Novel*, IV (1971), pp. 101–6.

'Mythic Imagery in Flaubert's *Oeuvres de Jeunesse*'. *Australian Journal of French Studies*, IX (1972), pp. 148–60.

Pradalié, G. *Balzac, historien.* 1955.

Praz, Mario. *The Romantic agony.* London, 1970.

Proust, Jacques. 'Structure et sens de l'*Education sentimentale*'. *Revue des sciences humaines*, n.s., fasc. 125 (Jan.–Mar. 1967), pp. 67–100.

Raitt, A. W. 'The composition of Flaubert's *Saint Julien l'hospitalier*'. *French Studies*, XIX (1965), pp. 358–69.

Rance, Nicholas. *The historical novel and popular politics in nineteenth century England.* London, 1975.

Reboussin, Marcel. *Le Drame spirituel de Flaubert.* 1973.

Reik, Theodor. *Flaubert und seine 'Versuchung des heiligen Antonius'.* Minden, 1912.

Riedmatten, L. de. *La Faillite de toutes les monnaies et dans tous les pays.* Versailles, 1947.

Roche, Anne and Delfau, Gérard. 'Histoire-et-littérature: un projet'. *Littérature*, no. 13 (Feb. 1974), pp. 16–28.

Rousset, Jean. 'Positions, distances, perspectives dans *Salammbô*'. *Poétique*, II (1971), pp. 145–54.

Sartre, Jean-Paul. 'La Conscience de classe chez Flaubert'. *Les Temps modernes*, XXI (May 1966), pp. 1921–51 and (June 1966), pp. 2113–53.

'Flaubert: du poète à l'artiste'. *Les Temps modernes*, XXII (Aug. 1966), pp. 197–253 (Sept. 1966), pp. 423–81, and (Oct. 1966), pp. 598–674.

L'Idiot de la famille: Gustave Flaubert de 1821 à 1857. 3 vols. 1971–2.

Schmidt, Charles. *Des Ateliers nationaux aux barricades de juin*. 1948.

Schwartz, W. L. *The imaginative interpretation of the Far East in modern French literature, 1800–1925*. 1927.

Seznec, Jean. 'Flaubert, historien des hérésies dans *La Tentation*'. *Romanic Review*, XXXVI (1945), pp. 200–21.

'Les Lectures antiques de Flaubert entre 1840 et 1850'. *Revue d'histoire de la philosophie et d'histoire générale de la civilisation*, fasc. 27–8 (July–Dec. 1939), pp. 274–82.

Nouvelles études sur 'La Tentation de saint Antoine'. Studies of the Warburg Institute, 18. London, 1949.

'Saint Antoine et les monstres. Essai sur les sources et la signification du fantastique de Flaubert'. *PMLA*, LVIII (1943), pp. 195–222.

Les Sources de l'épisode des dieux dans 'La Tentation de saint Antoine'. 1940.

Sherrington, R. J. 'Les Dangers de la correspondance de Flaubert'. *Bulletin des Amis de Flaubert*, no. 24 (1964), pp. 27–37.

'L'Elaboration des plans de l'*Education sentimentale*'. *Revue d'histoire littéraire de la France*, LXX (1970), pp. 628–39.

Gustave Flaubert: Three novels. A study of techniques. Oxford, 1970.

Shroder, Maurice Z. 'On Reading *Salammbô*'. *L'Esprit créateur*, X (1970), pp. 24–35.

Simmons, James C. *The novelist as historian. Essays on the Victorian historical novel*. The Hague and Paris, 1973.

Spencer, Philip. *Flaubert. A Biography*. London, 1952.

Politics of belief in nineteenth-century France. London, 1954.

Starkie, Enid. *Flaubert: the making of the master*. London, 1967.

Flaubert the master. London, 1971.

Suffel, Jacques, 'Sur les manuscrits de l'*Education sentimentale*'. *Europe*, XLVII (Sept.–Nov. 1969), pp. 5–12.

Suhner-Schluep, H. *L'Imagination du feu ou la dialectique du soleil et de la lune dans 'Salammbô' de G. Flaubert*. Zurich, 1970.

Swart, Koenraad W. *The sense of decadence in nineteenth-century France*. The Hague, 1964.

Szendrei, Julia V. 'A történelmi regény müfaji problémáinak kérdéséhez'. (With résumé in French: 'Sur la problématique artistique du roman historique comme genre littéraire'.) *Studia Universitatis Babes-Bolyai, Series philologia*, XIII (1968), pp. 53–62.

Taillart, Charles, *L'Algérie dans la littérature française. Essai de bibliographie méthodique et raisonée jusqu'en 1924*. 1925.

Tétu, Jean-François. 'Désir et révolution dans l'*Education sentimentale*'. *Littérature*, no. 15 (Oct. 1974), pp. 88–94.

Thibaudet, Albert. *Gustave Flaubert*. New edn, 1935.

Thorlby, Anthony. *Gustave Flaubert and the art of realism*. London, 1957.

Tillet, Margaret. *On reading Flaubert*. Oxford, 1961.

Toulet, Suzanne. *Le Sentiment religieux de Flaubert d'après la correspondance.* Quebec, 1970.

Trilling, Lionel. *The opposing self. Nine essays in criticism.* New York, 1955.

Tudesq, A. J. *Les Grands Notables en France (1840–1849): étude historique d'une psychologie sociale.* 2 vols. Bordeaux, 1964.

Viatte, Auguste. *Les Sources occultes du romantisme français. Illuminisme, théosophie. 1770–1820.* 2 vols. 1928.

Vidalenc, Jean. 'Gustave Flaubert, historien de la révolution de 1848'. *Europe,* XLVII (1969), pp. 51–67.

Vries, Jan de, *Forschungsgeschichte der Mythologie.* Fribourg–Munich, 1961.

Wells, G. A. *Herder and after. A study in the development of sociology.* 's-Gravenhage, 1959.

'Vico and Herder'. *Giambattista Vico: an International Symposium.* Ed. Giorgio Tagliacozzo and Hayden V. White. Baltimore, 1969, pp. 93–102.

Wetherill, P. M. *Flaubert et la création littéraire.* 1964.

'Une version manuscrite du premier chapitre de *Salammbô*'. *Les Lettres Romanes,* XXXII (1978), pp. 291–331.

White, John J. *Mythology in the modern novel. A study of prefigurative techniques.* Princeton, 1971.

Wilson, E. *The triple thinkers.* London, 1952.

Index